PETER HAIN

o

POLITICAL TRIALS IN BRITAIN

ALLEN LANE

ALLEN LANE
Penguin Books Ltd
536 King's Road
London SW10 0UH

First published 1984

Set in Monophoto Ehrhardt
Printed in Great Britain by
Richard Clay (The Chaucer Press) Ltd,
Bungay, Suffolk

BRITISH LIBRARY CATALOGUING IN PUBLICATION DATA

Hain, Peter
    Political Trials in Britain.
    1. Trials (Political crimes and offenses) –
    Great Britain
    I. Title
    344.105′231   HV6295.G7

    ISBN 0–7139–1339–8

FOR PAT, SAM AND JAKE — WITH THANKS

CONTENTS

PREFACE

Two images of the law in Britain are most striking: its majesty and its mystery. Both serve to invest it with a higher authority. But both also surround it with a great deal of mythology which this book attempts to expose.

My book is aimed at the general reader, being more of a popular political analysis than an academic or legalistic treatise (the notes, for example, are for reference purposes only and should not be allowed to intrude). For, while there is no shortage of learned legal texts, while there are a number of recent books on civil liberties, and while John Griffith's *Politics of the Judiciary* has broken new ground, there nevertheless remains a gap to be filled in our understanding of the law. This book tries to fill it by explaining the political basis of British law and the way it affects individuals and groups in our society.

The book's major theme is the role of political trials, and it is shown that these have occurred continuously throughout British history. While no pretence is made at an exhaustive historical analysis, it is impossible to assess or understand contemporary political trials except within an historical perspective. Thus each chapter describes modern developments in their historical setting.

The book does not claim to be comprehensive, nor can I claim any special legal expertise. Indeed, one of the problems of analysing the legal system is the fact that lawyers and legal protocol all too frequently act as barriers to the lay person's understanding – yet it is the lay person who is the consumer or the victim of the legal process.

I am grateful to Phil Kelly for his research assistance and for drafting Chapters 1 to 6, and to Penguin Books for providing a grant to enable him to do this. I am also grateful to Patricia Hewitt for her comments on the manuscript; to Alan Rushton for his help and ideas; to my parents for their assistance with editing; to Geoff Hodgson, Harriet Harman, Andy Harris and Alan Clinton for their comments on some chapters; and to Molly Turpin for typing. As always I am indebted to Pat, Sam and Jake, who had to bear the strain of my writing the book on top of the enormous pressures they normally face from my political activities. Finally, thanks to Neil Middleton who commissioned the book and encouraged me to write it.

PETER HAIN

Putney, April 1982

1

LAW AND THE PEOPLE

Commenting on Lord Denning's rejection of the G.L.C.'s transport fares reduction, the Prime Minister, Margaret Thatcher, rebuffed an accusation that the Court had made a 'political' judgement, not a judicial one. She said to shouts of 'rubbish' from Labour M.P.s: 'Judges give decisions on the law and the evidence before them. They do so totally impartially.'

(*Guardian*, 11 November 1981)

'Some counsel have described this trial as a political trial. I direct it is not a political trial.' So ruled Judge Alan King-Hamilton in the 1979 case of four young anarchists charged with various firearms and explosives offences. He continued: 'We do not put people on trial for their political views in this country. If what is meant by a political trial is someone on trial because of his political views it is completely untrue. One of the proud boasts of this country is that a person can hold any views he likes, subject only to the laws of libel, slander and sedition. Merely being an anarchist is not a crime.' [1]

The press, failing to respond to his certainty, had already dubbed the proceedings the 'Anarchists' Trial' or even the 'Anarchy Trial'.[2] Both the judge and press were right and, of course, both were wrong. But they were right in ways which suited their own purposes.

Judge King-Hamilton was right in the sense that no law in this country forbids the holding of any political opinion (though since 1974 it has been illegal under the Prevention of Terrorism Acts to organize political support for certain organizations, and several groups are banned in Northern Ireland). Yet the press on the one hand, and frequently the supporters of various defendants on the other, are often united in a belief that arrests, charges and trials occur for political reasons.

No one in this country has the slightest difficulty in determining when dissidents in the Soviet Union are being accused and tried because of their political beliefs – even when the charges themselves are for 'ordinary' criminal offences such as a breach of the peace. Yet there is a reluctance to admit that the British legal structure too is part of a system intended to preserve and advance certain political views and the interests of certain groups, and to oppose the views and interests of others.

In reality, everyone from extreme left to extreme right, from anarchists to Fleet Street leader writers, knows that political trials take place – they are merely the outstanding features of a legal landscape political in every detail. Judge King-Hamilton's denial is so compulsory a statement by a presiding judge at a political trial that one can formulate a handy layman's rule: 'It's a political trial if the judge (or the prosecutor) specifically denies that it is.'

But other trials too are political; indeed the whole operation of the administration of justice is a political matter. Constitutionally, there exists in this country a formal separation between the administration of justice by the police and the courts on the one hand, and the political system on the other. Political decisions are made as a result of political activity: elections produce parliaments, in turn producing ministers and governments which hold office by public consent – and parliamentary majorities allow the translation of the electorate's wishes into law, called statute law. Once policies are law, the police enforce these laws 'impartially' and the courts deal with alleged offenders – also 'impartially'.

Or so conventional wisdom would have us believe. In reality it is false from beginning to end. Elections and the parliamentary system do not necessarily translate people's wishes into law. Laws once made are not enforced impartially. Concentrating on the *enforcement* rather than the creation of laws, later chapters will seek to show that the origins of statute law and the methods of its enforcement are two sides of the same political coin.

For it is impossible to divorce the legal system from the political and economic nature of the society in which it operates. Indeed, an understanding of the operation of the law is impossible without acknowledging that British society remains rigidly stratified, with pronounced class divisions, most wealth in the hands of a tiny minority, and effective political power exercised by a few. Far from Parliament having the dominant say, our democratically elected representatives are forced for the most part merely to go through the motions of exercising power. Real decisions are taken by the City, in the board-rooms of the giant multinationals, the big corporations, the pension and insurance companies, the Common Market and N.A.T.O.[3]

·CIVIL SERVANTS·

Another group which removes power from the House of Commons is the Civil Service, and the manner in which it operates impinges directly on the theme of this book. Civil servants have been directly involved in major political trials, for example Ministry of Defence involvement in the 1978 A.B.C. case and Home Office instigation of Harriet Harman's prosecution for contempt in 1981. They also staff key legal departments such as those of the Attorney General, the Director of Public Prosecutions and the Lord Chancellor. Moreover, the judiciary is widely held to be an independent and impartial organ of the state, like the Civil Service. In several recent memoirs, the power of the civil servants to form policy and to thwart even their 'own' ministers has formed a major theme.[4] Drawing on his experience as a former civil servant, an M.P. and Parliamentary Private Secretary to Tony Benn at the Department of Energy, Brian Sedgemore has written:

Two things only can be said with certainty about Parliamentary democracy in Britain today. First, that effective power does not reside in Parliament. Secondly, there is little that is democratic about the exercise of that power.[5]

He locates the strength of establishment in its 'hierarchy of secrecy'. Prime ministers withhold information from their Cabinet colleagues, and many of the activities of the Cabinet are conducted through sub-committees whose very existence, along with their membership and the topics they discuss, are official secrets. The existence and deliberations of many such committees are kept secret even from those Cabinet ministers who are not members of them.

In addition, civil servants themselves use secrecy against their 'own' ministers, withholding information so as to place close limits on the possible range of conclusions which a minister can reach. Sedgemore quotes Sir William Armstrong, then head of the Civil Service, now Lord Armstrong and chairman of the Midland Bank:

Obviously I had a great deal of influence. The biggest and most pervasive influence is in setting the framework within which the questions of policy are raised. We, while I was in the Treasury, had a framework of the economy which was basically neo-Keynesian. We set the questions which we asked ministers to decide arising out of that framework, and it would have been enormously difficult for my minister to change the framework so to that extent we had great power. I don't think we used it maliciously or malignly. I think we chose that framework because we thought it the best one going.[6]

Brian Sedgemore concludes that Lord Armstrong slightly overstated the power of civil servants. He argues convincingly that the limits of political debate are set by the Prime Minister in conjunction with the Civil Service and that both act within a conventional political wisdom. The system continues to function because all prime ministers have held views which fell within this conventional wisdom, which is overwhelmingly corporatist, believing that good government should 'reconcile the interests of big institutions and corporations with each other when they are in conflict in the belief that if this can be done then everyone else will have no option other than to accept what has been done and in the belief that in such circumstances dissent in society can be contained'.[7]

The power of civil servants and of the Prime Minister is now so well documented that few can seriously dispute that the reality of parliamentary democracy in Britain falls far short of its textbook image. One authoritative recent analysis by a conservative historian showed that, since the early 1900s, the dominant force in British politics has been a corporatist momentum determined by industrial and economic factors, with the party holding government office by comparison having little real influence.[8]

Most of Brian Sedgemore's examples are drawn from the spheres of economic and energy policy. But it is abundantly clear that the absence of effective Cabinet control applies equally in all areas. For example, Tony Benn has cited as decisions which never come to Cabinet the 1977 deportations of American journalists Agee and Hosenball; the subsequent prosecution of Crispin Aubrey, John Berry and Duncan Campbell under the Official Secrets Act; and the decision by the Attorney General to proceed against three publications which named an anonymous military officer, 'Colonel B', who gave prosecution evidence against the A.B.C. three.[9]

Brian Sedgemore's account of the realities of political life describes the power of the Civil Service against individual ministers who attempt small reforms. He stresses the conservatism of civil servants, their reluctance to change, their belief in the virtue of continuity, and therefore their relegation of the policies of succeeding governments to a secondary position relative to the continuity of administration. But such power can only be exercised with the consent of the Prime Minister.

Before Richard Crossman, Barbara Castle, Joe Haines and Brian Sedgemore gave their insiders' accounts of the way in which government is carried on, at least one academic observer, Ralph Miliband, produced an account of the role of the state which anticipated the experiences of these practitioners. Civil servants, he wrote, cannot be neutral in the affairs which they manage, because no one constantly in touch with matters of state and government can fail to form an opinion. Such opinions are not formed at random, but are themselves conditioned both by the social and educational background of civil servants and by the selection and training processes which they go through before and after their appointment.

Higher civil servants in the countries of advanced capitalism may generally be expected to play a conservative role in the councils of the state, to reinforce the conservative propensities of government, in which these propensities are already well developed, and to serve as an inhibiting element in regard to governments in which they are less pronounced . . .[10]

Even when social democratic* governments come to power, their very moderation has been their undoing, as the more radical ministers and supporters have found to their dismay time and time again:

[Social democratic governments] have never attempted to implement a coherent set of policies so much at variance with conservative interests and modes of thought as to be utterly intolerable to them; and civil servants confronted with such governments have not therefore been forced to make a clear choice between serving what they viewed as the national interest and serving the government of the day.[11]

What they can and have done is attempt to hamstring ministers in social democratic governments who have attempted to stray into reforms which went beyond the Civil Service's conception of 'the national interest'.

In the face of the resources of the state, parliamentarians are more or less helpless. Prime ministerial patronage extends to nearly 100 ministerial appointments for M.P.s alone. Given that for each post there are within the ranks of the parliamentary party both an incumbent and at least one member who feels that he could do the job better and whose behaviour in voting and other political activity is directed towards attracting the

* An ideological description fitting post-war Labour governments rather than the Social Democratic Party.

favourable notice of the whips and the premier, 200 people – two thirds or more of a parliamentary party with a normal working majority – are influenced by the power of such patronage. The remainder are handicapped by the poverty of resources made available to them.

·THE SECRET STATE·

E. P. Thompson the historian has drawn attention to the growth in both power and size of the 'secret state' – the security services, the police, and the civil servants in the ministries concerned with the administration of justice and the running of internal affairs. These civil servants are chiefly the Home Office, the Attorney General's Office, the Lord Chancellor's Office and, last but not least, the Cabinet Office. They are able to conceal their activities from public gaze, and insulate themselves from public pressure, to a greater extent even than their colleagues in other ministries. Why? Because on crucial questions they are able not only to take refuge behind the Official Secret Acts – the bedrock of administrative practices designed to cut the public off from information on the workings of government – but are also able to hide behind the alleged need to preserve national security. Writing of the security services and the police Special Branch, E. P. Thompson remarks that

it would amaze many British citizens to learn that these and other organizations are only at the end of a long historical line of ruling-class institutions with agents or informants in trade unions, educational institutes, and political organizations (especially of the Left) and with direct access to the postal and telephone system of the country; that they are larger and more powerful, and less subject to ministerial or parliamentary control than they have ever been and that a large part of their function has been to invigilate the British people themselves.[12]

This, from inside and outside, historically and contemporarily, is the British state. The significance for political trials is that this secretive, self-appointing and virtually self-managing state determines the content and form of the machinery of justice, from the lowest police constable to the most exalted Lord Justice. And from this state too come the Acts of Parliament which the machinery of justice is intended to enforce.

Just as the constitutional fiction of democracy bears precious little resemblance to the reality of an elitist secretive state, so that equally durable fiction of the separation of the administration of justice and the government of the country does not survive inspection. As well as political considerations playing an important role in the appointment of judges and magistrates, the immense discretion of the police is increasingly directed, at the urging of the Home Office, towards political policing. In addition, when it thinks the issue at stake is important enough, the executive interferes with the functioning of the administration of justice so as to affect the outcome of individual cases.

· LAW AND SOCIETY ·

If then the operation of the law should be seen as part of the modern state, the wider picture should be taken account of as well. For part of the fiction of judicial impartiality is connected with the notion that the state is itself an impartial vehicle able to be steered in whichever direction an elected Parliament decrees. But as Miliband (among many others) has demonstrated, the state reflects dominant class and economic interests, whichever party is in power, and so does the legal system.

Even Dicey, the noted constitutional lawyer and proponent of *laissez faire*, conceded as much when he wrote:

Men legislate . . . not in accordance with their opinion as to what is a good law, but in accordance with their interest, and this . . . is emphatically true of classes as contrasted with individuals, and therefore of a country like England, where classes exert a far more potent control over the making of laws than can any single person . . . So true is this, that from the inspection of the laws of a country it is often possible to conjecture . . . what is the class which holds, or has held, predominant power at a given time. [13]

That he was writing of the nineteenth century does not detract from the timelessness of his argument.

Notwithstanding modern legal aid provision, the old adage 'one law for the rich and one for the poor' still holds true. On the whole the courts protect the rights of property as against those of individual citizens. Indeed, over 90 per cent of serious crime involves property and the whole law enforcement apparatus is directed at tackling it. Contrast this with the tiny team of factory inspectors trying to enforce health and safety regulations; and the fact that although several thousands of people are killed at work each year, prosecutions of companies are most unlikely and, if they occur at all, fines are puny.

Here, the law is not itself creating any particular social order but is rather sustaining and legitimizing one. In this role, as Miliband explains, the judiciary 'has no more been "above" the conflicts of capitalist society than any other part of the state system. Judges have been deeply involved in these conflicts; and of all classes it is certainly the dominant class which has had least to complain about the nature and direction of that involvement.'[14]

Research into the operation of the law during the 1970s in Britain's large conurbations confirms that class divisions are alive and well and entrenched in the whole way the law operates locally.[15] Profits, whether those of company owners or landlords, are protected at virtually all costs, often despite the letter of the law. 'Workers have found that there is no legal machinery open to them to challenge the exodus of industrial capital from their neighbourhoods. There is no protection against the consequent factory closures, redundancies and cuts in income.'[16] Whatever may be the rights of tenants, workers or those on welfare in *theory* (and in some respects these groups have been given more statutory protection since the Second World War), when they come hard up against the harsh realities of economic power, they are in *practice* overridden. Again we find this gap between received wisdom and life as it actually is. On paper the law seems eminently even-handed: in reality it is not. The inequality still experienced by women is further testimony to this, as is the lack of protection given to ethnic and sexual minorities.[17]

But it is not simply that British law reflects the ethos of British capitalism. With economic recession in Britain, there is evidence that the legal system is being used to control and manage the social consequences of that recession. This is to be seen clearly in the role played by the law as public expenditure cuts increase pressure on housing, welfare and jobs.[18] It is to be found in the frontline role adopted by the police as they are faced with social strife and tension in our inner cities. Tougher laws against trade unionists and on public order are all aimed at protecting the interests of the governors as against those of the governed. Political trials, too, are a feature of this process. Furthermore, the state has needed to play the 'law and order' card in an effort not just to quell dissent, but to firm up a new social consensus needed for stability.[19]

·THE STATE AND THE JUDICIARY·

But to speak of 'the state' and its relation to 'the law' is not to assume some simple mechanical relationship between the two, still less to pretend that either of them is monolithic. This is not the place to enter into a theoretical discourse on the nature of the state. Suffice to say that the judiciary forms an elite which is part of the state, but also one which has its own *independent political interests*. These interests are not in conflict with the broad objectives of the state and of modern capitalism. But they are distinct nonetheless and to understand how the judiciary acts as a political agency it is necessary to examine the *specific* forces and interests expressed within it.

Some judges may even act against apparently conservative initiatives by governments—for example in political trials brought by the state under official secrecy legislation. Judges don't always back up to the hilt strong police measures, as illustrated by Lord Scarman's report on the policing of inner cities in 1981.[20] Nor when judges act in tune with the dominant ideology do they always act in the interests of the socio-economic system as a whole; the law lords' judgement against cheap transport fares in London, discussed in Chapter 4, is a case in point. In short, there is no evidence of some central conspiracy acting on behalf of the ruling class, pressing buttons and pulling levers to manipulate politicians, civil servants and judges in concert.

Just as the official mythology – the idea of the independence and impartiality of the judiciary – is challenged in this book, so too is a different kind of mythology suggesting that there is a direct and uncluttered channel between the law and the perpetuation of ruling class interests. As the experience from the North of Ireland shows, for instance, both these theories are found wanting.[21] We need to examine the specific roles of the courts, the police and of government, since these different state agencies have their own political interests to pursue. And unless we are clear about this, we shall be in a weak position to identify the political remedies necessary to defend the rights of citizens.

Nor should it be suggested that the law can act in a consistently repressive way in a society like Britain's. Indeed, precisely because it is an inherently political instrument, the law can be responsive to reform and pressure. The legal system does not need to give any real ground when it acts prudently in response to public pressure – even to the extent of bending the rules as, for example, occurred when the official solicitor appeared out of nowhere to release the trade unionists known as the 'Pentonville 5'. Their incarceration under the unpopular Tory Industrial Relations Act in 1972 brought Britain to the brink of a general strike that would severely have damaged the interests of business and finance.

· LOCAL GOVERNMENT ·

However, the law has consistently been called upon to assist the ruling class in times of social and economic unrest. One of the areas which illustrates both this point and the argument that the state is a highly complex animal, is local government – itself increasingly on the frontline during the 1970s and the 1980s, as national governments have sought to clamp down on public spending. Here we find a series of trials for which there can be no description other than 'political'. The role of the judiciary in this will be described in more detail in Chapter 4, using the example of the clash over public transport fares between the courts and the Labour Greater London Council.

But although the law was increasingly used to restrict local government autonomy under the Conservative government in the early 1980s, the conflict between the centre and the locality has been an ever-present feature of the history of local government. Moreover, the reorganization of local authorities in the early 1970s represented a fresh drive towards centralization, with a clear political motivation that should be acknowledged in order to make sense of the recent role of the law. As Dearlove shows, 'the essential object of reorganization has been to make local government more functional for dominant interests, by restructuring it so as to facilitate their direct control of its expenditure and interventions'.[22] That is to say, the overriding purpose of the reforms effected by the 1972 Act was to bind local authorities – and particularly Labour-controlled ones – more closely to the national state and dominant class interests, cutting the scale and expenditure of local government and directing it towards supporting the private sector.

The major fiscal crisis facing the British state in the 1970s required the intervention of the law, for there was a clear conflict to be resolved between the policies of democratically elected local councillors and central government. Although Mrs Thatcher's government took new *political* powers directly to control local authority expenditure, these had to be supplemented by additional *legal* powers.

But a more traditional quasi-legal device re-surfaced in the use of the district auditor. A somewhat mysterious civil servant with the ability to determine whether elected local councillors have exceeded limitations on their ability to spend, the district auditor is not accountable to anyone, the criteria for his decisions are effectively secret, and his role has been described as 'tyrannical'.[23] In theory the district auditor is a watchdog against financial irregularity, mismanagement, or the possibility of local authorities defaulting on their obligations to provide services by going bankrupt. In practice, district auditors have manipulated their legal status to thwart policies deemed by the state to be objectionable. Invariably the targets have been Labour-controlled councils: their policies have either been shelved under threat of councillors being surcharged, or surcharges and the accompanying disqualification from office have actually been imposed.

The classic case involved the East London borough of Poplar, which in 1919 refused to implement a central government edict to reduce benefit payable to unemployed people already on the verge of starvation. George Lansbury and other Labour councillors were jailed for their decision. Later, in 1921, pressure from local ratepayers provoked the district auditor into surcharging the councillors for their policy of equal pay for women and their refusal to reduce the wages of council employees at a time of falling prices. As has been pointed out, 'the District Auditor was challenging the right of councillors to exercise a power actually conferred upon them by Parliament . . . [under] . . . Section 62 of the Metropolis Management Act of 1855 . . . The Auditor was thus attempting to stop the council doing something which by law it was specifically entitled to do.'[24]

When the Poplar case eventually went to the House of Lords on appeal in April 1925, the judges adopted a practice for which they have become historically renowned. By interpreting the law in a particular way, they reversed an earlier judgement and 'revealed' that the district auditor had indeed been behaving fully within his powers. One of the law lords in question, Lord Sumner, went so far as to state: 'I can find nothing in the Acts which authorizes them [the elected members of local authorities] to be guided by their personal opinions on political, economic or social questions in administering the funds which they derive from levying rates.' Generously, however, he conceded that they were still able to decide questions of 'policy', by which the noble lord meant 'such matters as the necessity for a urinal and the choice of its position, provided no public or private nuisance is created'.[25] Clearly, if that statement were to have been applied literally, local government would have come to a standstill.

Another celebrated case occurred more recently, in 1972, when Clay Cross councillors refused to increase council rents by £1 as stipulated by the 1972 Conservative government's Housing Finance Act. After the intervention of the district auditor, they were surcharged and disqualified from holding office for five years. Lord Denning delivered a ringing judgement rejecting their appeal, accusing them of breaking their electoral promise to fulfil their duties as councillors. This was an extraordinary accusation, since the local Labour Party had specifically campaigned in the election on a policy of low rents – and had received overwhelming voter endorsement, winning all the council seats.[26]

Roy Shaw, leader of the London Borough of Camden, commented on his council's experience of increasing intervention by the district auditor:

There is clear evidence that the district audit services are interfering in matters which are no concern of theirs. They are commenting not on particular decisions but on general levels of expenditure. If an individual decision is properly reached and there is no criticism of that, it is no business of the district auditor to comment on the general level of rates, or whether general levels of expenditure are right or wrong.[27]

This scrutiny of higher-spending councils contrasted with the district auditor's response to Conservative-controlled Epping Council early in 1982. It launched a special low-start mortgage scheme to help council tenants buy their houses, and let purchasers off paying interest on half the purchase price for between five and ten years. This was estimated to benefit each purchaser by £4,700 – which amounted to a total of £800,000 of ratepayers' money illegally spent by the council. Pointing this out, however, the district auditor said he was 'satisfied that the council's failure to observe . . . [the law] . . . was an oversight', and no further action was taken.[28]

By the early 1980s, the threat of being surcharged was now something that potential Labour council candidates had to face up to well before they considered putting themselves forward for selection, let alone when they were in power. Labour councillors on the G.L.C., for example, were constantly confronted by officials waving lawyers' briefs at them after their election in May 1981. Thus, for example, an election pledge to reduce school meal charges by 10p (or 28.5 per cent) was not implemented because it was decreed illegal on counsel's advice. The only comfort the Labour members could draw from this episode was that something like it had happened before. In 1912 the district auditor had ruled that the old London County Council (the G.L.C.'s predecessor) could not continue supplying such items of food as fruit, cod-liver oil and malt extract to poor children, because he decided these did not constitute 'food' within the terms of the Education (Provision of Meals) Act!

In February 1982 Lord Denning's Appeal Court unanimously endorsed the move by Michael Heseltine, Secretary of State for the Environment, to take over homes owned by Norwich City Council to speed up their sale to tenants. The Labour-controlled council had appealed against this move, but in rejecting it Lord Denning remarked: 'Local government is such an important part of the constitution that to my mind the courts should see that the power of the government is not overused.'[29] Perhaps the judiciary were becoming a little sensitive to the politically controversial position to which they were being exposed by constant recourse to the courts to settle political conflicts over local authority independence. In March 1982 a Divisional Court judge, Mr Justice McNeill, expressed resentment at the courts having become an arena for councillors of one party to score points off another. Rejecting a move by Conservative councillors on Kensington and Chelsea Council to challenge the Labour G.L.C.'s rate precept, he complained of 'issues for the hustings and not for the court', and 'party superficialities dressed up as points of law'. He added: 'The proper remedy on such issues is the ballot box, not the court.'[30] Whether such a sympathetic judgement would have greeted the G.L.C. had a different judge been sitting is another matter (as it happened, his son was a Labour councillor elsewhere in London).

But judicial concern at their exposure to charges of political bias was evident in another important case. In the spring of 1982 thirty-one Camden councillors were taken to court by the district auditor. They were accused of acting too 'generously' by voting to pay their manual workers a minimum of £60 a week just before a lower national settlement was reached in the 'dirty jobs' strike of 1979. The Labour council took the view that the position of their low-paid workers needed improving anyway. But they were also concerned at the dislocation of crucial local services caused by the strike. The council faced a situation where meals-on-wheels and home helps had come to a halt, 500 elderly people were at risk, dozens of bodies were awaiting burial and over 1,000 tons of refuse were piled on emergency dumps. So they wanted a quick settlement. They argued this before the Divisional Court which, to the surprise of many, upheld them. On 29 April 1982, the court dismissed the arguments of the district auditor, with Lord Justice Ormrod ruling: 'The question for this court is not whether Camden made a bad bargain or were precipitate . . . These are matters for the electorate at the next election. The question for the court is whether the evidence establishes that no reasonable local authority could have made such a settlement on those terms.' The answer was that it did not and the settlement was therefore within the law.

Welcome though this judgement was, however, the specific reasons for it given by the judges were no less political. They accepted as reasonable that the pay rise was not in fact as far above the norm as the district auditor had claimed (begging the question as to what is 'reasonable'). They also argued that Camden had not acted in a 'political' way in pursuit of 'socialistic philosophy', like Poplar, but rather in response to industrial action which threatened community services. Their interpretation of the law was thus every bit as ingenious as the contrasting interpretations from their colleagues which had earlier gone against local government autonomy. It merely responded to the growing political opposition to those earlier judgements, reflecting perhaps some element of prudence. Welcoming the decision, though only 'on balance', *The Times* conceded the next day that 'it would be wrong for the reasonable exercise of discretion which is central to local government to be progressively hemmed in by palisades of case law'. Meanwhile the political battle being fought out between the judges and Labour local councils remained unresolved.

· POLITICAL DISCRETION ·

For the problem here goes beyond the particular political preferences of judges. It is rather that their powers are extremely vague, not to say elastic. And this brings us back to the heart of the matter. For the whole of the British state, including the legal system, is shrouded in uncertainty, mystery and secretiveness. This is in itself a source of political power, protecting those in positions of authority, enabling judges and others to exercise political bias because it is difficult to pin down exactly what are the precise boundaries of their influence. E. P. Thompson graphically describes this:

If a private citizen tries to peer into the state today, it seems like nothing so much as a huge aquarium, filled with inky water and flourishing weeds. The weeds are the Official Secrets Acts, and the water is dark with 'confidential matter'.

He continues with a separate, though related, point:

It is simpler to act as if (some small pieces apart – the Monarchy, the House of Lords) we have no constitution whatsoever. What then becomes legitimate is whatever authority can get away with. Since governments and ministers are in the public eye, execution can more easily be carried out by surreptitious means. It is all done today by senior civil servants and the like, and by a new set of instruments – discretionary powers, enabling acts, guidelines, circular instructions, in camera decisions, orders in the law vacation. [31]

In other words, the legal system gives considerable scope for *discretion*, for the ability of public servants, from judges through to district auditors and down to police officers, to act and interpret the law as *they see fit*. Clearly there are limits on their freedom. But they are not as closely drawn as we are led to believe. And once you allow for discretion, you allow for political factors to be the determining ones in the way that discretion is exercised. To put it another way, choices are made all the time in enforcement and interpretation of the law. So it is not a *technical* instrument, but a *political* one.

For example, the emergence of a growing layer of administrative law over welfare matters, supplementing the traditional structure of the criminal law and its courts, tends to provide a legal cover for the reality of wide discretionary power exercised by various public officials. The allocation of housing and social benefits is basically dependent upon administrative discretion and is ultimately a political matter; yet it is now surrounded by a legal infrastructure with its own experts, tribunals, rules and precedents.

As a result, the distinction between 'pure' law and politics is increasingly blurred. A good example was the bureaucratic change in wording on the regulations governing abortion. In March 1981 the Department of Health and Social Security issued a new form to be filled in by the operating doctor within seven days of an abortion. Until this new form, one of the options open to the doctor was to give as reasons for an abortion 'non-medical grounds', as specified by the 1967 Abortion Act. The Act permitted account to be taken of a woman's 'actual or reasonably forseeable environment' in assessing any mental or physical risk she might run in continuing the pregnancy. But the new form removed these 'social' grounds, specifying only 'main medical conditions'. It amounted to a back-door method of changing the law: there was no public consultation and no prior parliamentary debate.

Two surgeons, including Professor Peter Huntingford, were referred by the D.H.S.S. to the Director of Public Prosecutions for failing to fill in the forms correctly. Professor Huntingford said he had put 'none' in the section requiring gynaecologists to detail the 'main medical condition'. However, the D.P.P. recommended early in 1982 that no proceedings should be instituted against him, leaving the whole matter desperately vulnerable to legal nuance and administrative discretion.

This incident highlighted another problem with the conventional wisdom on British law. One of its main virtues is supposedly its *certainty*. Yet again and again the operation of the law is found to be far from certain. It depends on the decisions of human beings – on the choices of men (rarely of women) – and is therefore prey to human fallibility or prejudice. And this in turn means that the mechanism of justice can be rather a lottery. For example, C. H. Rolph describes how human fallibility can play a part in the outcome of a trial:

... the greatest enemy of justice in the courts is drowsiness; or, not to put too fine a point upon it, downright slumber. In the afternoon it is sometimes impossible to keep awake, not merely in the jury box but on the judicial bench – many times I have seen judges and magistrates fast asleep during a trial, and more than once there have been appeals to the Court of Appeal on the grounds that the trial judge was asleep. (I don't remember that any of these has succeeded.) Sometimes the sleepers manage to perfect a private technique in concealing their condition; one well-known woman magistrate in London could not merely sleep sitting bolt upright but always woke up at precisely three-fifteen to make some loud observation she hoped was relevant (which it surprisingly often was). Once when she did this in a Juvenile Court she woke up at a moment when a young detective constable was in the witness box. She looked at him over her spectacles. 'You look a very big boy for fourteen?' she said. [32]

Acknowledging the scope for the unpredictability of human behaviour in the operation of the law helps to strip it of its aura, thereby confirming that the rule of law is not an abstraction. Though circumscribed by procedure, by precedent and by statute, it remains open to human interpretation and discretion.

Law cannot be 'above' politics any more than it can be above 'society'. To that extent, all trials are political in that they reflect a wider political structure. But, as one political scientist has pointed out:

In a sense, *all* trials are political. Since courts are government agencies and judges are part of 'the system', all judicial decisions can be considered political. Judges, who are usually lawyers, are politicians too, and every judicial decision, whether in contract or divorce, has the heavy hand of government upon it. Still, to call a case involving a traffic accident a political trial would rob that phrase of its usual meaning. [33]

He goes on to say that calling all cases political trials 'tends to muddle the play and befuddle the audience', noting that 'the perception of a direct threat to established political power is a major difference between political trials and other trials'.[34]

'Political trials' are thus predominantly those in which defendants have advocated social change, though the charges are the same as those which might be preferred against others without political motives. And it is in examining such political trials that the appearance of impartiality which the administration of justice affects becomes transparent. When the state is using judicial means against opponents of the status quo, the legal proceedings are usually part of a wider campaign mounted by other parts of the state, including carefully controlled leaks to an overwhelmingly conservative media.

In these instances the response by the defendants and those who support them has increasingly been to accept that the charges and the trial are simply part of a political campaign. Assertions of the innocence of the defendants from public platforms, leafleting and pamphleteering, even protests in Parliament, customarily accompany political trials now. Despite the denials of Alan King-Hamilton and other judges, both prosecution and defence in political trials know that it is a political struggle which is being fought out in a courtroom.

While those who seek social change frequently are accused of breaking only the laws they oppose, some of these laws are themselves described as 'political' – such as the Official Secrets Acts, the Incitement to Disaffection Act, or public order and conspiracy laws. That this happens in some political trials is more an additional indication of their political nature than an essential attribute. In many – probably most – political trials, the charges are those which might just as easily be brought against 'ordinary' defendants. The essence of a political trial is the use of the police and judicial apparatus against those who threaten the social and political status quo. It is therefore impossible to understand such political trials except in the context of this wider apparatus of justice which succeeding chapters describe.

POLITICAL POLICING

Britain's police *are* political, in that policing is a political activity in any
society . . . Both as individuals and as an occupational group, the police
have wide influence over the way life in society is conducted . . . They
cannot go on protesting ignorance when the nature and extent of their
political influence is now the subject of general debate.

(Irene Wilson, staff tutor at the Police Staff College,
Bramshill, quoted in David Watts Pope and Norman L. Weiner (eds.),
Modern Policing (Croom Helm, 1981), p. 127)

As the political character of the law comes increasingly to be recognized,
so too does the political character of the police. Since they are the ground
level agents of a system of law which is heavily dependent on *discretion*,
their role is critical. And it is through examining the exercise of discretion
by the police that we can begin to establish more clearly the foundations
of political trials in Britain.

For discretion lies at the heart of the British legal system. In a society
where the majority do not break the law and are not perceived as a threat
to the status quo, it is possible – indeed, normal – for many illegal acts to
be ignored by the authorities. Some 85 per cent of criminal offences are
not even reported to the police and, while 1 in 36 people in Britain are
arrested each year, most people break the law regularly, even if only by
speeding. Numerous Acts of Parliament give the police and various
authorities the power to prosecute, but the decision in each individual
case is not made by Parliament or the courts. It is made by a police
officer or another person legally empowered to do so. The authority of
the British police officer is uniquely derived. It does not come about
because he is an employee of the police, but from his own personal oath
of allegiance to the state – the Crown. Each police officer swears to
uphold the law as an individual and is responsible for his or her actions.
If he acts wrongly he can in theory be charged – as a civil servant often
cannot.

The office of constable is often claimed to be a continuation of the ancient parish constables and watchmen. But the creation of the Metropolitan Police in 1829, by the then Home Secretary Robert Peel, marked a sharp break from tradition, and it is more useful to view the contemporary police in the light of this.[1] The setting up of a police force was an attempt to resolve the problems faced by the British state during the Industrial Revolution. Problems of opposition from the growing urban proletariat – and, related to this, rising crime in the cities – could not be solved by the continual use of the Army, whose excesses served to provide radicals with further criticisms of the status quo.

An unarmed body of men was created which was intended to, and to a great extent did, win the confidence of the public. Unlike the continental police tradition, where the public are not expected to come into regular contact with the police, except as lawbreakers, the British police spend a great deal of time patrolling alone. They are not expected to enforce the law as a small elite capable of implementing the wishes of the government by superior force of arms and doing so, if necessary, against the wishes of large numbers of people. Instead, the police are supposed to act in accordance with the wishes of the majority, against a minority of lawbreakers. All of which implies a flexible, pragmatic role, as Lord Scarman pointed out in 1981 in his report on the Brixton riots when he stressed that the police need to maintain public respect.[2]

It follows that there are circumstances in which a police officer may decide not to make an arrest, even though a clear offence has been committed, not because he is physically unable to do so but because he judges that the matter would be made worse by an arrest. For example, a senior Metropolitan Police officer, Chief Superintendent Adams, told the Scarman inquiry into the demonstration against the National Front in Red Lion Square, London, on 15 June 1974: 'If you have a march escorted by police you are always going to get, if it is a march against one government policy or another party, provocative remarks shouted or voiced. If we were to take action over every provocative remark we would not have any policemen left at the end of the march.'[3]

Not only the need for good relations with the public dictates that some crime must go unpunished. There is recognition by the police themselves that 'working to rule' would disrupt the functioning of the police force and the criminal justice system. In the words of one uniformed police constable: 'If we worked to rule, the British people would not know what had hit them. My idea of a work-to-rule is this. You walk along the street and see people committing any number of offences. Instead of giving them a good telling off and letting them go their way, you report them rigorously as per book. You have cells full of the drunks you turn a blind eye to on Saturday night because all they're going to do is foul the cells up, stink the place out so it has to be disinfected. The courts would be jammed with people down for every motoring offence under the sun. Relations with the public would go [raspberry noise].'[4]

What one former chief constable termed 'discrimination and responsiveness to the public mood' requires particular flexibility over the enforcement of obsolete, controversial or unpopular laws, with the legitimacy of the law on drinking and driving depending entirely upon how 'reasonable' the police are in enforcing.[5]

Thus *discretion* is one of the cornerstones of British policing, as Lord Scarman acknowledged in his 1981 Report:

... the exercise of discretion lies at the heart of the policing function. It is undeniable that there is only one law for all: and it is right that this should be so. But it is equally well-recognized that successful policing depends on the exercise of discretion in how the law is enforced. The good reputation of the police as a force depends upon the skill and judgement which policemen display in the particular circumstances of the cases and incidents which they are required to handle. Discretion is the art of suiting action to particular circumstances. It is the policeman's daily task.[6]

But Lord Scarman fails to point out that such discretion is not amenable to legal or constitutional scrutiny. For example, there was no admission by the Red Lion Square police officer quoted above that the discretion he identified in choosing to arrest some demonstrators and not others has been extended by the police into a principle of disorder policing. The police have now trained 'snatch squads' directed at those they regard as 'ringleaders'. So a *tactic* permitted because of the scope for discretion is elevated into a *practice* without prior democratic sanction.

Interesting light is thrown on the political significance of this by the use of police in the industrial emergency of the 1978–9 'Winter of Discontent'. When ambulancemen went on strike in early 1979 the police maintained emergency services in areas where no cover was being provided. But although this was in fact the first occasion where police had performed strikers' work rather than simply maintained order, it was done entirely at the discretion of the relevant Chief Officer of Police. Section 15 of the Police Act 1964 enables the chief officer to provide what are termed 'special police services' at his own discretion. However, as one legal expert points out, 'It is unclear whether these "services" are limited to activities of a kind within the range of police duties.'[7] As she also argues, in performing the work of strikers police cannot possibly be neutral. On the contrary, in 1979 their role was politically significant. Yet it was dealt with at the time on a purely administrative and expedient basis. In short, right across the board of discretionary policing, the force can act with real political autonomy.

· POLITICAL ATTITUDES ·

The first political trial takes place on the street. A police officer sees a person or group of people and the way they are behaving and decides on a number of things: whether or not they are known to him, either personally, or because they are known to the police; whether the way in which they are behaving amounts to a crime, or seems likely to lead to one. He or she must then decide what to do: whether to intervene even if the behaviour does not actually amount to a crime, and if he or she thinks that it does, whether or not to make an arrest or to do something else. What happens will depend on the circumstances, and the police officer will be guided by training, by instructions from his superiors, both general and specific, and by his own social and political attitudes, influenced as they are bound to be by the attitudes of colleagues in the force.

It would not be surprising to find that the social and political attitudes of individual policemen, drawn to a service intended to uphold law, order and the status quo, were themselves conservative. Robert Reiner in his study of police attitudes, *The Blue Coated Worker*, stresses that views are not formed in the abstract, but in relation to the specific situations in which individuals, including police officers, find themselves. Reiner was not allowed by the Home Office to question police officers directly about their political views, in terms of support for specific parties. But their social attitudes were overwhelmingly conservative. In reply to an open-ended question about the problems facing the police, of Reiner's respondents, a sample of police officers from a large provincial English city,

Eighty-one per cent felt that things were getting worse, and this was often expressed in most emphatic, even apocalyptic, terms. Virtually none of the rest saw things as getting better . . . The healthy society was depicted as one based on a considerable measure of discipline and acceptance of authority. Various tendencies were undermining these preconditions of the good society. We were heading towards disorder, which not only made the police task vastly more difficult, but also threatened to undermine 'civilization' itself. [8]

While many socialists and civil libertarians might share this pessimistic assessment of a society fragmenting as capitalism declines, the remedies which the police offered were overwhelmingly right-wing:

The only solution to this was a reassertion of control by authorities in society which would involve giving the police more powers and backing them up by severer sanctions against offenders. This was more problematic by the degree to which authorities were under the sway of ideologies which aggravated the situation. Politicians were seen as, at worst, influenced by radical beliefs which made them anti-police, or at best as effete and naïve, albeit well intentioned men who were out of touch with the real condition of society. The courts failed to deal with offenders effectively because of the influence of 'do-gooders' with theories about the sources of crime which were over-indulgent to criminals. The shackles of 'due-process' law frustrated the honest efforts of the police. The policeman had to contend not only with his obvious enemy, the offender, but also with the other members of the system of authority, whose ignorance of the real life of the society outside the charmed circles they inhabited led them to emasculate police action. [9]

Such views were those held in 1973 and 1974, when Reiner carried out his surveys. Criticisms of politicians apart, they are virtually identical with sentiments voiced from Conservative Party platforms during the 1979 General Election campaign. The continual articulation of these and similar conservative views by the police officers' representative body, the Police Federation, and by senior police officers from the Commissioners of the Metropolitan Police, Sir Robert Mark and Sir David McNee, downwards, has almost certainly served to reinforce them since that time. It is hardly surprising therefore that police officers have increasingly come to see their role as a political one, filling in a vacuum left by 'weak' politicians.

· STEREOTYPING ·

The black community has been most vocal in its criticisms of the way police discretion affects police treatment of the people of this country. Reiner did not identify the city in which he conducted his 1973–4 survey. But it was in fact Bristol. In view of the violent resistance to police action in that city which erupted in 1980 and, on a lesser scale, in 1982, the following comment made to him takes on an alarming significance; 'S.P.', the immigrant area referred to by the police officer quoted below, is St Paul's, where those angry events took place.

S.P. (the immigrant area) is a terrible place, shocking. Whatever job you go to, you know you're going to have trouble. You always look out for a knife or a fist or something. It's a drunken Irish labourer or someone. They've got all sorts over there. West Indians, Indians. They're always fighting, at one another's necks. You've got Hungarians, Poles. And your local layabouts that mix in with them. Prostitutes. It's a right den of iniquity . . . We're here to be run around by the public today, rather·than a police *force* that could command people. [10]

Police use of discretion is thus highly distorted by their expectation that some sections of the community are 'anti-police', and the same actions take on a different significance depending on who is the actor and what are the circumstances. It might be thought that this sort of bias would be weeded out by training; but the available evidence seems to suggest that conservative attitudes are encouraged rather than reduced by this. In fact, the police belief that there are identifiable 'criminal types' forms an integral part of the shaping of police behaviour. In a booklet published in 1978, and used in the training of police officers, a serving Metropolitan Police chief inspector, J. F. Robinson, wrote: 'Because the criminal picks up the characteristics of his particular branch of crime, a criminal who is associated with cannabis will be recognizable as such, whereas a criminal who is associated with heroin will look different.' [11]

Another serving officer, the Deputy Assistant Commissioner of the Metropolitan Police, David Powis, reveals how important a basis for the exercise of police discretion is their stereotyping of individuals. He lists the following indices of suspicion:

young people generally, but especially if in cars (and even more so if in groups in cars);
people in badly-maintained cars, especially if they have a tatty, dog-eared licence;
people of untidy, dirty appearance – especially with dirty shoes (even manual workers, if honest, he says, are clean and tidy);
people who are unduly nervous, confident or servile in police presence (unless they are doctors, who are 'naturally' confident);

people whose appearance is anomalous in some way – e.g. their clothes are not as smart as their car;

people in unusual family circumstances;

political radicals and intellectuals, especially if they 'spout extremist babble', and in possession of a 'your rights' card (as supplied by the N.C.C.L.). These people are also particularly likely to make unjust accusations against the police.[12]

I well recall the role played by police stereotyping, spilling over into malice, when I was wrongfully arrested in 1975 on a charge of robbing a bank near my home. Although it became a celebrated example of a mistaken identity case (see my *Mistaken Identity*, Quartet, 1976), it might never have got off the ground had it not been for the fact that, as one of the investigating officers told me during the initial hours of my detention: 'You have caused a lot of trouble with your activities and protests and we are going to make sure this charge sticks on you.' It was obvious as they questioned me that being in their eyes a political 'troublemaker' was tantamount to being a 'criminal', and they were simply not prepared to examine the situation impartially. Had they done so it would have been crystal clear that the case against me was as bizarre and far-fetched as the jury and the general public accepted when it later came to court. Given the political bias involved from the outset of the prosecution process, it would be quite reasonable to regard my subsequent trial as a 'political' one – even though the charge of bank theft was nothing if not strictly 'criminal'.

Such encouragement of the perception of stereotypes, based largely on the existing prejudices of serving police officers, inevitably leads to the perpetuation of discriminatory attitudes. A young, working-class or black person would be regarded as more likely to be involved in the commission of street crime than an older, more affluent, white person, and their behaviour scrutinized more closely as a result. But this is not thought of as much of a problem by the police: 'I don't care if a police officer is racially prejudiced, as long as it doesn't affect the way he does his job,' an officer involved in training at the Hendon, London Police Training, School told Labour M.P. Arthur Latham during an official visit.[13]

The effects of this are documented. According to the Institute of Race Relations, black people coming into contact with the police, even on a voluntary basis as witnesses or victims of crime, are likely to find that:

(a) black people are often given no reason for being stopped and searched;

(b) unnecessary violence is used to arrest blacks;
(c) juveniles are particularly subject to harassment;
(d) the assertion of one's rights would seem to lead to arrest;
(e) witnesses or bystanders may also be at risk;
(f) repeated arrest is used to persecute individuals;
(g) black homes and premises are entered at will.[14]

· POLICE LEADERSHIP ·

The discretion of the police officer is of course guided by the instructions which he receives from his superiors. These take the form of a volume of 'General Orders' issued by chief constables and the Metropolitan and City Commissioners. These orders are secret; the only part which has been 'leaked' to the public was the section of the Metropolitan Orders referring to surveillance of political activity by the Special Branch.

But these are the orders which embody the chief constable's instructions on the way in which his force should be run. Although police authorities are nominally responsible for the police forces over which they are set, the law, in the shape of the 1964 Police Act, makes it clear that the 'direction and control' of the force is the sole responsibility of its chief officer: so chief officers begin with *statutorily based* powers of discretion which are very wide indeed. They are in sole control of all matters from strategic planning to the allocation of resources and the day-to-day activities of their force. Furthermore, the responsibility of chief officers for law enforcement has been repeatedly defined by the courts as one of accountability only to the law (as *they* interpret it) and not to their police authority or the Home Secretary. Thus while the distinction between 'operational' and 'non-operational' matters is not made in the 1964 Act, in practice the police are fully entitled to claim legal backing for their jealously guarded right to determine operational policing. In the face of this there are real limitations on the extent to which police authorities are able to influence the policing policy of their area.

While a great deal of police activity is in effect centrally directed by the Home Office, the chief officers of the 52 police forces of the United Kingdom retain a great deal of autonomy over policy matters. For example, although Sir David McNee, as Metropolitan Police Commissioner, regularly defended the use of the 'Sus' law (before it was repealed in 1981) to arrest people whom police officers think may be about to commit a crime, other police forces, such as the West Midlands, found it possible to manage without it, using more modern stop and search powers to achieve the same ends. The way in which the limited resources of each police force are used is up to the chief officer. Yet to commit extra officers to immigrant areas or to warn officers to be particularly on the alert for certain crimes is a decision which stems from political attitudes and has political consequences.

Indeed, it is necessary to underline the fact that police chiefs have more discretion than possibly any other section of the system of law administration and law enforcement. Even though judges, for example, have considerable discretionary powers, they at least are constrained by formal rules and procedures. The police are much less so, since their work in practice is heavily dependent on their personal feelings and political attitudes.

The political views of chief officers must therefore play a large role in the way in which their forces are run. Possibly the most notorious of Britain's breed of political policemen is Greater Manchester's chief constable, James Anderton. In June 1979, for example, he suggested that young offenders 'should be arrested, convicted, and placed in penal work camps where through hard labour and unrelenting discipline they should be made to sweat as they have never sweated before and remain until their violence has been vanquished by penitent humiliation and unqualified repentance'.[15] Mr Anderton has also suggested that the major police task of the future will not be basic crime but political dissent.

He typifies the more *activist* role assumed by today's police chiefs: one where they see their duty as being to go out, to mould public opinion and to put public pressure on politicians. In terms which can only be described as 'political', he explains: 'I'm looking for a mandate from the people out there. If I can win public support for my ideas, it will make my job easier.'[16] Whereas a traditional chief constable would have lobbied discreetly through conventional political channels to secure changes (including changes in public opinion prompted by politicians), Mr Anderton and his colleagues are openly short-circuiting this. Their political message goes directly to the people, actively seeking to mobilize political support.

In 1982 Mr Anderton was at the centre of a heated controversy which threw considerable light on modern political policing. In an outspoken statement he attacked what he saw as a sinister effort by police authorities to control chief constables. His target was self-evidently Labour-controlled police authorities, and the background to his outburst was the increasingly critical stance taken by more radical Labour members of such authorities. Two incidents in particular had led to tension with his own Greater Manchester authority: his support for the management of Laurence Scott and Electromotors in a police operation which enabled them to take out plant from the factory by helicopter, and what the authority regarded as his insensitive handling of the summer riots in Moss Side. On 19 March, the authority censured him for his handling of the Laurence Scott dispute and rejected a motion of confidence in him.

In his public statement issued a few days before this, he had said:

A quiet revolution is taking place around us and the prize is political power to be wielded against the most cherished elements of the establishment, including the monarchy. It is as much the duty of the police to guard against this as it is to guard against crime. I sense and see in our midst an enemy more dangerous, insidious, and ruthless than any faced since the Second World War.

I firmly believe there is a long-term political strategy to destroy the proven structure of the police and turn them into an exclusive agency of a one-party state. I am also convinced that the British police service is now a prime target for subversion and demoralization.

I recommend that police committees should be totally abolished, and replaced by non-political police boards, the members of which would surely be much more objective.

The time-honoured practice where police committees put aside internal political rivalry and invariably sought a consensus of opinion in the wider public interest has disappeared completely in some areas.[17]

He also spoke of a 'blatant use' of the police authority machinery to serve distinctively narrow political ends. But what he really meant by this was 'narrow political ends' different from his own. Looking back to the halcyon days when chief constables were not challenged in this unseemly way, Mr Anderton's call for 'non-political' police boards really meant ones that would not challenge the consensus determined by him and his fellow police chiefs.

His speech was denounced as 'inflammatory nonsense' by the Labour shadow Home Secretary, Roy Hattersley, and he was rebuked by a fellow chief constable, Devon and Cornwall's John Alderson. But that did not stop his tone becoming even more shrill. The next day he told *The Times*:

There are serious attempts now being made to undermine the independence, the impartiality and the authority of the British police service. I honestly believe we are now witnessing the domination of the police service as a necessary prerequisite of the creation in this country of a society based on Marxist Communist principles. The current concern over policing being expressed by certain political factions has got precious little to do with better community participation in police affairs, or the improvement of democracy – rather it is the first conscious step manifesting itself towards the political control of the police, without which the dream of a totalitarian, one-party state in this country cannot be realized.[18]

He went on to admit that no chief constable today could avoid being involved in politics, insisting that these were 'politics with a small p'.

Nevertheless it seems hardly coincidental that the sentiments he was expressing were exactly those which Labour Party election candidates found directed at them by Conservative opponents at the time. The whole thrust of his attack amounted to a thinly veiled smear on the Left of the Labour Party under the guise of an upright defence of police integrity. Mr Anderton's 'small p politics' were the reactionary ones of a status quo increasingly subject to stress by economic recession.

While his views are more robustly expressed than those of his fellow chief officers, the direction in which senior police officers would like to see society move and, specifically, the changes they want in legislation and police powers, are overwhelmingly authoritarian. But to understand the present-day politics of the police, it is necessary to make a short examination of their history.

· POLITICAL ROOTS ·

The creation of the Metropolitan Police in 1829 was an explicit intervention by central government in a locally organized system of policing which had degenerated in the face of the social dislocation of the Industrial Revolution. The 1829 Act is still the major statute governing the existence and activity of the Metropolitan Police; it was passed by a Parliament just three years before the first Reform Act of 1832 – the first faltering step on a road to parliamentary democracy which took nearly a century. 'The Bill provided for a complete separation of police administration in London from its centuries-old link with the magistracy and the parishes.'[19]

Peel declared that he intended, as the police became publicly accepted, to extend the area of operation of the Metropolitan Police beyond the districts around London to which the 1829 Act applied. But the hope of acceptance of a national police force was overtaken by the reform of local government in the form of the 1835 Municipal Corporations Act, which brought the rising middle class to power in many towns and cities. The new corporations were to appoint watch committees from among their members, and to take control of law and order from the multiplicity of watchmen, parish constables and private watches.

The results were patchy to say the least. The state took matters in hand in 1856, when some towns failed to create forces and none was able to provide a police force of the size or organization of the new Metropolitan force. In the counties, local government was still in the hands of the justices of the peace; there was to be no democratic local government until the 1880s. The 1839 County Police Bill provided for the magistracy to set up county police forces under their control.

The pressure for rationalization of the police came from the challenge of Chartism. But disagreement between central and local government about the best way of combatting the threat of democratic agitation meant that the central state had once again to intervene. The 1856 County and Borough Police Act made the creation of police forces compulsory, and set up an Inspectorate of Constabulary in the Home Office to supervise standards and operation of police forces.

The origins of the police thus lie in the state's resistance to the struggle for democracy, and the division between local elites represented in watch committees, and the central state in the form of the Home Office, represented the maximum amount of centralization which the local elites would tolerate. There is no doubt that the alternative of a single national police force would have been preferable to the Home Office had it been politically acceptable.

The central control instituted in 1856 gradually began to take effect, shaping the organization and direction of policing. Central government's share of police financing increased from one quarter to one half in 1874 when, as the Home Office put it, 'The very considerable addition about to be made to the contribution from Imperial funds in aid of local police expenditure affords government an opportunity of which it may be well to take advantage, of endeavouring to secure for the Secretary of State a greater amount of supervision and control over the police forces of Great Britain than he now possesses.'[20]

Police forces in boroughs were commanded by head constables, and chief constables commanded the county forces. Their relationships with their respective watch committees became even slenderer. The Acts of

Parliament creating the borough and county watch committees did not lay down what sort of orders the committees could give their police chiefs, but there are few recorded examples of serious conflict. The situation evolved gradually to the point where, in 1962, a Royal Commission on the Police reported 'that a situation was gradually coming about in the counties where, unregulated and probably unrecognized by Parliament, Chief Constables, able and intelligent men, growing in professional stature and public esteem, were assuming authorities and powers which their predecessors would formerly have sought from justices'.[21]

Chief constables of borough forces might have had to pay closer attention to their watch committees, but the late nineteenth and early twentieth centuries saw the emergence of a group of senior police officers who, under the guidance and direction of the Home Office, shaped the interests and the direction of policing and the allocation of police resources. In the shaping of the police force, the role of the chief constables was vital. The emergence of a group of professional policemen with common concerns guided by the central state not only shaped the police force, it also shaped the definition of crime.

Watch committees and police authorities at first preferred ex-Army officers and former Metropolitan detectives. But after 1920, the police were established with a strong enough tradition for a Royal Commission to recommend that candidates for the post of chief constable should be drawn from within the police. The history of the police is the story of the slow eclipse of the power of the local political elites and the establishment of a unified, national force – albeit divided into regional components – influenced by national government and commanded by a group of men with deeply political concerns.

The definition of police concerns was political from the outset. In the early years of the force, the social role of the police in restoring order to a society undergoing rapid change was directed principally at the working class:

Because the 'criminal class' came predominantly from the proletariat, detection was only possible through a first-hand knowledge of the matrix of working-class life. To apprehend these criminals meant that the communities had to be patrolled, bringing a real intrusion into everyday life ... Policemen were attacked or set upon by outraged groups attempting to frustrate an arrest, and many policemen resigned because of this. But by patrolling working-class communities the police also came to act on behalf of individual working-class people.[22]

Public acceptance of the police came in this way, for a large number of working-class people were given protection they had not previously enjoyed. Nevertheless,

> The violence against individual members of the working class used by the state . . . in this process was without precedent in British history. How can the cumulative effects of thousands of arrests, trials, fines and imprisonments over many decades be adequately described? It was, in short, a process of attrition. The class was also under ideological attack. The hard-working and law-abiding were praised while the poor and unemployed were attacked.[23]

By the time universal suffrage had finally been won in 1928, the police had, by this process of attrition, gained the acceptance of most ordinary people and were adept at isolating those who resisted. Many of the laws which were at the disposal of the force either dated from times when ordinary people had no say at all in running the country, or were revised and updated by a bureaucracy totally removed from the control of ordinary people. Crime – as defined by the state during the period when the police were consolidated as the principal counter-crime institution – was a working-class activity.

'Crime was one challenge to the police; the other was public order – the forgotten industrial and political disputes that made up the news headlines long ago,' records Critchley.[24] The disputes may have been forgotten, but Critchley, in documenting the history of the police from a conservative standpoint, deliberately seeks to obscure their importance. The content of those disputes which occupied the police in their formative years were the struggles for basic rights and dignity at work and for the right to vote and organize politically. The pressure on the police is illustrated by the fact that, during one period, between 1872 and 1908, the army had to be called in 'to quell political and trade union demonstrations on no less than twenty-four occasions. Not until the 1920s could the police alone maintain public order in Britain.'[25]

Despite the fact that the police have always sought to present themselves as standing between conflicting social forces or 'extremists', this is not now, and never has been, the case. There is no recorded example of the police helping a movement for progressive social change. Critchley gives away the falsity of the 'man in the middle' image so carefully fostered by the police and their supporters when, referring to the nineteenth century, he writes: 'They stood (as they sometimes do today) at the storm centre of the conflict between two natural antagonistic and mutually uncomprehending systems of virtue – radicalism and authority.'[26] Possibly it is the British love of compromise which leads the police and their supporters to seek to portray themselves as *par excellence* the referees of society's disputes, the machinery by which compromise between extremes can be reached. But 'authority' in the late nineteenth century, before the advent of democracy, was little more than the power of businessmen and landowners. It is an insult to democrats to suggest that a balance should have been struck between this 'authority' and 'radicalism'. But the creation of a police force was a response to the inability to maintain the existing law and order by the existing means. So the police did not then, and do not now, stand between radicalism and authority; they are part of that authority.

· POLITICAL SURVEILLANCE ·

In defining the direction of policing, the absorption by the police of the functions of political surveillance previously carried out by other state departments was of great importance. In 1883, in response to a series of bombings carried out by the Irish nationalists, the Fenians, twelve Metropolitan Police detectives were formed into the 'Special Irish Branch'. The significance of this was twofold. Twelve men may not seem many, but the Criminal Investigation Department of Scotland Yard was at the time both small and known to be stretched in the detection of 'ordinary' crime. Only a few years previously, in 1877, three of the four chief inspectors of the C.I.D.'s predecessor, the Detective Department, had been convicted of corruption. The C.I.D. itself was thus only five years old, having been effectively re-founded in 1878 in the wake of the corruption scandal.

Twelve of its 250 men were diverted to tracking down the Irish bombers. But bombs were not their only target. In 1886, the Special Irish Branch arrested five Irish Nationalist M.P.s when they arrived to attend the House of Commons. The charge was 'sedition' – in this case the advocacy through Parliament, by elected members, of Irish independence. The five were handed over to the Royal Irish Constabulary and served terms of imprisonment. Thus the Special Branch started as it was to go on. Established at a time of crisis, in apparent response to violent activity which threatened the normal life of the community, it directed its efforts at eliminating the threat, not simply by trying to find the 'criminals' but by amassing information on, and ultimately curtailing the political activities of, those who supported political aims similar to the supposed perpetrators of the violence.[27]

The Special Branch exhibited a further characteristic common to laws and institutions created to meet what is alleged to be a new threat to the state. Formed in emergencies, such new institutions outlive the circumstances of their creation. The activities of plain-clothes spies and provocateurs, working for the Home Office among radicals, trade unionists and Chartists, had produced by the middle of the nineteenth century a widespread distrust of political policing, a feeling held also by those not particularly in favour of social change. Thirty years later, the Irish emergency allowed the appearance of a political police – indeed the Special Irish Branch was to have been named the 'Political Branch', but this was thought too controversial.

When the threat of Fenian bombings subsided, the Special Irish Branch, which had found for itself more than enough tasks to perform, simply dropped the 'Irish' and is still with us today. Trade union activists and political groups of the Left are its main targets. The technique of surveillance, harassment and arrest of supporters of causes which are perceived as a threat to the status quo serves several purposes. It warns off the general public by identifying protest movements as 'criminal'; it dissuades the less enthusiastic from continuing or increasing their support; and it provides the Special Branch with more information on the political activities of those arrested or associated with them.

The Special Branch expanded from the Irish to other foreigners, and from them to British anarchists and socialists. The First World War provided a welcome fillip for their activities. Sir Basil Thomson, head of Scotland Yard's C.I.D. and thus in charge of the Special Branch, was a close confidant of the Prime Minister, Lloyd George, and provided him with regular information from spies: 'Pacifism, anti-conscription and Revolution are now inseparably mixed,' wrote Thomson. 'The same individuals took part in all three movements. The real object of most of these people, though it may have been subconscious, appeared to be the ruin of their own country.'[28] The practice of attending political meetings was commonplace and Special Branch officers were often discovered in embarrassing circumstances – hidden under the stage of a theatre where the Communist Party was holding one of its conferences, for example – and this often led to questions in Parliament. Such questions went unanswered – successive Home Secretaries have claimed that such matters must continue to be considered 'operational', and thus solely the prerogative of the Commissioner; a clearer illustration of politically motivated police discretion it would be difficult to conceive.

In the thirties, the National Unemployed Workers' Movement was heavily infiltrated by the Special Branch. The movements and activities of leading members were kept under constant surveillance, and when the newly founded National Council for Civil Liberties protested, the Special Branch was able to provide the Metropolitan Commissioner with material for a report to the Home Secretary of the day, describing Ronald Kidd, N.C.C.L.'s founding Secretary General, as 'well-known for his antipathy against the police and their methods'.[29]

After the Second World War, the Special Branch paid special attention to Communists who they thought were fomenting industrial unrest; to the mass movement for unilateral nuclear disarmament in the 1960s; and to the growth first of student protest and then of increasing union militancy in the 1970s. The activities of the Special Branch as the overtly political section of the police play an important part in events which lead up to political trials.

In gathering information on political activities, the Special Branch monitors openly published material in the newspapers and bulletins of political and trade union groups; indeed, most of its information comes from open sources. But there remains the ability to tap telephones and to open mail. In 1980, *New Statesman* writer Duncan Campbell revealed the existence of a massive phone-tapping centre operated by the Post Office – now British Telecommunications – on behalf of the police, the Special Branch, the security services (MI5), and H.M. Customs and Excise.[30] Only ten per cent of the estimated capacity of 1,000 lines, it was alleged, were used by the police in the detection of 'ordinary' crime – the vast bulk were used for political and customs investigations. How many people are affected by this? Partly in response to the revelations in the *New Statesman*, the Conservative government issued a White Paper, *The Interception of Communications in Great Britain*.[31] This said that in 1979, 411 warrants for tapping telephones and 52 for opening mail were signed in England and Wales; the figures for Scotland were 56 and none. But, as the White Paper admitted, one warrant would cover *all* the communications of an organization, such as a political party or campaigning organization. All individuals in contact with that organization thus have their activities revealed to the police. Labour's former Home Secretary, Merlyn Rees, admitted that while he was Home Secretary 2–3,000 telephone lines were tapped, and that 250–400 warrants were in force at any one time.

Legally, the position is that a Secretary of State must sign a warrant authorizing the interception. But the relationship between civil servants and ministers means that those seeking to intercept have the initiative. Even senior Secretaries of State are unlikely to have sources of information independent of the Special Branch and MI5. This is in part out of choice; a Labour Secretary of State could choose for himself to ask fellow Labour supporters and trade unionists whether the allegations made by the security services stemmed from genuine apprehension or political bias. So far, none has chosen to do so – as far as can be ascertained from their own evidence. Official files on such matters, of course, are subject to remaining secret for 100 years rather than the customary 30.

So when the Special Branch allege that the conditions for the issue of a warrant have been met in any particular case – that is, that the offence is a serious one; if the person under suspicion has no criminal record, that other methods of investigation have failed; and that a conviction must be thought likely to result from the interception – then they are unlikely to be resisted by civil servants, nor in turn by the Home Secretary. For strictly political investigations, the criteria laid down for MI5, which no doubt apply to the Special Branch, also require that other methods of investigation shall have failed and that there must be major subversive or espionage activity likely to injure the national interest. For their part, the security services, commonly known as MI5, are even more closely insulated from democratic scrutiny than the Special Branch. As a leading legal textbook points out, MI5 'is neither established by statute nor is it recognized by common law. It has no defined status. There is no mention of its existence in the Official Secrets Acts and it has never been the subject of a full debate in Parliament.'[32]

It is on the concept of 'subversion' that the security services and the Special Branch rely to justify their surveillance of those involved in political activity which is neither directed towards violent ends nor for the benefit or at the instigation of a foreign government. Introducing a Parliamentary debate on the activities of the Special Branch in 1978, the Labour M.P. for Central Edinburgh, Robin Cook, drew attention to the widening of the definition of 'subversion' which had taken place.[33] Subversion, he pointed out, had shifted from being something strictly illegal, 'capable of clear, precise and narrow interpretation based on statute and common law'. Under the revised Home Office definition, first offered in 1975 and repeated by Merlyn Rees as Home Secretary in

1978, subversion was 'in no way restricted to illegal activities', and was 'an invitation to the police forces who police this concept of subversion to stick their nose into any form of political and industrial activity'. Mr Cook went on to say that it was quite improper for Mr Rees, 'by executive decision', to create a new class of quasi-crimes such as subversion, 'which would not in themselves lead to conviction in any court in the land, but render the suspect liable to police surveillance and being placed on police records. That is the road to the thought police and the closed society.'

The constitutional doctrine of ministerial responsibility meant that Mr Cook had to talk of the new definition of subversion as the responsibility of the minister concerned. But Mr Rees was not even Home Secretary when the new definition was first enunciated by a junior minister, Lord Harris, three years before. Its origins are more likely to lie in Home Office departmental policy than in any decision by an elected politician. The Special Branch, for example, had been operating on the wider definition of subversion for many years. John Alderson, Chief Constable of Devon and Cornwall, confirmed this in an interview in April 1982:

I've found, by making checks on the activities of my officers, that there is this innate tendency to want to record almost anything, however remotely connected it may be with activity which might in the loosest sense be regarded as subversive. This word 'subversion' needs to be defined . . . Some people would regard subversion as anything which is designed to change society.[34]

The public revision of the definition gives an insight into the overwhelmingly pragmatic nature of the British state. Administrative practices by the police and civil servants come first. They remain largely hidden, until forced into the open by diligent pressure like that exerted by Robin Cook over the Special Branch. Where the convenience of the police and administrators runs counter to existing laws, then they exert pressure, usually covert, to change the law.

The political autonomy of the Special Branch is also illustrated by the evidence that mail has been intercepted and telephones have been tapped for years on a far wider basis than is officially acknowledged. Most tapping takes place on the basis of an informal request by local police or Special Branch officers to head postmasters or telephone managers. The Home Office circular 'Consolidated instructions to the police (1969)'[35] allows officials to assist the police on request in cases where they are investigating any indictable offence, where an investigation has been authorized by the Director of Public Prosecutions, or where the police are acting on behalf of a government department in relation to a document 'missing' from such a department. In such circumstances, the Post Office or British Telecommunications officials can 'help' the police without the existence of a warrant. It would be an unusual P.O. or B.T. official who, faced with police assurances that the matter concerned terrorism or subversion, would refuse such 'help'. And the police could hardly be expected to explain that their real interest was merely the contacts of, say, a local official of the Labour Party or the Anti-Nazi League.

During the Grunwick dispute, the offices of the strike committee were tapped.[36] The work was done at the local telephone exchange, and although a sympathetic engineer disconnected the tap, it was replaced. British Telecommunications maintains a special team of engineers to install tapping devices; they are said to be very unpopular with colleagues, and the story is told of a member of the special team, working at a local telephone exchange, who found himself surrounded by the exchange's own employees who regaled him with a chorus of 'Land of Hope and Glory'.[37]

In February 1982 the *Guardian* reported the existence of secret guidelines on the police use of surveillance devices which mean that members of the public can be covertly taped or filmed without the need for a Home Office warrant. The 'bugging code' allows a chief constable or his deputy to authorize the covert use of listening, transmitting and recording equipment, with visual equipment requiring the authority of a chief police inspector. This revelation followed an incident at Talysarn, North Wales, where the police had planted a radio device in a public call box, apparently to monitor conversations by Welsh Nationalists. It was discovered by a local resident in January 1982, but was snatched out of his hand by two men driving a white estate car; later the vehicle's registration number was 'not available' from the national police computer on a 'Home Office directive'.[38]

The gathering of information about political activity occupies a fair amount of time of other police officers outside the Special Branch. In this, as in many other aspects of police organization, the discretion of the constable is guided very closely. The 'General Orders' for the Metropolitan Police, which tell each and every officer in considerable detail how he will do his job, are of course secret. But part of them was leaked to the London magazine *Time Out* in 1974. The published extracts

confirmed that the Branch is informed by local police stations of all
political meetings known to the local police, and says that a report should
be forwarded to the Branch if its own officers do not attend. Only
political activities concerned with parliamentary and local council matters
appeared to be excluded. But in view of the events which have followed
the candidacy of openly racist organizations in such elections, this limita-
tion has in all probability been removed since. After a person has been
arrested on a demonstration, the Branch must be informed:

> Whenever persons are arrested for minor offences connected with political
> activities including minor breaches of the peace and cases of slogan-daubing,
> etc., inquiry is always to be made of Special Branch to ascertain whether anything
> is known about the accused before the case is dealt with at Court. This inquiry
> will be in addition to any other searches made. Results of all cases are to be
> submitted to the Special Branch.[39]

Commenting on this in his book *The Political Police in Britain*, Tony
Bunyan writes:

> Firstly, it appears that in addition to the usual check through the Criminal
> Records Office to see if there are any previous convictions, the Branch records
> are also to be checked. These records include information on people previously
> unconvicted of any offences as well as much criminal data. All this of course
> begs a question. Are the records of the Branch supplied to the prosecution
> solicitors at the trial? And if they are is this not likely to increase the prosecution's
> chances of getting a conviction, particularly when used by the prosecution in
> examining defence witnesses? Secondly, it appears that *every* incident however
> minor resulting from political activity is recorded.[40]

For some time, the Metropolitan Police have issued a form to local
stations on which the names and addresses of people organizing political
meetings are to be recorded for onward transmission to the Special
Branch. Scotland Yard described the form as being 'like an accident
report'. It asks for names and addresses of speakers, chairman, subject,
organizers and information about future meetings. The form is 'to simplify reporting on small public meetings and demonstrations', and is now
'routine procedure' in London.[41] The existence of this form came to
light when the organizers of a women's meeting on Ireland were shown a
copy. Uniformed police questioned women leaving the meeting in
Greenwich, in April 1979, and told the organizers that 'people above
them' had requested the information. The police also claimed that they
should have been notified in advance of the meeting – there is of course

no such requirement. Although the police have been pressing with some success for prior notification of demonstrations, not even they have demanded that indoor political meetings should be cleared with them first. That, no doubt, will come in the future. Nevertheless, the police asked for, and were naturally refused, details of future meetings planned by the organizers. The Greenwich Commander's office said: 'We try to check on every political meeting in the area.'[42]

Similar efforts to extract information on political activities seem a frequent occurrence, and the police often claim that they have powers to demand information which they do not legally possess. An anti-cuts rally in Wandsworth, London, in March 1979, for example, was attended by police officers who claimed that they had a right to know the speakers' names under the Public Order Act – which is not true.

The files built up in this way are the basis of political policing. In reacting to an incident, the individual police officer is guided by what he learns about the people involved from his local station, or from the records of the force, or from national records usually held on computers. In deciding how to police a meeting, picket or demonstration, the police are influenced by the information they hold about the organizations and people concerned. The additional dangers of computerization are mentioned below. But it is important to remember that, in principle, computers are simply a method of storing and referring to large quantities of information.

What is this information which is so important to the police?

As far as can be ascertained, about one fifth of the population has a police record, much of which consists of inaccuracies, gossip and hearsay. Anyone approaching the police for help stands a good chance of ending up on a file for life.

In 1979 a detective working in the Brixton area in London lost several files, which were found and given to the left-wing press. The files provided 'a unique and chilling view of police methods of getting information', wrote Duncan Campbell in the *New Statesman*.[43] Information filed on one woman included the fact that her car was seen outside a house being watched by the Serious Crimes Squad, though she had in fact no connection with the person who lived there – her car had been borrowed by someone else. Also noted on file was the fact that she had stood bail for someone, had moved house, and that her sons had been in contact with the police. One of the sons' files starts with a minor conviction for which he was fined £1, and records several brushes with the police, none of which resulted in arrest or conviction. One incident, in which he claimed to have been roughly treated by plainclothes police officers, seemed a classic sequel to his status as 'known to the police'. Once a person has been in contact with the police, they are naturally likely to regard his or her activities with greater interest than those of someone they do not know.

The other son of the woman in question has a number of convictions for theft and burglary. But his file also contains the names of others, without convictions, who are now on police files because they are his 'associates', in police terminology. This amounts to no more than that they were with him on an occasion when he was stopped by the police. Another man, who lodged with the woman in the files, has a file which claims that he is the father of a certain child – which he is not.

The routine vetting and influencing of juries by the authorities and the police is referred to at great length later. In the most notorious recent case, that of the four anarchists, referred to as the 'Persons Unknown' case, a check was made in police records on 93 potential jurors. Leaving aside for the moment their role in the particular case, and taking them as a fairly representative group of citizens, it should cause surprise that 19 of the 93 – about one fifth – were 'known to the police'. Yet only eight had convictions. The information was printed by the *Guardian*, after it had been handed over by the prosecution to the defence in the case on the orders of the trial judge. The records which were handed over, like the files lost by the Brixton detective, contained the results of the activities of local, divisionally based officers of the Metropolitan Police. Such files are maintained by a collator or local intelligence officer and they are quite separate from Special Branch files. Typical 'information' on the files of the potential jurors was that one person's address was 'believed to be a squat'; that one had made a complaint against the police; five had been victims of crime which they had reported to the police, and had won themselves a place in the files as a result; four were associates of criminals, which might mean no more than that they were extremely casual acquaintances; and of the eight who had criminal convictions, four were 'spent' under the Rehabilitation of Offenders Act, and therefore in theory not relevant for any public purpose.[44]

As far as can be ascertained, the 'criminal intelligence' files at Scotland Yard are no more accurate than such local files. They contain the results of such local work, plus material from other police forces. These files too are apparently full of hearsay and opinion. It should be borne in mind that the decision to create and maintain 'criminal intelligence' files was a conscious extension of the techniques of intelligence gathering perfected by the Special Branch on political activities to 'non-political' criminals and suspected people. At the Old Bailey in 1979, a former Metropolitan Police officer, Chief Superintendent John Groves, was accused of corruption and Official Secrets Act offences. The prosecution alleged that he passed on to the property dealer the late Sir Eric Miller files which he had obtained from C11, the Scotland Yard Intelligence section. The file on Sir Eric Miller himself dealt with his alleged relationship with M.P.s Sir Harold Wilson, Reginald Maudling and Bob Mellish. According to the file, Sir Eric had provided helicopters for the Labour Party's 1974 election campaign and laid on hospitality for Labour leaders at a London hotel owned by his company, Peachey Properties. The file contained the comment that Sir Eric was 'a very unpleasant person who would screw anyone for a buck'. The existence and content of the file was not contested by the defence, though Mr Groves was later acquitted. Its accuracy may have been indicated by the fact that Bob Mellish M.P. employed a barrister to record before the court that allegations in the file that he, Mr Mellish, had attended Sir Eric's daughter's wedding and knew him closely, were not true. He had never met him.[45]

Yet the police continue to compile such records and to trade them between different forces. In 1979, the London *Evening Standard* reported that:

Police in F Division, which has Chelsea, Fulham and Queen's Park Rangers in its area, are compiling a special black-list detailing the wild ones. The index will identify all known trouble makers, those who go away to matches, the way they travel, and other details. Before each away match police will pass information to other London districts and provincial forces. Eventually they hope to open files on problem fans in the other 19 clubs in the Second Division.[46]

Effectively, there is no right of privacy for someone who the police have decided is 'of interest' to them, and no one has any right to correct mis-statements and biased comments on records which form the basis of local policing. Yet such files are a major influence on the way in which police officers use their discretion in dealing with members of the public. They effectively institutionalize the basis for bias and political prejudice in the way police officers exercise their discretion.

When such files are computerized, their dangers are multiplied. They become more permanent and the ability to cross-refer between them is increased. Computers, it has been well said, operate on the Ri-Ro principle – Rubbish in, Rubbish out. Thames Valley Police is one of the forces which has been first to computerize its criminal intelligence files; the computer, based at the force headquarters at Kidlington, Oxfordshire, has been operational since the end of 1976. An early note of caution was sounded about the activities of the police collators by *Police Review* in May 1972:

Since 1966, the Service has collators in most Police divisions and they have amassed information which in both quantity and quality would surprise most people on their books. Police intelligence is both forward looking, anticipating who is going to commit what, when and where – and because it is so purposeful, it is also frequently libellous . . . Much of the information stored in collators' files is tinged with the calculated guesswork of the officer who has provided it. Much of the information is personal detail [and] it may seem a trespass on the freedom of the individual . . . There is a serious danger that once a person is in the system, he may remain there – and there is no way of opting out until the Police consider he has reached the age of criminal ineffectiveness.

These worries were borne out in 1978 by remarks of two F.B.I. visitors whom the Home Office had invited to inspect the Thames Valley system. During the inspection, the visitors were shown the record of one man about whom it had been noted that he 'fancies little boys'. This record was based on a conversation overheard by a policeman's wife in a local village shop, after which it had been entered by the policeman in an 'occurrence book'. *Police Review* commented that the allegation was untrue, and that although much information going on to such a computer was 'valid intelligence', 'a substantial proportion is unchecked bunkum'.[47]

In an extensive survey of the impact of computerization on police behaviour, Duncan Campbell drew attention to the dangers posed. In particular, he criticized the refusal of the police and the Home Office to contemplate any overseeing of police computer applications by an outside body, and he showed how the rapid development of computerized policing has occurred without prior parliamentary debate, let alone approval.[48] This is a classic example of the police extending their powers and their role on purely operational grounds according to priorities which *they* determine. Despite their obvious interference with individual rights and privacy, new techniques and sophisticated technology employed by the police have been introduced on a basis which allows for no public debate or democratic accountability. Specifically as far as political surveillance

is concerned, 'the police and the security services operate almost entirely
outside the law. This is not to say that they *break* the law: quite simply,
there are hardly any laws for them to break. The methods of surveillance
. . . are effectively uncontrolled by the law. The terms within which the
political police operate are a matter of executive, not Parliamentary or
judicial, decision-making.'[49] So here we have the foundations, not just
for police discretion, but for their *political discretion* and hence one of
the springboards for political trials.

· A POLITICAL FORCE ·

As well as policing politics, the police have their own political views
which these days they lose no opportunity to bring to the attention of the
public. The striking feature of the last ten years is the *organized* way in
which police views have been articulated and pushed before the public
by representative organizations of the police themselves. Two bodies in
particular have 'gone public' with a police view of affairs: the Association of Chief Police Officers (A.C.P.O.) and the Police Federation.

A.C.P.O. was formed in July 1948. Membership is open to all police
officers in England and Wales above the rank of chief superintendent.
There is a separate Association of Chief Officers in Scotland; Royal
Ulster Constabulary senior officers have been eligible for A.C.P.O.
membership since 1970. Since 1968, A.C.P.O. has had a paid secretariat,
based at Scotland Yard, with a full-time general secretary who has always
had experience in a senior police position. It has both a national and
a regional structure.

A.C.P.O. is the forum where views of individual senior officers can
be refined and presented to authority. The status of senior police officers
has been much enhanced by the reforms in policing which followed the
1962 Royal Commission on the Police. Rejecting the idea of a single
national police force, the Royal Commission recommended instead that
the 117 police forces then existing in England and Wales should be
reduced by amalgamations. Under the 1964 Police Act, which gave statutory effect to many of the Royal Commission's recommendations, the
then Labour Home Secretary, Roy Jenkins, set about creating what were
in effect regional forces. A particular goal was the creation of single
forces for each of the large conurbations. But when the Labour government decided to go ahead with the reorganization of local government in

1966, by appointing a Royal Commission on Local Government, the Home Office decided that police reorganization could not wait. On 18 May 1966, Home Secretary Jenkins announced that he would use his powers under the 1964 Police Act to compel amalgamations which would further reduce the number of police forces from 117 to 49.

The effect was drastically to increase the separation of the police from public control and to strengthen the hands of the chief constables. Traditionally, police forces – particularly those serving medium-sized urban areas with the old status of 'county borough' – had been distinctly local forces. Their small size – many under 300 men – meant that they were more likely to be known to the community which they served. The chief constable was well known through his social contacts with a local elite of businessmen, solicitors and councillors. The watch committee of councillors and magistrates was drawn from the local community. All this was swept away.

The arguments used by the Royal Commission and accepted by the Home Office for the reduction in the number of police forces were similar to arguments which later led to the reorganization of local government and the National Health Service into larger units. From the point of view of central government, and of the police, they were pressing. The needs of modernization, of the introduction of new technology and new methods of policing, and the need to make the police service attractive in career terms, were basically the same as those used to justify the reorganization of other local functions. In all these cases, the then existing arrangements were not satisfactory. But the chosen solution represented a giant step along the road to centralization which the Home Office had espoused virtually since the creation of the modern police force.

In the case of the police, there were two additional effects. The new police authorities came into being before the reorganization of local government, with members drawn from several local councils. Many people who had served on the old watch committees retired and their experience, which allowed them to criticize police activity from an informed standpoint, was lost. The new authorities' members owed allegiance to different local councils, and there was an inevitable tendency for the police authority to be a less cohesive and less effective body in scrutinizing the police than the old watch committees. Not for the first time, cohesive police arrangements were made before democratic institutions had been created to oversee them.

The new local authorities did not come into being until the reorganization of the early 1970s, and soon attracted criticism for being too large and remote from the people whom they serve. Political decision-making is now effectively in the hands of senior officers and a handful of councillors, with 'backbench' councillors having little influence. When the new county authorities were created, there was a further reorganization of police forces so that they coincided with the new counties and metropolitan counties. This saw a further reduction in the number of forces in England and Wales to 42.

By the time democratic institutions which covered their areas were elected and functioning, the police forces were already cohesive units. The net effect was to strengthen the position of the police and particularly the chief constables, and to weaken outside local influence. As a consequence the importance of A.C.P.O. increased. Fewer chief officers meant that it was easier for them to achieve a consensus; the greater area, numbers of officers, and financial strength of the new police forces enhanced the status of A.C.P.O.'s members.

But before examining the role of A.C.P.O., it is worth noting that the momentum for centralization of the police by no means subsided with the reorganizations of the 1970s. Two major factors have been behind this: the desire for an 'efficient', 'streamlined' force; and the centralizing imperatives of modern technology. And underpinning both has been a growing consensus among police chiefs that their political role in a time of political crisis, industrial strife and street disorder would be strengthened by a more unified police service.

In 1979 a joint conference of the Association of Chief Police Officers, the Association of Metropolitan Authorities and the Association of County Councils discussed the question of a 'fully national police force' along the lines of most countries of the European Common Market. The Chief Constable of Lancashire, Albert Lougharne, explained the rationale behind a national force: 'In days of widespread unrest and protest, of terrorist violence and the like, when every force may be under great pressure, a lack of cohesive command could become a serious, perhaps crippling weakness.'[50] Another chief constable, Greater Manchester's James Anderton, in 1981 called for a streamlining of the police service down from 42 into 10 regional forces.[51] The present structure, he complained, was like a 'torpid bureaucracy'. He reserved particular contempt for administration and liaison procedures with government departments which he felt were 'much too unwieldy and stolid and belong to a bygone age'. While he was concerned with freeing police chiefs from paperwork and enabling them to 'concentrate on chasing criminals', Mr Anderton was equally anxious to free the police from government control which he saw as inhibiting police activity. In other words, with almost all of his fellow chief constables, he sees in more centralized policing the opportunity for the police force to become even more independent, organizationally and politically. This was underlined by the explicit rejection by A.C.P.O. of the 'liberal' policing ideas of Devon and Cornwall's chief constable, John Alderson.

·THE ASSOCIATION OF CHIEF POLICE OFFICERS (A.C.P.O.)·

A.C.P.O., unlike the Police Federation, is not a statutory body. It is consulted on all aspects of policing and serves as a channel of all communications, not only for a police view to the Home Office but as a means of standardizing practices and facilitating the reduction of conflict in the application of Home Office directives to chief constables. It has a more powerful voice in the direction of policing than the Police Federation, yet it has the freedom of manoeuvre of a voluntary organization. A.C.P.O. made it clear in its evidence to a Home Office committee of inquiry in 1979, under Judge Edmund Davies, that it would not want any change in this.

'The Association of Chief Police Officers is the one authoritative body the government will go to to seek views,' commented one senior police officer.[52] Others are less convinced of A.C.P.O.'s importance; its views 'can be and are safely disregarded if they do not accord with ministerial wishes, since legislators can rely on the traditional silence of the police', Sir Robert Mark has written.[53] Mark himself spearheaded the breaking up of the tradition of silence. But he reflects the probability that senior civil servants' views (or 'ministerial views' as Mark calls them), which can be channelled through A.C.P.O., have rather more influence on the police than do senior police officers on the Home Office, using the same channel. But it is clearly intended that the general public should have no idea how the balance lies in policing between the police and the Home Office, and no access to or ways of influencing this process either in general or over particular details.

It was probably the influence and example of Sir Robert Mark that led A.C.P.O. to forsake the 'traditional silence of the police' and to add to its backstairs lobbying the full-scale public relations exercise which it has mounted since the mid-1970s. Initially A.C.P.O.'s opinion-making function was largely confined to confidential exchanges of opinion with the Home Office and the submission of evidence to government in-quiries. They told the 1962 Royal Commission on the Police that a police officer 'must be part of the community, and yet at the same time it is always dangerous to become on too intimate terms with people to whom at any time he may have to apply the due process of law'. It is perhaps not surprising that since the reorganization of the police, A.C.P.O. has taken the opportunity to enlist public opinion in its campaigns for the continued autonomy of the police force from democratic or community control.

It was the industrial relations proposals of the 1974–9 Labour govern-ment which enraged A.C.P.O. into public action. Proposals were before Parliament to regularize picketing by giving pickets the legal right to stop vehicles in order to communicate with their occupants. A.C.P.O. chose a dramatic and publicity-worthy method to 'consult' its member-ship, sending telex messages to each chief constable. Their predictable response – outright opposition – attracted the desired publicity. The proposals vanished and the determination of the police to exercise the maximum freedom of action was rewarded.

Since then, A.C.P.O. has taken each opportunity – the submission of evidence to official inquiries, the meeting of its annual conference, the sitting of parliamentary committees – to publicize its views. In June 1976 it used the telex stunt again to dramatize its opposition to the strengthening of the police complaints procedure by the introduction of an outside element; this time it was not successful. Efforts by the local authorities to make chief constables more accountable provoked strong opposition at the 1978 A.C.P.O. conference. In 1977, following the disturbances at Notting Hill and Lewisham, A.C.P.O. announced that 'the police can no longer prevent public disorder in the streets' and called for greater powers for the police by the passing of a new Public Order Act, giving the police the power to control marches and demonstrations, 'similar to police powers in Ulster'.[54] The 1979 conference called for police officers to be provided with extra protection such as body armour when policing demonstrations. All these matters, it should be noted, were politically sensitive and in no sense could A.C.P.O. claim to be 'above politics' in its public campaigns.

The 1979–80 Royal Commission on Criminal Procedure provided A.C.P.O. with another opportunity to demand greater police powers. Along with the Metropolitan Commissioner, Sir David McNee, A.C.P.O. called for general powers of search where the police suspected serious crime or danger to the public, including powers to set up road blocks and to fingerprint whole communities; powers to hold suspects for up to three days without charging them, with further three-day extensions if the police thought it necessary. The proposals as such were rejected by the Royal Commission.

The switch in tactics by A.C.P.O., following Sir Robert Mark's example of influencing the authorities by shaping public opinion, was almost certainly made with the approval of the Home Office. Sir Robert Mark's own career indicates the approval of the Home Office for his reforming zeal, and examples abound of political lobbies mounted with at least tacit approval from the Civil Service to support or oppose demands which they themselves approve or otherwise. Such collusion between the police and civil servants reached a pitch during Labour's period of office in the 1970s, when both exerted pressure on an elected government which in theory controlled them.

This is not, however, to deny the police the right to use pressure group tactics to express their views. The central problem is a different one: the belief that they are 'non-political', which in turn lends their views a spurious authority. Ironically, the decision by police chiefs to 'go public' has helped to push policing squarely on to the political agenda and has begun to destroy the mythology of a 'non-political' role which the force has traditionally claimed. Their political pressure campaigns have also enormously strengthened the case for bringing them under democratic control. So the underlying theme of this chapter is not that the police should be silenced, but instead that policing in its entirety is a political matter; and any lingering doubts on this should be dispelled by the recent activities of the Police Federation.

· THE POLICE FEDERATION ·

Like A.C.P.O., the Police Federation (which represents constables, sergeants and inspectors) has displayed two main concerns in its efforts to influence public opinion: it has shared with A.C.P.O. a demand for greater police powers and tougher treatment of suspects and criminals; but whereas A.C.P.O. has defended its own members' interests in opposing any greater outside interference in police activity, the Police Federation has stood up for its members on matters such as pay and protection on demonstrations.

'The Federation was a consciously fashioned government device to smash the independent police union which had developed during the First World War.'[55] As an official alternative to trade unions, the Police Federation was charged by law with representing the opinions of constables, sergeants and inspectors on matters concerning wages and conditions. Its fortunes, the support which it has received from ordinary police officers, and its effectiveness on their behalf, have varied a great deal over the years since its establishment in 1919. In the past fifteen years it has come into conflict with both Conservative and Labour governments (but mainly with the latter) over pay restraint policies and restrictions on government spending applied to the police. Clashes occurred in 1970, in 1975 and in 1977-8, being resolved on the third occasion by the creation of a committee of inquiry into police pay under Judge Edmund Davies. In 1971 and 1979, incoming Conservative governments were prepared to relax restrictions on police pay and expenditure imposed by their Labour predecessors and so to reduce confrontation.

In the Federation's view, greater powers and larger resources for the police have been the way in which the pay and conditions of its members could be best increased. 'In 1965 a document called "The Problem" was launched by the Federation at a press conference to support its pay claim. This was intended to show that "owing to manpower difficulties, the police forces of Great Britain are in grave danger of losing the fight against crime".'[56] The Federation saw the opportunity to make life easier for its members in two ways: higher pay for the police which would have the dual effect of attracting more recruits to ease the burden of each individual officer and of course raising the pay of officers already in service; and, second, greater powers coupled with tougher sentencing which they claimed would make the tasks of the police easier.

Home Secretary Roy Jenkins responded by including Federation representatives in three working parties set up in 1966 on police manpower, equipment and efficiency. But relations soured over pay, particularly after 1968. As Reiner argues:

The late 1960s and the 1970s show mounting police concern about what they perceived as a trend to lawlessness, disorder and increasing violence, manifest not only in rising rates of crime but also growing problems of crowd control arising out of political demonstrations, industrial militancy and the spread of terrorist tactics. Concern with these social issues pervades Federation meetings, documents and actions in the 1970s . . . Pay demands come to be seen as morally justified by the danger and difficulty, as well as crucial social importance, of police work.[57]

In a sense, therefore, pay became a vehicle for more overt political intervention, and the Police Federation emerged as one of the central institutions of the law-and-order lobby. In November 1975, in response to the general police dislike of the direction of penal and sentencing policies, the Federation launched a major law-and-order campaign, 'to harness', as they put it, 'the public's growing concern about the state of crime and public order in Britain into a programme for positive action'.[58] Members were urged to write to M.P.s opposing lenient sentencing and permissive legislation, and the Federation wrote to trade unions, the C.B.I. and political parties, nationally and locally, seeking talks to put its point of view. Twenty-five Labour M.P.s tabled a Commons motion regretting the campaign and the political activities of the police.

The impending General Election in 1979 galvanized the Federation into a large-scale effort to make law and order a key electoral issue. Federation chairman James Jardine asked political parties to state their solutions on the problem of law and order and, as the Federation put it, '. . . It is clear that [our] campaign involves criticism of the present Government's political and economic policy towards the police and the administration of justice.'[59] In other words the police were opposing the Labour Party.

As *State Research* pointed out:

But in seeking directly to mobilize the 'silent majority', the Federation is making a political intervention into the law-making and legal process. The danger is that the distinction between law-making (the job of parliament), law-interpreting and sentencing (the judiciary and the courts) and law-enforcement (the role of the police), will become blurred. Unless the Government rejects this type of political campaigning by the traditionally and theoretically neutral police in Britain, civil liberties in areas such as detention may be eroded simply because it would make the police job easier.[60]

The Police Federation took newspaper advertisements during the

General Election campaign, urging greater police powers and harsher sentencing as well as the return of the death penalty for the killing of police and prison officers and terrorist offences. Similar sentiments were voiced by the Conservative Party in its successful campaign, and the antagonism of the police towards Labour in office in the 1970s spilled over into outright hostility in the early 1980s as Labour Councils, notably the G.L.C., pressed Party policy for greater democratic control of the police.

An anti-Labour bias has increasingly surfaced in the public comments of police spokesmen. While James Anderton, for example, would doubtless deny this, the whole thrust of his public comments has been critical of the Labour Party. For his part, Sir Robert Mark made it clear that he saw the police as a bulwark against socialism:

The police are . . . very much on their own in attempting to preserve order in an increasingly turbulent society in which Socialist philosophy has changed from raising the standards of the poor and deprived to reducing the standards of the wealthy, the skilled and deserving to the lowest common denominator.[61]

Leaving aside his extraordinary misrepresentation of the purpose of socialism, it was clear that he was speaking for most of his colleagues. Their views, it should also be noted, have coincided not with any centre or consensus political position associated with, say, the left of the Tory Party. They are firmly on the Tory right. Just in case we hadn't guessed, the Police Federation chairman, James Jardine, said in 1982 that he was 'a great admirer' of Mrs Thatcher.[62]

Around that time the Federation was in the thick of another political campaign, concentrating on bringing back capital punishment. It spent £30,000 on newspaper adverts and as a spin-off obtained a great deal of news coverage. Shortly afterwards, on 10 March 1982, Scotland Yard broke with its previous practice and published a racial analysis of those responsible for street robberies. The Yard's analysis showed that 55 per cent of the victims of robbery and other violent thefts identified their attackers as black. (The Yard made no mention of the finding of a Home Office report the previous year that Asians are 50 times and other blacks 36 times more likely than whites to be the victims of mugging attacks.) Saturation media coverage of this single isolated fact for types of crime that formed a tiny percentage of the total whipped up public pressure on the Tory Home Secretary, William Whitelaw, seen by the media as a 'moderate'. As New Society put it: 'Scotland Yard, which is supposed to be accountable to the Home Office, is engaged in nothing less than a political campaign which might end in the removal of the Home Secretary.'[63]

The Police Federation was quick to capitalize on the controversy, seeing an opportunity to further its campaign against the recommendations of Lord Scarman's report into the summer riots the previous year. Scarman's criticism of 'fire-brigade' policing and his support for softer 'community policing' had not been accepted by the Federation. And, commenting on the release of Scotland Yard's crime figures, Mr Jardine blamed rising crime on the official reaction to the riots and in particular the Scarman report. Young people now thought they could commit crimes and get away with it: 'They are laughing at the law,' he said.[64]

The previous week, a former Labour Home Office minister, Alex Lyon, had accused senior police officers of 'fighting back'[65] against Lord Scarman, who had himself been involved in a public difference of opinion with Scotland Yard's Deputy Assistant Commissioner, Leslie Walker; Mr Walker had suggested that the Scarman report was making it harder to control street crime.[66] On behalf of the Police Federation, Mr Jardine followed this up with a ringing call on politicians to 'get your priorities right . . . A parliamentary democracy that does not maintain the rule of law will degenerate into a shambles in the span of a generation. We are giving this warning to the public that anarchy could be the order of the day before very long.'[67] In the same speech he criticized both demands for more consultation between police and public, and the abolition of the 'Sus' law. So far as the latter was concerned, a quick response followed from the beleaguered Home Secretary – Mr Whitelaw promising new powers to deal with street crime. Police pressure had succeeded. Indeed the Metropolitan Police had never really accepted the change in the law which had abolished 'Sus' as from 27 August 1981. On 15 February 1982 the High Court had been forced to make a ruling that the Met was acting illegally in continuing to bring 'Sus' prosecutions. Three months later, however, and amid growing public pressure from the police and the right of the Tory Party, the law lords ruled that the police did have the power to arrest without warrant for a host of minor street offences. Giving judgement on 26 May 1982 in the case of Susan Ann Wills, their Lordships interpreted Section 28 of the Town Police Clauses Act 1847 to immensely strengthen police powers of immediate arrest for suspected street offences. In so doing they did not exactly revive 'Sus', but they supported the use of police powers on the street which will doubtless have a similar effect to the old law.

· TYPES OF POLICING ·

The 1970s fashion for the police to enlist the assistance of the media in putting their demands for changes in the law has been taken up by individual senior police officers philosophizing on the role of the force. The public has been presented with an apparent debate between the 'consent' formula which, the police claim, allows 'preventive' policing, and 'reactive' policing, also called 'fire-brigade' policing, in which the police, using modern technology, simply respond to incidents. This latter form of policing, which it is generally alleged has replaced or is replacing the consent model, was attacked by the then Chief Constable of Devon and Cornwall, Mr John Alderson, as 'quasi-military'.[68] The powers which some police chiefs were asking for, he has also said, would turn the police into an 'occupying army'[69] or a 'third force'.[70]

Mr Alderson has put forward instead the concept of 'community policing'. This he sees as a refinement of preventive policing which he also calls 'pro-active' policing. 'Whereas preventive policing tends to put the system on the defensive, pro-active policing seeks to penetrate the community in a multitude of ways. It seeks to reinforce social discipline and mutual trust . . . it strives to activate all possible resources in support of the common good.' He has argued that the police are probably 'better placed than most other organizations for providing social leadership of this kind'.[71]

Successful pro-active policing, Alderson argues, involves the breaking down of barriers between police and other agencies such as social and probation services, an 'open and trusting' relationship with the media, and a high level of police involvement by appropriate officers in education from primary school to higher education.

A good example of the way in which Alderson has put his ideas into practice in Devon and Cornwall is an experiment in Whitton, a district of Exeter. The central role in this exercise lay with the Crime Prevention Support Unit. A research project was commissioned into the area and, armed with its findings, the unit enlisted the help of youth and community workers and the local Social Service Department to call several public meetings. Within a year, a community association had been formed which had the active support of the police. The end results were two-fold; the police gained close and informative links with the community, and the community gained the benefit of an active community association.

In superficial contrast to Mr Alderson, Greater Manchester Chief Constable James Anderton has emerged as the most notorious public advocate of the tough, coercive model of policing; indeed the two clashed publicly in speeches delivered within days of each other in March 1982. Mr Anderton has advocated the introduction of identity cards. He has spoken out against 'subversion', in which he apparently includes a great deal of legal left-wing political and trade union activity. In his 1978 annual report, Mr Anderton described the work of his Special Branch as the gathering of intelligence on both 'terrorist activities' and 'public order situations' – pickets, demonstrations and the like. He has publicly voiced his feeling that the police should seek to stifle left-wing political activity:

There are at work in the community today ... factions, political factions, whose designed end is to overthrow democracy as we know it. They are at work in the field of public order, in the industrial relations field, in politics in the truest sense. And I think that from a police point of view my task in the future, in the ten to fifteen years from now, the period during which I shall continue to serve, that the basic crime as such – theft, burglary, even violent crime – will not be the predominant police feature. What will be the matter of greatest concern to me will be the covert and ultimately overt attempts to overthrow democracy, to subvert the authority of the state, and in fact to involve themselves in acts of sedition designed to destroy our parliamentary system and the democratic government in this country.[72]

The different approaches of the two men naturally relate directly to the way in which they use their *discretion* as chief constables and point up the very broad nature of that discretion. A demonstration in Exeter against a South African touring rugby team in October 1979 passed off with little disturbance after Mr Alderson's police consulted extensively with the organizers. A National Front election meeting in Plymouth during the 1979 election campaign had to be called off by the organizers after Devon and Cornwall police decided that the Representation of the People Act required that the meeting be genuinely open to all members of the public. By the time National Front supporters and speakers arrived at the meeting, the hall was full of people opposed to the National Front;

the local Anti-Nazi League had organized this 'occupation', unhindered by the police. The organizers decided they did not want a real public meeting in those circumstances, and called it off after unsuccessfully appealing to the police to evict their opponents.

Mr Anderton in contrast deployed hundreds of men in order to enable the National Front to march through areas of Manchester where many black people lived and to prevent local residents from objecting to the demonstration. His interpretation of the issues involved was echoed by many other police chiefs during 1978–9 when mounting National Front activity was countered by the Anti-Nazi League. On a number of occasions – for example during the 1978 Ilford North by-election and in Brixton and Southall during the general election – N.F. meetings went ahead, guarded by thousands of police.

The point is that Mr Alderson approached the question in an entirely different way. He effectively sided with the anti-racists, whereas his colleagues from other areas protected the racists. His role gives the lie to the conventional view that the police in such circumstances are simply enforcing the law 'impartially', in the only way that is open to them: by allowing National Front meetings to go ahead. The fact is that there *are* alternatives: the Alderson option or the Anderton option. Persistently to adopt the latter course (as mostly occurs) means that the police are using their discretionary powers in a politically partisan way which undermines their proverbial claim to be anti-racist. Mr Alderson exercised his discretion in another unusual way in 1981 when he refused to evict demonstrators from the planned site of a nuclear power station in Cornwall – the implications of which are discussed in Chapter 11. Despite the qualification invariably made by sneering colleagues from other parts of Britain that Devon and Cornwall is a 'different kettle of fish' from tough inner city areas, the advantage of Mr Alderson's approach is that it involves far less, if any, violence. In the wake of the Brixton riots of 1981 and the Scarman report's endorsement of 'community policing', it is clear that at least some sections of authority have begun to come round to Mr Alderson's views.

But there are things in common between the two approaches and, as far as the public is concerned, what the two different approaches have in common is probably far more important.

Both, after all, are concerned overwhelmingly with social control. The 'hard' strategy of social control contains elements such as computerized surveillance, the Special Patrol Group and 'fire-brigade policing'. But there is a 'soft' strategy as well which seeks to co-opt dissent rather than to put it down, to involve the community without removing the causes for social grievances. In that sense the two approaches are opposite sides of the same coin of social control. Neither offers any 'solution' to the disturbances they seek to police: a genuine solution is excluded since it would involve a fundamental redistribution of power and resources to communities in need. It is imperative to note that (perfectly worthy and admirable) public participation schemes for greater community involvement in practice became mechanisms for co-opting the poor in general and blacks in particular, in the U.S.A. in the 1960s and in Britain during the 1970s.[73] While the Alderson approach is unquestionably preferable to the Anderton approach, and while the liberalism of Lord Scarman is preferable to the reactionary views which generally prevail among judges, it is important not to see them in isolation from the system of state power they ultimately serve.

Indeed, the appointment of Sir Kenneth Newman in March 1982 as the new Metropolitan Police Commissioner exemplifies the essential unity of these 'hard' and 'soft' strategies. The former Chief of the Royal Ulster Constabulary, he was responsible for extremely 'hard' and high technology policing in Northern Ireland. Yet on his appointment it was made known that he was simultaneously an advocate of community policing, even if not strictly in the Alderson mode. The implication was that hard tactics would be used for public order or violent crime while soft tactics would be employed to harness community support and involvement. As John Alderson put it in a lecture, the task of community policing is 'to reinforce our control'.[74] While it would be unfair to compare Mr Alderson with the view of a Thatcherite Secretary of State for Social Services, Patrick Jenkin, who described the police as 'our first social service', the criticisms of Mr Alderson made by a former Labour Home Office minister, Alex Lyon, should be noted. He suggested that community policing could become 'benevolent authoritarianism' unless it was accompanied by firm democratic controls.[75]

Both policing approaches also require the collection of large amounts of information on the community and its storage in a way useful to police officers. This has been done in both Devon and Cornwall and Greater Manchester. In the latter, a computer has been installed in order to centralize all the information currently held on manual files, so that it is available faster to constables on patrol. The management consultants who recommended the system warned that the present public opinion climate would probably not tolerate the inclusion of 'intelligence' – unverified police gossip – in the computer, but 'it is possible that this climate may change. A generally open mind should be maintained.'[76]

Regardless of recent interest in community policing following the Scarman Report, the British police force continues to be changed into a national force for the protection of the state and the status quo – and this without public discussion or prior parliamentary approval. A survey of official reports from chief constables and from the Home Office Inspectors of Constabulary in England and Wales, and Scotland, concluded: 'The present "debate" between preserving policing by "consent" . . . or the adoption of "fire-brigade" (or reactive) policing has, in practice, *already been resolved* in favour of the latter.' It continued:

Nor can the British police be viewed as an unarmed force . . . more than 12,000 rank and file officers are trained in the use of firearms . . . Another 'debate' about whether or not Britain should have a 'third force' (comparable with the French C.R.S. or the West German Border Guard) 'to deal with strikes, demonstrations and terrorists', *has also been resolved* . . . there are already at least 12,000 riot-trained police 'hidden' in the ranks of the uniformed police, mainly organized as Police Support Units.[77]

· POLICE INDEPENDENCE ·

In the drive for greater computerization of police activities, the separation of the police from democratic control has been increased. Police forces have gradually turned to the purchase of their own computers. During the 1970s and 1980s they have been able to secure Home Office finance for technological development in spite of central government pressure on local authorities drastically to reduce expenditure. Such separate facilities give the police greater operational autonomy, and they have resolutely opposed the application of data protection measures involving civilian oversight of their computers.

The growing independence of the police from democratic accountability is also emphasized by the role of the Special Patrol Groups. As far as can be determined from the reports of chief constables, at least 27 of the 52 police forces in Great Britain have Special Patrol Groups. The Home Office claims that the main role of the S.P.G.s is 'to assist hard-pressed local police in the fight against crime'. They are units which do not come under the command of any of the geographical police divisions, but are answerable to the force's central headquarters. The fact that 24 chief constables did not bother to mention whether or not their forces have such groups does not necessarily mean that they do not have them; chief constables' annual reports vary a great deal in the amount of information they divulge; at any rate all forces covering major conurbations have them. As *State Research* concluded: 'The evidence is irrefutable. In Britain, there are now at least 27 elite S.P.G. groups with a para-military capacity which are also being used in everyday policing in the community.'[78]

The other main police units which have been trained in crowd control duties, including the use of riot shields, are known as Police Support Units. These differ from S.P.G.s in that the officers forming them are normally attached to a division, and are formed into the unit when needed for an operation. The creation of the P.S.U.s was a Home Office initiative. After the Second World War, police civil defence duties were reorganized. The plans envisaged that in an emergency about a third of the police would be withdrawn from normal duties and formed into self-supporting mobile columns, called Police Support Units, which would be held in reserve for use wherever necessary.[79] In the Home Office *Police Manual of Home Defence* issued in 1966, the formation of P.S.U.s is laid down as being one for each police division, consisting of 34 officers.

Publicly, all emergency training and organization of the police is discussed solely in relation to home defence in the wake of nuclear war. But in 1972 the Home Office told local authorities: 'It is considered that there is much common ground between war planning and the preparations required for, and the organization appropriate to, a major peacetime emergency.'[80] *State Research* discovered that 28 police forces had formed P.S.U.s in the six years up to 1979, and a further 14 forces reported that the officers had undergone training in crowd control, public order or the use of riot shields.

Bearing in mind that chief constables are not required to divulge any information, it is a reasonable assumption that all police forces have formed or are engaged in forming P.S.U.s, whose major role will be in crowd control.

The national nature of police organization is underlined by the role which P.S.U.s play in 'mutual aid' operations, where officers are sent into the area of another force as reinforcements. 'Mutual aid' was formally instituted in 1925, in the wake of the Desborough Committee's report. The ability of police officers to serve in areas outside their own force area was extended by the 1964 Police Act, which provided that a police officer could exercise the powers of a constable throughout the country, and not, as previously, only in the area of his own force and immediately contiguous areas.

Home Secretary William Whitelaw announced in August 1980 that the police would review command structures and operational plans for dealing with spontaneous disorder, and the chief officers would consider invoking mutual aid at 'an early stage in an incident'.[81] He also called for a report from his officials into the disturbances in St Paul's, Bristol, on 2 April 1980, a disturbance which occurred when police officers raided a café searching for illegal alcohol and escalated to a point where police were forced by a hostile crowd to withdraw from the district. Much criticism was directed at the fact that it took six hours for the Avon and Somerset Constabulary to organize an operation to retake the St Paul's district.

It later became clear that the delay was necessary because reinforcements were required from neighbouring police forces – Devon and Cornwall, and Gloucestershire and Wiltshire. It was P.S.U.s from these forces, along with the Avon and Somerset P.S.U.s and Task Force, as the local S.P.G. is called, which reoccupied St Paul's.

Thus the political climate and the connected dictates of national policing are shaping the internal structures and policies of regional and local police forces.

As far as public order is concerned, a series of regional police forces already exists. Several chief constables have been named as regional police commanders designate in the event of a national emergency such as large-scale industrial action. The regions are those set up in the 1920s by the Home Office under its then permanent secretary, Sir John Anderson, for the contingency planning which was used to break the General Strike.

In a total emergency, such as a general strike or the aftermath of nuclear war, regional commissioners – who would be ministers – would take over all executive, judicial and police functions in each of the twelve regions in the United Kingdom. In such conditions, the regional police commanders would be immediately subordinate to the regional commissioner. But the regional emergency planning structure is activated for any large-scale emergency – for example, a national strike by economically key groups, such as miners or transport workers. The regional emergency planning organizations are flexible; they include

representatives of different ministries, of local authorities, of the police
and the armed forces, as required. The boundaries of the regional areas
were adjusted on 1 April 1974 to coincide with the reorganization of local
government under the 1972 Local Government Act. The boundaries for
the 52 local police areas in the U.K. were adjusted at the same time.

The centralization of policing has proceeded apace. Meanwhile it is
evident that the official image of the police as a neutral agency playing a
referee function in our society does not square with the facts. The police
have considerable discretion. Inevitably they exercise it either according
to their own political preferences or according to the constraints determined by the dominant interests of a society for which they are the
major agency of social control. Equally, the force is increasingly adopting
the role of a democratically sanctified but nevertheless extra-democratic
agency, well able to pursue its own political objectives. The police have
become an independent political force in their own right.

THE PROSECUTORS

It is of paramount importance that I have and must jealously maintain
a position of complete independence from political influences whilst
accepting my answerability to Parliament through the Attorney General.

(Sir Thomas Hetherington, Director of Public Prosecutions,
Guardian, 2 June 1980)

On 30 November 1975, members and supporters of the National Front
violently broke up a meeting in Manchester organized by the National
Council for Civil Liberties. Shouting 'Jewish maggots' and 'People like
you should be exterminated', they arrived in combat jackets and began
throwing lumps of concrete at the platform and chairs at the audience,
causing numerous injuries. One man who suffered a broken arm and a
severe eye injury was off work for four months; an elderly lady was hit
on the head with a chair and was badly cut; another man was attacked
with broken glass and needed 19 stitches in the face.[1]

The main culprits were eventually brought to trial in January 1978
and although one was acquitted, four were found guilty of threatening
behaviour, with one of them also being convicted of affray, disorderly
conduct and damage to property; the latter was sent to prison for six
months. Several individual policemen gave crucial evidence for the prosecution.

Yet it was a *private prosecution* sponsored by the Students' Union of
the University of Manchester Institute of Science and Technology, on
whose premises the meeting had been held. Despite investigating the
matter sufficiently thoroughly to produce the kind of evidence able to
mount a successful prosecution, the local police and the Director of
Public Prosecutions had refused to proceed.

How could this happen? The answer, simply, is that those responsible
for prosecutions in the name of the Crown – whether police, the D.P.P.
or the Attorney General – have extensive powers of discretion. This is
the second layer of discretion in our legal system, the first being the

operational discretion exercised by the police. And potentially it allows for political bias to enter into the decision over whether or not to prosecute.

This was seen most clearly in the seventeenth and eighteenth centuries when nearly all prosecutions were brought by *private* parties and where, as a result, 'The entire legal fabric, from prosecution to punishment, was shot through with discretion.'[2] Operating against a background of massive inequality, it also meant that prosecutions could be manipulated by property owners so that they became a 'selective instrument of class justice'.[3]

By the early nineteenth century, however, this system was beginning to break down. It had been subject to widespread abuse and corruption and, as industrialization occurred, crime and disorder grew, placing an impossible burden on maintenance of the rule of law. This led to the setting up of an organized police force, beginning in London in 1829. The police were charged with bringing prosecutions to restore order, later assisted by the Director of Public Prosecutions, whose office was set up in 1879 – a system which remains basically unchanged to this day.

· POLICE PROSECUTIONS ·

In England and Wales in 1980, 507,000 people were prosecuted for indictable offences, 1,370,000 for motoring offences and 502,000 for other summary offences. That means that over 5 per cent (or one in nineteen) of the population are now prosecuted for breaking the criminal law each year. In one sense we are a law-breaking society, with most people breaking the law almost daily: parking meter feeding, speeding, drinking and driving, cheating on bus or tube fares, tax evasion, customs dodging, avoidance of buying dog and television licences, fiddling insurance company claims – all are crimes. Yet most either go undetected or the individuals concerned are not proceeded against even if they have been identified by the police: in 1980, for example, police cautioned but did not prosecute 101,000 people for indictable offences and 45,000 people for summary offences; and written warnings for motoring offences were sent to 240,000 individuals.

Thus, while decisions were made to prosecute, there were also a comparatively large number of decisions made *not* to prosecute. By contrast, a different aspect of this discretionary role is shown by evidence from

Crown courts that, in 8 per cent of Birmingham cases and 6 per cent of London cases surveyed, the police proceeded when there was insufficient evidence to reach the minimum legal standards required for prosecution, i.e. there was 'no case for the defendant to answer'.[4]

Then there is the choice faced by the police and other prosecuting authorities about *which* charge to bring; for it is possible to bring in charges for particular offences which are either more, or less, serious than the ones normally chosen. The police may wish to dispose of a case quickly and so bring a lesser charge, heard in a magistrates' court; another reason for choosing a magistrates' court may be greater confidence on the part of the officers that they can secure a conviction, especially in public order or 'political offences' where juries could be more critical of the Crown case. Yet in 1952 a judge with the agreement of the Lord Chief Justice stated that if there were a choice of charges, the police should prefer the more serious.[5] By contrast, after the acquittal of Jeremy Thorpe and others of conspiracy to murder in 1979, there was wide public debate on whether a conviction would have resulted if the lesser charge of conspiracy to intimidate had been preferred, a suggestion given credence by an interview conducted after the trial with one of the jurors.

Furthermore, in their role as prosecutors, the police are required to exercise discretion in areas of acute social sensitivity. For example, the crime of incest produced prosecutions in nearly all known cases earlier this century. But these days only about 40 per cent of those known to the police reach the courts.[6] The reason for this is that it is increasingly felt that prosecutions in less serious cases do more harm than good. So, on *social grounds*, law enforcers collude in ignoring the letter of the law – albeit in a way most people would regard as desirable.

But it is not just the discretion evident here which is at issue. As important is the point that it is relatively unfettered discretion. One study showed how, in criminal prosecutions, 'the police have been able to establish a considerable measure of autonomy and independence. There is, in practice, no real judicial supervision of their activities and they are accountable only in a remote sense.'[7]

· THE DIRECTOR OF PUBLIC PROSECUTIONS ·

The office of Director of Public Prosecutions (D.P.P.) was created in 1879, to take over functions of instituting and supervising the prosecution

of serious offences on behalf of the state. The interest of central government in law enforcement had previously been expressed by the role of
the Treasury Solicitor and the Attorney General in determining what
charges should be brought in cases of interest to the government of the
day. As the newly formed police forces expanded their activities, they
referred serious cases to the Home Office for advice, which in turn
passed the papers on to the Treasury Solicitor.

The government wanted the decisions made about prosecutions to
appear to have a measure of independence from the state. In 1879 the
Prosecution of Offences Act created the office of the D.P.P., which was
charged with supervising prosecutions for serious offences as prescribed
by regulations made at the time. Various Acts of Parliament since have
required that in many cases prosecutions may be brought only with the
consent of the D.P.P. He was also required to advise chief officers of
police, justices' clerks and others, including civil servants, about the
bringing of prosecutions.

Despite the intention to give a measure of independence to the prosecution process, the D.P.P. remained closely attached to other institutions
of government. For instance, between 1884 and 1908, the D.P.P., Sir
Augustus Stephenson, was also the Treasury Solicitor. The D.P.P. is
a civil servant and is answerable to the Attorney General who may be
questioned in Parliament about decisions on prosecutions – though the
sub-judice rule, which prevents M.P.s raising matters where a charge
has been brought, operates to limit the topicality of such questioning.

Nevertheless, the work of the Attorney General and the Director of
Public Prosecutions must overlap very closely in matters which are 'in
the public interest'. Bluntly, issues of general public concern which have
produced a situation in which criminal charges might well be brought are
also likely to have political (that is, at least in part electoral) repercussions.
In 1967 the then Speaker of the House of Commons gently rebuked
Labour M.P. Reginald Paget for suggesting that questions to the
Attorney General about the possibility or otherwise of charges being
recommended by the D.P.P. amounted to the bringing of political
pressure to 'decide a judicial point one way or the other'. Mr Paget
rightly asked: 'Is it not a fact that the decision whether or not to prosecute,
even if that prosecution is unsuccessful, is a decision to inflict a severe
penalty?' The Speaker had no difficulty reaffirming the rights of M.P.s
to hold the Attorney General responsible for the actions of the D.P.P.:

'It has been the custom of the House for a long time that the action of the Director of Public Prosecutions in not instituting a prosecution, or in instituting one, is something which is to be raised in the House with the Law Officers.'[8]

But the matter is not as simple as that. It is clear that vigorous and detailed questioning of the Attorney General about the activities of the D.P.P. would be resisted. As one generally conservative commentator put it: 'The noticeable restraint exercised by Members of Parliament in not pressing too hard when dealing with matters relating to the administration of justice shows a commendable desire not to let it be thought that they are trying to bring political pressure to bear.'[9]

The seemingly impossible feat of the man who is Attorney General – a party politician who nevertheless puts all and every political and party consideration aside when carrying out most of his duties – will be considered below. But the D.P.P., whatever the Speaker of the House of Commons might think, does not himself consider his post the equivalent of that of a mere civil servant. In 1980 the D.P.P., Sir Thomas Hetherington, said: 'The D.P.P. is not a member of a minister's staff, not the Attorney's civil servant, in the sense that even top civil servants are members of their minister's departments.'[10]

He went on to describe the situation as one where 'I have and must jealously maintain a position of complete independence from political influences whilst accepting my answerability to Parliament through the Attorney General . . . In practice this works because all Attorneys General, certainly in my experience, respect the need for the Director to be free from political influence and because, although by statute his consent is necessary for certain types of prosecution, he does not in practice seek to exercise any direct control over the decisions and advice of myself and my officers in other cases.' Thus the D.P.P. considers himself to be even freer of democratic control than the most senior civil servants; yet he has just as much of a policy-making role as any of them, and probably exercises more power too.

The growing centralization of the state prosecuting system is shown by the fact that the number of applications to the D.P.P. trebled between 1949 and 1970.[11] The D.P.P.'s office presently employs about 70 professional officers (either barristers or solicitors) and about 15 non-professional staff. It has always operated a rule (known as the '50 per cent rule'), in deciding whether or not to prosecute in a particular case, that the evidence available means that 'there is a reasonable prospect of a conviction, that is to say that a reasonable jury is more likely to convict than to acquit on the evidence that the prosecution are in a position to present.'[12]

The D.P.P.'s operation of this rule has caused particular controversy in cases of police officers accused of corruption. Sir Thomas has said: 'It is sometimes alleged that when we are considering prosecutions of police officers, we apply a different standard to that adopted when considering ordinary prosecutions.'[13] But, he said, this is not the case. The conviction rate is lower in cases involving police officers than in others and 'this may be just a reflection of the traditional reluctance of juries to accept the word of a citizen with, perhaps, a criminal record against that of a police officer'. Whereas the D.P.P.'s overall conviction rate is about 67 per cent, of the 37 policemen charged with assault in 1977, only 43 per cent were convicted.[14] Therefore the evidence offered against a police officer must be more solid than that offered against an ordinary citizen. Where the evidence might be thought sufficient to convict an ordinary citizen, it would not suffice as a basis for a charge against a police officer.

The result is that it has been very difficult for police officers to be prosecuted; and the D.P.P. proceeds in only 2 per cent of complaints of assault by police referred to him.[15] Four cases of violent deaths in which the police were involved in the 1970s have highlighted the problem of prosecuting police officers: those of Liddle Towers, James McGeown, Jimmy Kelly and Blair Peach. In each of these cases, there was no question but that police officers had been involved in violence; inquest juries considering all these deaths decided either that the violence used by police was justifiable or that there was insufficient evidence that any police officer had been responsible for the deaths. But in no case did the Director of Public Prosecutions consider the bringing of any lesser charges. Operating the 50 per cent rule – with due consideration given to the alleged difficulty of securing convictions against police officers – has meant that police officers are aware that their wrong-doings must be better documented than those of members of the general public if they are to be convicted: there is one law for the police and one for the ordinary citizen.

Moreover, the police complaints procedure – as created by the 1964 Police Act and modified by the 1976 Police Act which introduced a Police Complaints Board to make final adjudication on complaints – provides the police with a protection afforded to no one in any other occupation. If the chief officer, on making his investigation into complaints, is satisfied that a criminal offence has not been committed, he is of course at liberty to proceed as he wishes: to do nothing if he feels that the complaint has no substance whatsoever, or to take suitable disciplinary action if he thinks that the complaint amounts to a breach merely of internal discipline. But the legal requirement that any suspected criminal offence must be brought to the attention of the D.P.P. means that no action is taken until the D.P.P. has considered the case. If he decides that there is *insufficient evidence* to prosecute, as often occurs, then no disciplinary proceedings will normally follow. But the D.P.P. may decide not to prosecute because it is 'not in the public interest' or that the matter would be better dealt with by disciplinary charges – in which case disciplinary action can and often does follow. Thus the police are protected against wrong-doing in their work in a way which employees of other organizations are not. While the government announced late in 1982 proposals to reform the complaints procedure, this whole matter underlines again the reality of discretionary power in the prosecuting system, with the D.P.P.'s role being critical.

The D.P.P. has also played an important role in shaping police practice. The now widespread use by the Metropolitan Police of criminals known as 'supergrasses' – those involved in serious crime who agree to help the police in return for sentences reduced in comparison with what they might otherwise receive – became possible because the D.P.P.'s office agreed to the practice. The first 'supergrass' was Bertie Smalls, arrested in 1973 in connection with a series of armed robberies. An agreement was reached between the police, Smalls' solicitor and the D.P.P. Smalls gave the names of 27 men with whom he had been associated in robberies; between them, they subsequently received 315 years of imprisonment. The Director of Public Prosecutions agreed in writing that: Smalls would be granted immunity for all his criminal activities other than homicide; he would have his application for bail supported by the Crown; he would be able to retain the proceeds of his crimes; and he would be protected by the police from attempts by former accomplices still at large to harm him.[16]

When those convicted of being Smalls' associates in one of the robberies appealed in 1975, Lord Justice Lawton expressed the hope 'that we will not see the undignified sight of the Director of Public Prosecutions making agreements with professional criminals again'.[17] But such arrangements became the core of the Metropolitan Police strategy against armed robbery, and one can readily understand why this happened.

A policy emerged after Smalls. A number of men who gave the names of their alleged accomplices in armed robbery received sentences of only five years for crimes which would normally have merited far longer terms. The five years, with parole granted after only twenty months, and allowance for time spent in police custody before trial, meant that super-grasses served very little time in prison, if any. Many were kept in police custody for their entire sentences and there were reports that many of them received favourable treatment in comparison with that afforded other prisoners.

The actions of the D.P.P. in agreeing to the procedures adopted in the case of Smalls and others were not those of an independent legal official impartially enforcing the law, but of a state servant carrying out a policy agreed between his department, the Home Office and the police – but never agreed by Parliament. Part of the agreement for the treatment of supergrasses involved the assistance of other government departments in manipulating regulations to help the informer and his family remain incognito after he completed his sentence, even including passports and National Insurance numbers in false identities.[18] Supergrass Charles Lowe was protected by the police to such an extent that he made court appearances in Southend under an assumed name while London courts were told that police could not trace him.[19] Eventually, Lowe stood trial for armed robbery and was promptly freed in April 1978, after serving 17 months of an $11\frac{1}{2}$-year sentence, by Home Secretary Merlyn Rees on the advice of his Home Office civil servants. 'It is right to make use of every available means to fight crime,' Rees said.[20]

But the use of supergrasses marks a radical break with past legal custom. Moreover, it is part of a wider trend towards devolving legal decisions away from the open adjudication of the courts towards state officials deliberating in private. One can fully understand why the authorities wish to use all means available to prosecute gangs of armed robbers. But the political implications were almost casually tossed aside when the practice began. Who is to say that the same rationale of admi-nistrative convenience could not be used in sensitive political trials in the future? Suppose, for example, some of the practices uncovered by 'Operation Countryman' were applied to political activity through use of agents provocateurs?

In 1978 allegations made by some men arrested for armed robberies suggested that some detectives in the Metropolitan and City police forces had been involved in criminal activities. The result was the creation of the inquiry into the two London forces, headed originally by Dorset Chief Constable Arthur Hambleton, known as 'Operation Countryman'. Allegations made to the Countryman inquiry included those that

detectives from both the City forces and the Met have been involved in setting up robberies by telling criminals of the movement of millions of pounds; facilitating robberies by making sure there were no police around when they took place; steering inquiries away from the real culprits to innocent men [naturally with criminal records and therefore likely candidates]; helping criminals to get bail; deliberately offering feeble evidence in some cases; framing criminals in others by planting evidence such as shotguns and 'verballing' [inventing supposed confessions].[21]

It was the D.P.P.'s insistence that evidence be presented against police officers accused of crime which led to a number of officers against whom allegations had been made not being charged. To assist the Countryman team, a barrister from the D.P.P.'s office was seconded to work full-time with them. But a recommendation which he supported that six senior officers should be charged was turned down by the D.P.P.[22] Further evidence that the D.P.P. had not supported the Countryman investigation came from its former chief, Arthur Hambleton, who, in Granada Television's *World of Action* programme in August 1982, spoke publicly for the first time about the obstacles he had faced. He claimed that his inquiry had been obstructed both by Scotland Yard officers and by the D.P.P.

The role of the D.P.P. has recently come under fire in a number of political trials or cases with political implications. After my own mistaken identity case, concluded in 1976, there were calls from M.P.s (including Liberal leader David Steel) for the resignation of the D.P.P. on the grounds that he should never have allowed the prosecution to proceed; he took it over from the local police after the initial charge had been brought. There was also public debate and criticism over the D.P.P.'s role in the prosecution of Jeremy Thorpe and his associates, it being suggested that the D.P.P. could have brought an alternative charge which might have secured a conviction.

Some insight into the discretion of the D.P.P. was revealed in the case of the Vietnam Information Group, who in 1967 mounted a campaign encouraging American soldiers stationed in Britain to defect from their country's war effort in Vietnam. The question arose as to whether the group should be prosecuted, and the matter was referred to the D.P.P. When it came up in the House of Commons, the Attorney General made it clear that the D.P.P. had been the one to decide what the 'public interest' was in the circumstances: 'I do not know that it is appropriate for the Attorney General to give the reasons why the Director has, in any given case, decided not to prosecute, but he came to the conclusion that, in this case, the public interest would not be served by a prosecution.'[23] We can only speculate as to what criteria were used for determining what such a notoriously political matter as the 'public interest' was in this case – whether, for example, the demonstrations at the time would have been further inflamed had the state decided to proceed as it would have had the legal power to do.

By contrast, the decision in 1973 to charge the three Shrewsbury building pickets with conspiracy to intimidate, resulting in relatively heavy prison sentences being imposed, 'was initiated at a level higher than that of chief constable, after two separate police forces had advised against prosecution'.[24] At one stage the Tory Home Secretary had made a speech advocating that charges be brought.

The authorities had the satisfaction of convicting the Shrewsbury trade unionists. But they were less successful in the case brought the same year against five building workers and three members of a television crew filming their sit-in at an employment bureau in Birmingham alleged to be involved in 'lump' labour. They were all charged with conspiracy. But on the second day of the trial the defence made a legal challenge on the basis that their action was in furtherance of an industrial dispute and was therefore protected by section 3 of the 1875 Conspiracy and Protection of Property Act. The judge directed an acquittal after prosecuting counsel had conceded this legal point: 'The prosecution's concession . . . suggests the disturbing possibility that this section had previously been overlooked by the D.P.P.'s office.'[25]

A political judgement by the D.P.P. was also evident in his refusal to prosecute oil companies for breaking sanctions against the illegal white Rhodesian regime in the 1960s and 1970s. Despite the fact that sanctions busting was an offence and despite conclusive proof that British oil chiefs had knowingly allowed oil to get through,[26] the D.P.P. maintained that the evidence was not sufficient to sustain a prosecution.

· THE ATTORNEY GENERAL ·

The D.P.P.'s political master is the Attorney General. Just as the D.P.P. is reluctant to concede that the Attorney General has anything but the most general responsibility for his actions, so the Attorney General, while obliged by constitutional tradition to answer M.P.s' questions, has always insisted that his decision to prosecute must be made without any regard for his party colleagues.

A former Attorney General, Lord Shawcross, expressed the orthodox view when he wrote:

In deciding whether in any particular case the public interest (considered always in a non-party political sense) requires a prosecution, the Director may consult with a Department or take specific instructions from the Attorney General. Similarly, the Attorney General is entitled to (but rarely does) seek the view of colleagues as to matters of public interest involved in a prosecution. The eventual decision, however, and the responsibility for it lies with the Attorney General alone and it is very well understood that no one may seek to influence him on political grounds. In my own experience no one ever does and no Attorney General worth his salt would tolerate any such intervention in his quasi-judicial duties.[27]

The effect of the Attorney General's perception of what does and what does not constitute political influence on him serves to obscure, and thus facilitate, political pressure from the civil servants of his department, while picking out, and so impeding, those from party colleagues. For the Labour movement, this has serious implications. 'The public interest (considered always in a non-party political manner)', seen from the position of Lord Shawcross, proves to be remarkably close to the interests of the state and the government of the day. As so often happens, right-wing pressure is invisible because it is built into the system.

Attorneys General may therefore be perfectly sincere when they maintain that they are not subjected to political pressure in making their decisions, or that when they see such pressure, they are quite capable of resisting it. The problem is that they do not see most of the pressure to which they succumb, for they are part of what amounts to a state consensus.

But this consensus has not been neutral. For example, in 1912 a number of syndicalists, including Tom Mann, were prosecuted and jailed for 'inciting' soldiers not to attack strikers. But there was a totally different response to Ulster Unionists who used blatantly illegal methods to oppose the British government's policy of home rule for Ireland. They were involved in gun-running and organizing armed resistance through the Ulster Volunteer Force. With the support of leading Tory M.P.s they also incited the Army to mutiny (the Curragh mutiny in 1914 being the most notorious example). As a result of all this resistance the Home Rule Bill was defeated in Parliament in March 1914. Amongst those engaged in such illegal activity was Sir Edward Carson M.P. But far from being prosecuted (the Liberal Cabinet had considered such a course, rejecting it on grounds of political expediency), the following year Carson was actually appointed Attorney General in Asquith's coalition government! He was later to serve in the War Cabinet and was appointed a law lord in 1921. His fellow conspirator, F. E. Smith, was appointed Solicitor General in 1915 and became Lord Chancellor four years afterwards. As has been pointed out, the 'assertion of the right to break the law in order to maintain the status quo clearly distinguishes Carson's philosophy of direct action from that of the syndicalists, who were far from satisfied with the existing social order'.[28]

Therefore, despite Lord Shawcross's assurances, Attorneys General have often acted to use the law to defend the state and many have done so as members of the government of the day. In 1915 the government decided to suppress a daily newspaper – the *Globe* – which persisted in declaring that the then War Minister, Lord Kitchener, had resigned. (He was in fact absent overseas.) At a meeting of the Lord Chancellor, the Attorney General, the Director of Public Prosecutions and the Permanent Under-Secretary at the Home Office, it was considered how to resolve the problem through silencing the government's political opponents by legal action. This was rejected, not because the government lacked the legal means – wartime emergency powers could have been used – but because such means would have taken time. The meeting therefore instructed the head of the Metropolitan Police Special Branch, Basil Thompson, to stop the *Globe*, which he did by walking into the paper's offices and stealing a small but essential part of the printing machinery. The political object was achieved: '. . . the *Globe* was suppressed until such time as the directors of the newspaper had come to an agreement with the Government.'[29]

It is worth considering this incident because of the light which it throws on incidents in more normal times. It might be objected that this event is not typical; in particular that it occurred in war-time when opposition could be thought to be illegitimate. Without the circumstances of war, a government must either reply to damaging criticism, possibly alter its policies or decide to weather the political storm in the hope that the critics will run out of steam. Cynical political observers feel that by far the most common reaction is to appear to be doing something to mollify critics without actually making any real changes. Be that as it may, there is no doubt that national security in war *or* peace presents a powerful weapon to the authorities to de-legitimize, and even to criminalize, political opposition.

The temptation to use the law against political opponents is one to which successive British governments have succumbed. Any political movement seeking to act outside the channels of the established parties runs the danger of finding its leaders brought before the courts. Throughout 1960 and 1961, central London and several American and British military bases in various parts of the British Isles were the scene of demonstrations by the Committee of 100, supporters of unilateral nuclear disarmament who mobilized large numbers on demonstrations with the aim of non-violently disrupting the functioning of central government and military activity connected with nuclear weapons. In April 1961, 874 people were arrested after sitting down in Whitehall in protest against nuclear weapons; in September 1961, 1,350 people were arrested after a similar protest in Trafalgar Square. The Committee of 100 planned a further demonstration at the American Air Force base at Wethersfield, Essex, in December that year. On the day before the demonstration, six leading members of the Committee were arrested and the office of the Committee and the homes of the six arrested were searched by the Special Branch.

The demonstration took place anyway; any possibility that the demonstrators might enter the base was ruled out by the deployment of large numbers of police; one estimate was that 850 police from Essex, Hertfordshire, Southend and the Metropolitan Police confronted some 400 demonstrators. Although the two previous, and much larger, demonstrations in central London had been broken up by mass arrests, there was little fighting, the disarmers offering only passive resistance as they were being carried and dragged away. But the Wethersfield protest erupted into violence: 70 people were arrested and 34 were subsequently sentenced to imprisonment. Shortly afterwards, the Attorney General announced that the six arrested leaders would be charged with conspiracy to contravene Section One of the 1911 Official Secrets Act – the first ever use of Section One of the Act against people acknowledged not to be at all involved in espionage on behalf of another country. The Act does not limit its use to this, but, as was pointed out in Parliament at the time, the relevant section is accompanied by a marginal note: 'Penalties for spying'. Nevertheless the Attorney General replied uncompromisingly: 'In considering whether or not to prosecute, I must direct my mind to the language and spirit of the Acts and not to what my predecessors said about them many years ago in an entirely different context.'[30] His answer gives little support to the theory that the reasons for requiring prosecutions to receive the consent of the law officers is to ensure that the real intentions of Parliament are implemented.

Tony Bunyan commented:

As it was admitted that the prosecution did not involve espionage or the civil service, the application of the [Official Secrets] Act took on a new meaning, that of curbing political rights. For there is no doubt that at this time the state was facing a serious challenge from C.N.D. and the Committee of 100, a challenge which embraced hundreds of thousands of people.[31]

The decision of the Attorney General to use the Official Secrets Act in such a novel way can thus be seen as part of a political offensive by the government against its opponents.

The function of the Attorney General in the state's use of the law as one of its weapons against its political opponents is often clarified in matters which concern 'national security'.

The same Attorney General who ordered the prosecution of the Wethersfield Six was one of several who consented to advice from his civil servants and those in the security services not to bring a prosecution against Professor Anthony Blunt who, during his years as a member of the security service, MI5, had been a spy for the Russians. He had confessed his involvement to the security service, but was still permitted to pursue a lucrative and prestigious career – even being employed by the Royal Family. Yet in 1970, while Professor Blunt was enjoying the results of the immunity granted to him, an elderly Labour M.P., Will Owen, had his career brought to an abrupt end when he was charged under the Official Secrets Act with divulging details of government expenditure (to which he had access as a member of the House of Commons Estimates Committee) to Robert Husak, a Czech diplomat alleged by the prosecution at Owen's trial to have been a spy. Owen was acquitted on eight separate charges; like Blunt, he said that he had had political reasons for his contacts with the Czechs. Blunt claimed that he had acted because he felt that the Soviet Union had been the strongest bastion against fascism. Owen said at his trial that he felt himself to be a teacher giving the Czech diplomat lessons in Britain's democratic way of life; he was ordered to pay the costs of his acquittal, an effective fine of about £2,000.

No doubt the security services felt that they had good reason to charge Owen. Though he had already decided to resign as an M.P. for health reasons, the prosecution and acquittal meant that it was impossible for him to be granted any honour in recognition of his public services. The issue is not just the differing treatment of Owen and Blunt, but the pressures which led to the decisions. In both cases (in Blunt's, judged from his later public statements) there seems to have been enough evidence to meet the criterion that there should be a 50 per cent likelihood of a conviction. But in the case of Blunt, the security service, MI5, pressed the government not to prosecute largely in order not to discourage other possible spies to defect; in the case of Owen, the decision to prosecute has to be seen in the light of persistent MI5 fear that sections of the Labour Party were too close to diplomats from Warsaw Pact embassies, and even fear that some of Sir Harold Wilson's closest advisers were covert Soviet sympathizers. Close contacts between Labour M.P.s and communist diplomats were to be discouraged, and others no doubt took note of Owen's fate.

The decisions in each case were clearly made on broader criteria than mere legal considerations. Equally, they were not, as far as can be ascertained, made under the pressure of elected politicians like the Attorney General's colleagues. Rather the politics of the Attorney General's decisions are the politics of convenience for the state – the permanent civil service, and in the case of 'security', the security services and the military.

There are other examples of initiatives by the Attorney General which illustrate the political role he plays. In 1970 the Palestinian activist, Leila Khaled, was involved in an unsuccessful attempt to hi-jack an Israeli airliner and was later detained by police in London. She had committed a clear offence under English law. But the Attorney General, Sir Peter Rawlinson, decided to release her as part of an international bargain involving the release of hostages held by Palestinian guerrillas. At the time some legal experts and politicians protested that the government's action was illegal, but Sir Peter was unrepentant. He had consulted the Foreign Secretary and had been told that there was great danger to the lives of the hostages if Ms Khaled was not released. So he decided not to prosecute her, maintaining: 'That was my decision and mine alone.'[32]

But constitutional nicety over the Attorney General's independence has not been so evident in other cases. In 1940 miners striking during war-time were prosecuted only 'after Cabinet backing had been assured'.[33] There was also the rather murkier example of the prosecution of John Campbell. As acting editor of a Communist Party paper, he had published on 25 July 1924 an article encouraging soldiers to align themselves with the working classes of the world: '. . . let it be known that neither in the class war nor in a military war, will you turn your guns on your fellow workers,' it said. There was political uproar, not least because he had an excellent war record, having been decorated for gallantry. As a result the D.P.P. backtracked and withdrew the prosecution. But this provoked even greater political uproar, causing Ramsay MacDonald's Labour government to fall. Although MacDonald insisted that the decision to withdraw the charge had been that of the Attorney General alone, the evidence is that the Cabinet directed the prosecution to be withdrawn.[34] Campbell was eventually convicted with others of sedition and incitement to mutiny, and imprisoned.

In a revealing epilogue to the affair, it later emerged that the Labour Cabinet had agreed a motion that in future 'no public prosecution of a political character should be undertaken without the prior sanction of the Cabinet being obtained'. And although the succeeding Tory Prime Minister, Stanley Baldwin, castigated this as 'unconstitutional, and subversive to the administration of justice',[35] in doing so he begged still more questions. For MacDonald's Labour Cabinet was not consulted *before* the initial proceedings – it was merely saddled with the consequences which, in the event, proved fatal to its future. It is likely that any Labour government – particularly one pursuing the kind of radical socialist policies decided by Labour conferences in the 1970s and 1980s – could find itself in conflict with the D.P.P., possibly with the Attorney General caught between the two. Indeed, albeit in a different context and under a Labour administration that was far from radical, there appears to have been some conflict between Harold Wilson's Cabinet and the prosecuting authorities over the decision to proceed in 1970 under the Official Secrets Acts against the journalist Jonathan Aitken and the *Sunday Telegraph* for revealing information about the Biafran war. While there were allegations that Harold Wilson had instigated the prosecution, this was emphatically denied by one of his senior Cabinet ministers, Richard Crossman, who claimed that the Prime Minister was keen 'to avoid the charge of political interference', adding that 'next time' he should 'be more ready to smack down his legal advisers in the cause of common sense'.[36]

At the very least, therefore, the basis for prosecuting, especially in political cases, is shrouded in secrecy. But we have enough glimpses of light to reveal that politics can play a crucial part, even if not the overt party politics of the government of the day, then most certainly the politics of the ruling elite. In a much more parochial context, some politicians and police officers have been quite prepared to acknowledge the room for political manoeuvre in the prosecuting system. For example, Greater Manchester's Chief Constable, James Anderton, complained in 1981 that over the years he had been asked by local politicians to pervert the course of justice: 'I have been approached on more than one occasion in my time as a chief officer of police by elected members of local communities using their privileged position and influence in a barely subtle way hopefully to obtain some advantage or benefit for themselves or a friend, usually in connection with a pending prosecution.'[37]

While it may well be that in the vast majority of cases which are perfectly straightforward the prosecuting system progresses in a mechanical fashion, at its heart remains the exercise of discretion. And as a former Chief Constable of Hertfordshire so aptly points out: 'Nobody . . . has been able to formulate rules fettering discretion. The reason is not far to seek: discretion means the freedom to break rules.'[38]

4

JUDGES AND THEIR COURTS

'When *I* use a word,' Humpty Dumpty said, in
a rather scornful tone, 'it means just what I
choose it to mean – neither more nor less.'
'The question is,' said Alice, 'whether you *can*
make words mean so many different things.'
'The question is,' said Humpty Dumpty,
'which is to be master – that's all.'
(Lewis Carroll, *Through the Looking-Glass*)

'Be careful about criticizing the judge,' I was advised by lawyers and journalists alike after my mistaken identity trial in 1976. Yet I had good cause to feel aggrieved at the judge's handling of the trial, particularly his extraordinary summing up in which he did his level best to dress up a thin prosecution case with some semblance of respectability.[1]

Judges are among the most powerful of all public officials. But they are also perhaps the most insulated from public criticism and democratic accountability. They are seen by the public almost as higher beings – so much so that Lord Hailsham hinted during the 1979 general election campaign that any criticism of judicial decisions amounted almost to treason; he was re-appointed Lord Chancellor by Mrs Thatcher after the Tory victory.

Although under 2 per cent of cases in Britain are tried by judge and jury, they are the more important ones from the standpoint of public policy and invariably the ones where overtly political trials occur. Judges and their courts, however, are keen to assert their 'independence' from political bias. So how does this view compare with reality?

· POLITICS AND JUDGES ·

Judicial independence is real in this country to the extent that judges are not under real pressure to conform to every detailed wish of the government of the day. There are notable examples of the wishes – and indeed the explicit intentions of governments, even as reflected in laws which actually reach the statute books – being overturned by judges. But the fact remains that all judicial officials are appointed by politicians: from the Lord Chief Justice to the newest magistrate.

High Court and Circuit Judges, Recorders, stipendiary and lay magistrates are appointed by or on the advice of the Lord Chancellor who is a member of the Cabinet. Appointments to the Court of Appeal, to the Judicial Committee of the House of Lords, and to the offices of Lord Chief Justice and President of the Family division (of the High Court) are made on the advice of the Prime Minister after consultation with the Lord Chancellor, who himself consults with senior members of the judiciary before making his choice or consulting with the Prime Minister.[2]

There is of course considerable variation in the personal involvement of individual prime ministers in judicial appointments. In *The Politics of the Judiciary*, from which the above passage is taken, Professor John Griffith cites the example of Winston Churchill, who promised Sir Walter Monckton the post of Lord Chief Justice if he (Monckton) condescended to take a minor ministerial role in the 1951 Conservative government.[3] Veteran socialist lawyer D. N. Pritt cites examples of more direct intervention for party political ends. Lloyd George extracted from one man whom he appointed to the post of Lord Chief Justice an undated letter of resignation which was put into effect when the Liberal leader wanted to replace the Lord Chief Justice with his Attorney General who coveted the post after his retirement from politics.[4] This transition from political to judicial activity is also evident in other ways. It is by no means uncommon for legally qualified politicians to be appointed judges after service in the House of Commons or as parliamentary candidates, while Lord Chancellors continue to serve as Lords of Appeal after the termination of their political appointment, many playing an active role.

Between 1832 and 1906, half the judicial appointments went to barristers who had been M.P.s in the ruling party of the day, 'with an eye not only to past services rendered in political life but also to future services to be rendered in judicial life'.[5] Lord Salisbury, when premier in 1895, wrote to a colleague on an issue of judicial appointments suggesting that the idea that a leading politician should be refused a judgeship was 'at variance with the unwritten law of our party system; and there is no clearer statute in that unwritten law than the rule that party claims should always weigh very heavily in the disposal of the highest appointments . . . It would be a breach of the tacit convention on which politicians and lawyers have worked the British Constitution together for the past 200 years.' [6]

But the system by which Whigs and Tories, and then Liberals and Conservatives, appointed themselves to the Bench was threatened after 1920 by the rise to power of the Labour Party. The response to this by the legal establishment, aided no doubt by the Civil Service in the Cabinet Office and the Lord Chancellor's Department, was interesting. Haldane, Liberal Lord Chancellor from 1912 to 1915 (and reappointed by Labour in 1924), defended the value of experience in the House of Commons for a judge. But Lord Sankey, appointed by Ramsay MacDonald's Labour administration as Lord Chancellor in 1929, 'replaced five Law Lords who had had political backgrounds by others whose reputation rested on their professionalism as lawyers'.[7] In this way the judiciary was able to deflect a potential threat by substituting 'professional' for 'political' as the criterion for selection to its highest levels.

Although this switch really made itself felt during the 1912–40 period, its origins lay well before this. The pressure for democracy in the nineteenth century had encouraged the state to move towards a system of law less blatantly political; the thrust towards professionalism and expertise was thus partly an attempt to secure renewed legitimacy for a legal system that had come increasingly under attack for being an unadulterated instrument of the ruling class. As early as the 1760s and 1770s, Wilkite radicals had attacked the judiciary for being a mere tool of the Crown and the administration; they were particularly critical of the discretionary powers of judges.[8] As the pressure for political and labour reform grew, with judges often resisting this, there was a clear danger that they would be discredited along with the law as a whole. This provoked some anxiety in official circles, one historian suggesting for example that 'a de-emphasis on judicial activism' could be detected as a prudent response to the political turbulence of the 1870s and 1880s.[9] Of course judges continued to play a political role, and one with a clear bias. But increasingly it came to be recognized that there were advantages to the state in seeming to place the judiciary 'above politics', one bonus being that 'the depoliticization of the judiciary gave the government an important new political weapon. When a political crisis was peculiarly complex and difficult to solve, an "impartial" judge could always be appointed who would come up with an "objective" solution.'[10]

So it is important to understand that the shift away from political patronage towards a more professional basis in the selection of the judiciary did not alter the basic truth that judges are political agents. It has simply enabled them to claim a higher mandate of expertise and objectivity for decisions which remain fundamentally political. In recent decades an additional source of legitimacy has been marshalled on behalf of the judiciary. By now thoroughly professionalized, the judiciary is projected as being a repository for the public 'consensus'. Armed with the official mythology of their 'independence' and 'impartiality', judges are seen as expressing a consensus view. Thus for example, while Lord Hailsham asserted that 'We have a non-political judiciary', at the same time he argued: '. . . judges, like everybody else, are influenced by the economic and political climate of their time. If they were not, they would be considered either revolutionary or reactionary, and they would become political judges.'[11] One may take issue with his denial that judges can be reactionary, but the point is that Lord Hailsham here is claiming a different basis for judicial legitimacy – that the judiciary performs a 'middle' role – as if there were no disagreement about the 'consensus' itself. In practice the 'middle' role turns out to be a rather narrow one which reflects the interests of those in power: 'consensus' becomes synonymous with 'status quo'.

The switch away from party political judicial appointments came at a timely moment. For if Labour prime ministers and Lord Chancellors had continued the patronage system which had suited the Liberals and the Conservatives, then it is just possible that one or two of those appointed to the Bench would have been socialists, much as one or two ministers in Labour governments have turned out to be socialists. Such pluralism is tolerated in government, where errant left-wing ministers can be controlled by the combination of Civil Service and prime ministerial power. On the Bench such diversity would be distinctly unwelcome. A judge sits alone and, while his idiosyncracies can be smoothed out by the appeal system, he wields considerable power and discretion.

Of course there are those within Labour's ranks who feel that there are genuinely non-political criteria which fit a person for public office in specialized sectors such as the law. It is not shared by Conservatives who have always been ready to act on Mao Tse-tung's exhortation to 'put politics in command'. For instance, during the Conservative tenure of office in the fifties, 'being an M.P. came once again to be regarded as a qualification for appointment to a judgeship'.[12]

Lord Gardiner, Lord Chancellor in the 1964–70 Labour governments, returned to the 'non-political' criteria, which in practice meant conservatism without the Party label. Many supporters of the Labour Party and others on the left are familiar with the way in which areas of public life retain the curious 'non-political but equally non-socialist' flavour. It is the same corporate consensus which informs the policy formation processes of the Civil Service, so well described by the Labour diarists, and closer inspection of the basis upon which judges are appointed reveals an inherent political bias.

· APPOINTMENT OF JUDGES ·

The conservatism of the judiciary is built into the appointments system. If the selection of judges as a recognition of services to the Conservative Party is in decline, the choice which might be available to the most radical Lord Chancellor and Prime Minister operating within the existing conventions is severely limited. Judges are drawn from the ranks of practising barristers – of whom there are but 4,000 in the entire country. They must have achieved a level of success in the eyes of their fellow lawyers, barristers and judges, within a legal profession which is as antiquated as it is conservative. A potential senior judge will almost invariably already have been raised to the rank of Queen's Counsel – itself bestowed by the Lord Chancellor's Department. So they cannot be too young, nor, because judges now retire at 75, can they be too old to hold judicial office for a significant period. The possibilities for appointment to a particular vacancy on the bench effectively reduce themselves to a handful. E.P. Thompson graphically describes the process: 'Judges, after all, do not suddenly appear, bewigged and fullblown, *ex nihilo*. They go through a caterpillar stage before, as lawyers. Then they pupate for a while in silk. And finally they blow in ermine.'[13]

But apart from the bare facts of the appointment procedure – and notwithstanding Professor Griffith's seminal analysis – we know very little about the internal organizational politics of the judiciary, precisely because it is shrouded in secrecy. How *exactly* is an Appeal Court judge chosen? What criteria are used for the advice given to the Prime Minister by civil servants? A 1977 report in the *Observer* gave a rare insight into the unguarded thoughts of the senior officials in the Lord Chancellor's Office over the future appointment of a successor to Lord Denning as Master of the Rolls (i.e. head of the Appeal Court). Doubtless influenced by these officials, three Lord Chancellors – Gardiner, Hailsham and Elwyn-Jones – had 'hinted to Lord Denning that he might think about retiring', but he 'failed to take the hint'. This presented a dilemma, for Denning's natural successor, favoured by reforming lawyers, would be Lord Scarman. But if Lord Denning stayed on too long, Lord Scarman would be ruled out on age grounds, 'and then the safety-first men in the Lord Chancellor's office will sigh with relief and appoint a conventional successor'.[14]

Nor do we know much about the choice of a particular judge for a particular case. The official line is that it is more or less a random process. At the Old Bailey, for example, judges will take cases according to when they are free on a rota arranged by court clerks. But this is not the whole story, for there is evidence that the process is not as random as the establishment would have us believe.

For example, after the storm over Judge Neil Mackinnon's handling of the trial of the fascist leader John Kingsley Read in 1978 (discussed more fully in Chapter 12), Lord Elwyn-Jones, the Labour Lord Chancellor, stated publicly that the judge would not in future try comparable Race Relations Act or Public Order Act cases. Lord Elwyn-Jones had clearly given an instruction to that effect, but a public face was put on it by the following, rather delphic, explanation in his public statement: 'The judge does not choose the cases that are listed before him but he has told me that in the circumstances which have arisen he would prefer that cases raising issues comparable to those which arose in the Read case were not listed before him. I have no doubt that those responsible for listing cases in the Central Criminal Court will give effect to the judge's wishes.'[15]

During my 1976 Old Bailey mistaken identity trial, I was reliably informed by senior members of the legal profession that Judge Alan King-Hamilton had been eager to try the case and that the court's administrators had been more than happy to give it to him. He did his best during the trial to influence the jury in favour of a conviction, to the extent that one journalist covering it accurately predicted after his summing up that the jury would take a long time to reach a verdict instead of bringing in the immediate not guilty result most observers expected. The judge was also a member of the Marylebone Cricket Club, for whom I had been a particular *bête noire* in the 1969–70 campaign which stopped the South African cricket tour; but then he subsequently showed a more general appetite for controversy in handling political trials, for example the 1979 'Persons Unknown' case.

The fact that the choice of a judge for a specific case is not as random as some would have us believe means that the defence invariably considers it, in political trials at least. In both my Old Bailey trials the defence team weighed carefully the implications of appearing before certain judges. It was half-jokingly said before my 1972 conspiracy trial over apartheid in sport that if I found myself up against Justice Melford-Stevenson (then notorious for his reactionary behaviour in court), I should simply 'plead guilty and go straight to appeal'! (In 1976, he volunteered to hear a libel action against the *Socialist Worker* newspaper.) There is also a well-known practice where solicitors can to some extent avoid certain judges by so arranging things that counsel they have instructed are not 'available' at the time a particular judge may be sitting; this is something more easily done at the High Court than the Old Bailey. But as important as any political calculation in the matching of judges to cases is the element of *chance* built into the system which exposes the myth about it being technical and predictable: justice for a defendant can quite literally depend on which judge he or she gets, especially in a political trial.

·ATTITUDES OF JUDGES·

Because of their restricted background and education, judges can only with difficulty understand the lives and attitudes of people from other social backgrounds, which has serious political consequences. The evidence is quite overwhelming.[16] In broad terms about four out of five full-time professional judges come from public schools, and from Oxford and Cambridge. Almost all are middle- or upper-class, male and elderly: the average age being 60 years for all judges, 65 in the Appeal Court and 68 in the House of Lords. (No English judge has ever been removed.)

They move in restricted social circles, not least being their inevitable long period of service at the closed system of the Bar as defence counsel or as prosecutors. Not surprisingly therefore, there have been numerous instances of judges appearing to be quite out of touch with the contemporary life of ordinary people. One famous occasion was in 1961 in the trial involving the book *Lady Chatterley's Lover*, when the prosecuting counsel (who later became a judge) asked the jury: 'Is it a book that you would ever wish your wife or your servants to read?' [17]

As recently as February 1982, Alex Lyon M.P., a barrister and former minister of state at the Home Office, criticized judges for being poorly informed, especially so far as young people were concerned. [18] The backwardness of the judiciary over social mores is shown by an examination of decisions on the adoption and custody of children since 1926. It found that, despite the legal principle that the 'welfare of the child' should be paramount, there are notable examples where judges have ignored medical and social work advice and favoured a highly traditionalist view giving natural parents pre-eminence. [19] In 1978 Justice Melford-Stevenson described the Sexual Offences Act 1967 as a 'buggers' charter' (he was later reprimanded by the Lord Chancellor). [20]

The great constitutional writer, Dicey, wrote of judges that they 'are for the most part men of a conservative disposition'. [21] That was at the turn of the century. But little has changed. In 1964 the Lord Chancellor, Lord Gardiner, said, 'I think all lawyers are conservative.' [22] More recently, John Griffith found 'a remarkable consistency of approach . . . concentrated in a fairly narrow part of the spectrum of political opinion. It spreads from that part of the centre which is shared by right-wing Labour, Liberal and progressive Conservative opinion to that part of the right which is associated with traditional Toryism – but not beyond the reaches of the far right.' [23] Significantly, this assessment was based upon the way judges operated in *practice*, not on a survey of their personal opinions. Similarly, Miliband has shown that 'judges in advanced capitalist societies have generally taken a rather poor view of radical dissent, and the more radical the dissent, the greater has been judicial hostility to it'. [24]

Although Lord Reid wrote in 1972 that judges should not take sides on party political issues, thus appearing to dispute the evidence listed above, his full argument in context actually supports the proposition that judges are inherently conservative by virtue of their function in supporting the status quo as determined by dominant interests:

Everyone agrees that impartiality is the first essential in any judge. And that means not only that he must not appear to favour either party. It also means that he must not take sides on political issues. When public opinion is sharply divided on any question – whether or not the division is on party lines – no judge ought in my view to lean to one side or the other if that can possibly be avoided. But sometimes we get a case where that is very difficult to avoid. Then

I think we must play safe. We must decide the case on the preponderance of existing authority.[25]

·JUDGES AS LAW MAKERS·

The political bias of the judiciary is most critical when it comes to their function in 'making' the law. Britain has a unique common law legal system. This means that, in addition to interpreting statute law passed by Parliament, it is the task of judges, where principles are not to be found in the statute book, to find the principles of common law which are nothing more nor less than generally accepted principles of social behaviour, and to codify them and apply them to specific cases under consideration. This 'judicial creativity' is accepted by the whole judiciary as a political role: Lord Scarman, for example, appears to regard all questions, legal or otherwise, as being 'ultimately political'.[26] And the interpretation by judges of their judicial creativity is on the whole deeply conservative; a classic example being conspiracy law, where over many centuries judges effectively invented new law to curb political or social movements they found objectionable. For judge-made law, in the form of rulings and especially in the decisions of the Court of Appeal and the House of Lords, is as binding as statute law. Decisions are binding until Parliament passes legislation to change them. The conservatism and rigidity of the arrangement has even become too constricting for the House of Lords, which has now decided that it has the power to reverse or alter the principles of earlier decisions. The tension between Parliament and the judiciary is an historical one, but is still apparent today in the reluctance of judges to accept parliamentary legislation of which they disapprove. Lord Scarman puts it, rather diplomatically, this way: 'The modern English judge still sees enacted law as an exception to, a graft upon, or correction of, the customary law in his hands ...'[27] Lord Scarman has been dubbed a 'political judge' by virtue of his role in arbitrating and inquiring into public order and race matters, notably Red Lion Square in 1974, Grunwick in 1977 and Brixton in 1981. But while he has had a higher public profile than most judges, his more activist role should not obscure what is in many ways a much more serious, consistent and regular process of day-to-day political decision-making by all judges.

One legal expert has written of another leading judge, Lord Denning, that his judicial career 'illustrates the power possessed by our senior judges. His decisions, and his influence, have had almost as profound an effect on the nature of our society in the last 30 years as the enactments of Parliament.'[28] Lord Denning himself gave the game away when he addressed the Mansfield Law Society at the City of London Polytechnic on 20 October 1977. He opened by expressing the hope that 'there are no reporters present', although his speech was videotaped with his full knowledge. He reviewed such controversial cases as the Grunwick strike (in which he played no small part), remarking at one point, 'By and large I hope we are keeping the [Labour] Government in order.' He also criticized Labour's Attorney General, Sam Silkin, for refusing in 1977 to prosecute the Union of Post Office Workers over its planned one-week ban of mail and operator calls to South Africa. And on his role and that of his judicial colleagues Lord Denning said: 'We have ways and means of getting round the law.'[29]

· JUDICIAL DISCRETION ·

Indeed, the evidence of judicial *discretion* (or 'ways and means') is overwhelming. One study of the law explains: '. . . judges have a creative role which involves the exercise of discretion . . . they are to a degree lawmakers.'[30] There are sensible reasons for such discretion. They include the fact that the law cannot possibly be drafted to take account of every eventuality and the fact that if it were applied uniformly it would be unduly rigid. But the very existence of such discretion against a background of the system of common law gives judges enormous scope to exercise it in a *political* manner. And when it is acknowledged by legal experts that the law is 'innately conservative',[31] it is apparent from the outset that such discretion will tend to be in one particular political direction.

Judicial discretion is perhaps most sharply to be seen in the way judges have absolute control over the courtroom, with clear political consequences. For example, an anti-apartheid demonstrator successfully appealed against a conviction for assaulting police during the anti-Springbok protest at Twickenham in December 1969. But despite getting his conviction quashed, he was denied costs, the judge in the case arguing that 'it was not a social thing to demonstrate, and that being on a demonstration was by itself likely to cause a breach of the peace'.[32] Judges have also used their sentencing powers over the years to attack political activity of which they disapprove, jailing trade unionists (as in the case of the 1973 case of the Shrewsbury building pickets), black people and 'teaching a lesson' to radical activists of various kinds.

This could be contrasted with the much more lenient treatment accorded to other defendants: to take just one example, that of a police constable who crashed into a young boy cyclist in Oxford in 1981, killing him. The officer had been driving a transit van at about 60 miles per hour after receiving a call for assistance. He had crossed over two red lights and swerved round the wrong side of a bollard in the middle of the road, crashing head on with the boy and killing him instantly. When it came to court, he was fined £100, provoking the understandable response from the boy's father: 'If it had been any other driver, apart from a policeman, he'd have had his licence taken away for a long time, and he'd have got a heftier fine. He might even have gone to jail.' There was much the same reaction from the father of another young man after a drunken policeman in Nottingham had crashed into him as he jogged home, killing him instantly; the officer was fined £160 and his licence was endorsed.[33]

Judges have also gone along with the well-oiled legal practice of finding loopholes in the law to avoid tax and estate duties, setting up special trusts to protect inherited wealth, assisting property developers to overcome planning regulations and enabling top companies to pay little if any corporation tax – all of which has been very lucrative for the legal profession from where judges hail.

In 1973, for instance, an accountant indulging in the 'middle-class crime' of defrauding the Inland Revenue was found guilty on eight counts of conspiracy, yet fined only £600 – a fraction of what it cost the Inland Revenue to bring him to trial, let alone the amount he had made for his clients. 'You get judgements like this, and you wonder whether it's all worth it,' said a tax inspector. 'The courts just don't seem to care about the sums involved.'[34] By the early 1980s it was officially estimated that tax evasion was running at approaching £4,000 million each year. Yet the courts, with the active blessing of the Thatcher government which hired special staff for the task, were enthusiastically prosecuting social security 'scroungers' for a total figure of £50 million lost each year – just $1\frac{1}{4}$ per cent of the tax loss. Meanwhile, in 1973 it emerged that a former Recorder of Bristol had escaped prosecution for fraudulent tax evasion because it had been feared that a criminal prosecution would undermine public confidence in the judiciary: 'We were simply told that a prosecution would not be in the public interest,' said a tax official.[35] The judge in question died in 1971, having been forced to retire six years earlier and to pay a 'heavy penalty' as part of 'an agreed settlement'. Not all of this bias is to be laid at the door of judges, of course: the state as a whole must shoulder the blame. But the judiciary has hardly played a neutral role, still less one of fearlessly applying the full weight of the law against tax evaders.

For judges are nothing if not kings in their own courts, as they never cease to remind everyone when it comes to political trials. In March 1975, for example, Mr Justice Melford-Stevenson openly censured three leading Q.C.s defending in a bomb conspiracy trial for what he called their 'insulting suggestions' of malpractice by the police. The defence had alleged police planting of evidence, including planting one of the defendant's fingerprints on an incriminating object, and John Platts-Mills Q.C. had given a demonstration to the jury with a piece of transparent adhesive tape to show how it could be done. The judge also issued guidance to the taxing officer that the three counsels' fees should be rigorously taxed, as a result of which their fees were indeed cut by one third.[36]

Judges have been very careful to control the course of political trials in the courts. While Lord Hailsham only grudgingly admitted as Lord Chancellor in October 1973 to the existence of 'cases with political overtones',[37] most judges have been insistent in their denial of the existence of any such thing as a political trial. They have been equally anxious to 'keep politics out of their courts' – or to be precise, defendants' politics, because judges' politics continually surface. Thus in 1972 Judge Bernard Gillis insisted that his court would not be turned into what he called 'a public meeting', during my conspiracy trial over South African sports protests. His intervention came during the defence case, whereas the prosecutor had been able to say quite freely that, among other things, my conviction might prevent loss of money to businessmen through some future protests I might have planned against trading links between Britain and apartheid South Africa. Similarly, in another political trial, the Cambridge 'Garden House' trial in July 1970 (where students were charged with various public order offences over a protest against the Greek junta), Justice Melford-Stevenson permitted the prosecution to probe the political views of the defendants in a hostile way. But when the defence sought to place the defendants' actions in the context of their detestation of the tyranny then operating in Greece, the judge stopped them, saying, 'I am not going to allow the court to be used as a vehicle for political propaganda.'[38] In other words, the courts have been prepared to treat political cases in a discriminatory fashion.

Nor has judicial discretion been immune from criticism on

'non-political' grounds. When Lord Denning finally announced his retirement in May 1982, one of his fellow Appeal Court judges told the *Sunday Times*: 'It has become impossible to connect anything he says or does with any known jurisprudence. He now makes it up as he goes along.' In a devastating critique of 58 cases decided by law lords between 1979 and 1980, Murphy and Rawlings punctured another judicial myth: that of the certainty and inviolability of judicial interpretation. In the authoritative journal *Modern Law Review*, they showed that the arguments of the judges were sometimes superficial, simplistic, casual, evasive or irrelevant. That is to say, their analysis challenged the logic and quality of judgements by their lordships.[39] This being accepted, there is even more scope for discriminatory political decisions by the judiciary than might have been supposed.

· WOMEN AND THE LAW ·

The general political thrust of the judiciary, the role of discretion and the extent of bias is evident in abundance in the treatment of women.

When Mrs Elizabeth Butler-Sloss was appointed a High Court judge in 1979, she joined one of the most exclusive male clubs in the country. No doubt conscious of this, she reassured readers of the *Sunday Telegraph* that she was still 'very much a housewife'.[40] (Perhaps more relevant to her appointment was the fact that her brother, Sir Michael Havers, was the Tory Attorney General, her father had been a High Court judge, and she had been Tory candidate in the 1959 election.)

In theory, barriers against women in the judiciary and the legal profession have now been lifted. But in practice male domination has hardly changed. Women make up half of all the persons concerned with providing legal services in this country, and a third on the bench of all courts from magistrates' level upwards. But virtually all those involved in legal work are secretaries, and all but a few female judicial officers are unpaid magistrates. Of about 1,000 professional full-time judges, county court registrars and stipendiaries, just 3 per cent are women.

The history of women and the law is in part the history of judicial resistance to equal rights. In the nineteenth century there were a number of legal battles around the admission of women to various public institutions. For example, Sophia Jex-Blake and her companions tried to enter the University of Edinburgh Medical School in the 1860s with results that bore strong similarities to the battle to admit black students a century later to colleges in the Deep South of America. After a protracted legal battle the courts excluded her.[41] Subsequently there were a number of court cases revolving around whether or not in law a woman was a 'person'. During progress through Parliament of the 1867 Second Reform Bill, John Stuart Mill had tried to extend votes to women by substituting 'person' for 'man' in the Bill. But he was unsuccessful. Women were equally unsuccessful in getting the judiciary to concede that basic citizenship rights accrued to women by virtue of their being 'persons', the term used in much other legislation: judges refused to concede that in law they were 'persons'. Thus, for example, women council candidates in London were prevented from standing for election. In 1889 Lady Sandhurst was actually elected to the London County Council. But her defeated male candidate applied for a court order on the grounds that she was not a 'fit person of full age' because she was a woman – and the Court of Appeal found against her.[42] Judges also barred women from entering the legal profession, declaring in one celebrated case in 1901 that a 'person' was really a 'male person'.

The law lords were also mainly responsible for blocking the entry to the Lords of ladies with hereditary titles. In a case involving Lady Rhondda in 1923 they gave a judgement against women being peers which was to last for forty years. The decision in her case was made despite the fact that in 1918 Parliament had granted votes to women together with their right to stand as M.P.s; and also despite the 1919 Sex Disqualification Removal Act, which barred discrimination against women exercising public functions. So from this period onwards, judges were flouting the will of Parliament: previously they could claim to be reflecting the general anti-feminist view of Parliament, even if their interpretation was overly narrow and rigid.

It was not until 1929 that judges declared women to be 'persons'. However, the interesting aspect of the judgement in question was that it could not have been delivered on 'technical' grounds, since the meaning of the word 'person' had not changed at all.[43] What had changed in the intervening period was the social attitude towards women together with the balance of political power, notably through the rise of the Labour Party. It was Labour which appointed as Lord Chancellor Lord Sankey, the judge who delivered the crucial 1929 'persons' judgement. From then onwards, there were several decades in which judges drew back from using the common law as an instrument against women's rights. But the whole

experience of women has served to expose the myth of judicial impartiality: judges have been 'dogged defenders of male supremacy'.[44]
For example:

A century after the courts had decided that it was unlawful in England to use
force to keep a slave in the house, lawyers were still maintaining that it was
permissible to use force to keep a wife in the house. An Englishman's home was
his castle, and her prison.[45]

While one can point to changes in the law on the family as signs of
progressive reform, it is important to view these against the background
of economic changes. Thus the law on the family in the nineteenth
century was reformed in tandem with changes in the nature of property
produced by industrialization. It had produced new forms of wealth
other than land, so that middle- and upper-class women had independent
means apart from any land ownership. Similarly, modern reforms giving
women more rights, in the sense of marriage being seen as a contract
from which both partners could draw equally, reflected the modern
middle-class home with no servants. Sachs and Hoff Wilson conclude
from their detailed study of women and the law:

The great changes in gender status have come about not through the harmo-
nious unfolding from within of legal concepts, but through vigorous attacks
against the legal system from outside. Contrary to common assertion by lawyers,
the law and the judges did not stand on the side of equality and individual
rights, nor were they even neutral. By and large, they acted as a barrier to, rather
than a guarantee of, equality between men and women.[46]

A more recent analysis of the position of women in family law confirmed
that while their legal rights may have been advanced, this has been
achieved in a way which actually reinforces women's dependency on an
individual male 'head of the household'.[47] The subordinate position of
women continues today.

Despite the introduction of the 1970 Equal Pay Act and the 1975 Sex
Discrimination Act, many inequalities still remain, not least those caused
by economic factors such as unemployment which undermines the right
of women to work and thereby to gain independence and the power that
goes with this.[48] In July 1981 a judge dismissed a claim by two feminists
under the 1975 Act against El Vino's wine bar in Fleet Street. It refused
to serve women at the bar, but the judge found against the women on the
grounds that no 'reasonable' woman would object to such treatment and
that activists in the women's movement were clearly not 'reasonable'

people.[49] The suffragettes who had been similarly patronized would not have been surprised: they had denounced the courts as organs of male oppression. (However, the Appeal Court did reverse the judgement in November 1982.) Further indifference to women's rights occurred when Greater Manchester's Chief Constable, James Anderton, called in October 1979 for the government to exclude women police officers from the Sex Discrimination Act because of the dangerous nature of certain types of police work. He claimed: 'I am exercising the full and proper discretion of a chief constable in the interests of the community.' But the *Police Journal* denounced him for what it termed 'this publicly declared contempt of the law of the land by a senior police officer'.[50]

In the early 1980s the issue which has most sharply focused women's discontent with judicial prejudice has been rape. In January 1982 there was public uproar when Judge Bertrand Richards said that a victim was partly to blame for being raped because she had been hitch-hiking home late at night, and on these grounds fined a rapist £2,000 rather than sending him to prison: 'I am not saying that a girl hitching home late at night should not be protected by the law, but she was guilty of a great deal of contributory negligence.'[51] There was no question in the case of the man not being guilty – only the 'contributory negligence' factor saved him from jail. In May 1982 a Scottish judge, Lord Ross, told a jury in a Glasgow rape case: 'If a woman voluntarily consumes alcohol to such an extent as to be virtually insensible, it is not rape to have intercourse with such a woman, just as it is not rape to have intercourse with a sleeping woman.' Summing up at a Cambridge rape trial in December 1982, Judge David Wild argued: 'Women who say no do not always mean no. It is not just a question of how she says it, how she shows and makes it clear. If she doesn't want it, she only has to keep her legs shut.' At an earlier trial, Justice Melford-Stevenson had said in one of his typically notorious statements: 'She was asking for it.' At the Old Bailey in 1976, Judge Sutcliffe had directed a jury to be sceptical of the evidence of a rape victim: '. . . it is known that women in particular and small boys are liable to be untruthful and invent stories,' he said.[52]

Although other judges have been more sympathetic, generally the behaviour of the judiciary has been to undermine the position of the woman and to place her in the position where as the victim she feels *she* is on trial. For example, while the 1976 Sexual Offences (Amendment) Act restricted the obnoxious practice of barristers questioning rape victims about their previous sexual experience, judges have effectively undermined this. They have used their discretion under the Act to allow such questioning almost as a matter of course, as a study of a sample of contested rape trials at the Old Bailey in 1978–9 showed.[53] The normal defence of the man is that the victim 'consented', and in 60 per cent of such cases the defence applied to the judge for permission to cross-examine the victim about her sexual past. The study found that three-quarters of such applications were successful, and that quite frequently questions were put to the victim about her sexual past without prior permission being sought from the judge, who normally did not intervene; sometimes the judge asked such questions even when the defence had not asked for permission to do so.

An investigation by London Weekend Television in February 1982 concluded that men could commit rape with 'something approaching impunity'.[54] The programme found that if the figure of at least 5,000 estimated rape cases each year was taken (police say only 2,000 cases are reported annually), then the yearly conviction of rapists (which stood at 450 in 1980) represented a conviction rate of under 10 per cent. In actual rape trials, the accused is acquitted in 60 per cent of *contested* trials and 24 per cent of all cases.[55] This latter figure of 24 per cent for rape compares with an 18 per cent acquittal rate for defendants in *all* Crown cases.

But while various reforms have been suggested – ranging from police chiefs calling for better training for their officers, to women's groups demanding structuring of juries in rape trials to include at least four women – the problem is really a much deeper one: the way society treats women and the way a male-dominated culture of violence reflects itself in discretion within the courtroom. But the specific culpability of judges was underlined when, in an unusual step, ten jurors signed a protest letter to the *Daily Telegraph* in 1978 after Judge Crichton had directed them to acquit in a Manchester rape trial. The jurors' letter complained that the judge 'had seemed unsympathetic from the start' to the victim and that they had felt there was 'a substantial case' to answer.[56]

All too frequently lawyers have further loaded the scales against women. In 1969, the Bar Council told the Monopolies Commission: '. . . the profession of barrister requires the masculine approach (however fallacious it may be) to reasoning and argument, and women only succeed in such activities if they have a masculine disposition.'[57] Such 'masculine disposition' was certainly evident in the comment of a male barrister prosecuting in a case early in 1982, where a fifteen-year-old girl was attacked by her boyfriend: 'Women can be difficult and tiresome at times, but no young man should act in the way that he did.'[58] Another example of legal male chauvinism came from Nicholas Fairbairn Q.C., Solicitor General for Scotland between 1979 and 1982, who remarked: 'Rape is a crime I've never been forced to commit. It is part of the business of men and women that they hunt and are hunted and say "yes" and "no" when they mean the opposite.'[59] Fairbairn resigned in January 1982 over his handling of a case where he defended an official decision not to prosecute three men accused of raping and slashing a Glasgow woman on the grounds that a trial might emotionally disturb her (she wanted a prosecution to proceed and later this was permitted).

In November 1975 Mr Justice Caulfield made it clear that a solicitor had been guilty of professional negligence through consulting a wife rather than a husband. *The Times* précised his judgement: 'Even in present times, where there was a movement by women for equality with men, a sensible wife, certainly in a united family, did not generally make the major decisions. Most wives sensibly left such decisions to their husbands. A solicitor should not take instructions from a wife when a husband was also available.'[60] Commenting on the case, one legal analysis argued that 'similar attitudes are to be found in hundreds of courts and tribunals sitting in judgement every day on cases where the rights of women are involved'.[61]

For example, women have often faced unsympathetic courts when assaulted by their husbands. Late in 1981 a woman who was beaten by her husband was refused permission to petition for divorce within three years of her marriage. Three Appeal Court judges decided her experience did not amount to 'exceptional hardship'; one of them, Lord Justice O'Connor, argued that physical violence between young married couples was not uncommon and so 'Before such assaults are said to inflict exceptional hardship, there must be something out of the ordinary in what happened.'[62] In other words he was virtually legitimizing violence against young wives as 'ordinary'.

In another case of husband's violence an extraordinary new notion of 'contributory negligence' was produced in Chester County Court on 15 March 1982 over the case of a wife who had been battered by her violent husband and had gone to live in a Women's Aid refuge. She was driving back to the refuge in the early hours one Sunday after attending a concert with several male friends, when her husband forced her to stop by swerving his car in front of hers. He pulled her out, punched her, and as she ran for safety he leapt into her car and chased her up the pavement, at one stage driving through a hedge into someone's garden. Eventually he was apprehended and sentenced to two weeks in prison. But in passing sentence Judge Seys Llewellyn also reprimanded his wife: 'Running about in cars in the early hours of the morning, with other men in the car, is likely to attract the kind of response it did on this occasion.' He also told her barrister to advise her not to behave like that again.[63]

The all too thin dividing line between violence and rape in marriage has exposed another feature of the law prejudicial to women. As one study pointed out, 'According to the law, sexual intercourse within a marriage is a man's conjugal prerogative and a woman's conjugal duty,' and thus rape in marriage can become a husband's right.[64] A legal precedent from the 1650s ruled: 'The husband cannot be guilty of rape committed by himself upon his lawful wife, for by their mutual matrimonial consent and contract the wife hath given herself in this kind unto her husband which she cannot retract.'[65] This basic principle remains in force today, slightly amended to prevent the husband using 'physical violence' to enforce his right and to give some limited protection while a separation process is going through; even then a judgement in 1954 stated: 'The mere fact that the wife has left her husband and has presented a petition for divorce does not infer revocation of the yes consent to sexual intercourse.'[66] In October 1981 a man who admitted to smashing his way into a woman's house and raping her was only convicted of 'entering premises with violence' and 'assault'; no rape charge could be brought because, although they were living apart, they were not yet legally separated, and he received only a £100 fine from a Reading court.[67]

This messy state of the law has provided a field day for judicial discretion. In 1980 Mr Justice Holdings granted a judicial separation to a man on the grounds that the refusal of his wife to have sex more than twice a week was 'unreasonable behaviour'.[68] In another case, involving a white woman who was the victim of two black rapists, the judge allowed defence counsel to introduce evidence that she had had black boyfriends in the past and also had a black child. This 'showed she had a predilection for having sexual relations with black people', remarked the Judge[69] – as if that had anything at all to do with the fact that she was raped.

Such cases are not unusual. Indeed, the evidence suggests they are the *norm*, a further twist being given by the tendency to treat with leniency violence by husbands who claim they have been driven to it by persistent 'nagging' or some similar stereotyped domestic provocation.[70] And the problem runs right up to the top of the judicial tree, as was confirmed in 1976 when the House of Lords ruled in the Morgan case that the man was not guilty of rape if he honestly *though unreasonably* believed the woman had consented.

It follows that womanhood itself is politically on trial all the time women come up against a legal system which reflects a dominant male culture.

· JUDGES VS. PUBLIC TRANSPORT ·

What may prove to be the most important political trial of the 1980s occurred over the Greater London Council's cheap fares policy for public transport. A series of legal judgements in the winter of 1981 forced the reversal of the policy, the whole episode highlighting a number of key issues: the political bias of the judiciary; their discretion; the ability of judges to overturn parliamentary legislation, in this case for subsidizing public transport; and their willingness effectively to overturn a democratic election result just a few months previously.

The story began with the manifesto produced by the London Labour Party for the May 1981 G.L.C. elections. It pledged: 'Within six months of winning the election, Labour will cut fares on London Transport buses and tubes by an average of 25 per cent.' The manifesto also made it quite clear that this would have to be funded by rates increases. During the election campaign, the low fares policy was the main plank of Labour's appeal to the electorate and Party candidates were quite open about the need, not just for public subsidy through the rates, but specifically for a 'supplementary' rate rise which it would be necessary to levy that autumn in order to bridge the gap to the following spring when the authority's rates would normally be due for review.

So Londoners knew full well what they were voting for that May, and when they returned Labour to power at the G.L.C.'s headquarters, County Hall, the new Labour team quickly set about implementing their promise on fares and deciding on the rates rise needed. But by this time another factor had entered the picture, in the form of the Conservative government's new powers to control local government expenditure. The government took unprecedented controls over local authority finance, with the effect on the G.L.C. amounting to a special government penalty tax on its low fares programme, doubling the rates rise which would otherwise have been needed to finance it. This was because the £110 million extra expenditure needed to subsidize the fares cut resulted in the government imposing a £50 million penalty on the authority. So instead of a 6.1p in the pound rate rise, an amount of 11.9p was necessary to make up for the loss in central government grant.

It was this unplanned-for consequence of the fares cut which Lord Denning seized upon when the London Borough of Bromley took the G.L.C. to the Appeal Court in November 1981. The fares cut had meanwhile been implemented from 5 October, amid an outcry from Tory Party leaders, businessmen and ratepayers; public transport users of course felt differently.

Lord Denning's judgement, delivered on 10 November 1981, said that the fares cut was injuring ratepayers 'far more severely' than voters had realized before the election, because of the government claw-back, adding: '. . . nevertheless the majority of the Council determined to go ahead with the cut of 25 per cent irrespective of the penalizing hardship on the ratepayers.' The burden of his opposition to the G.L.C.'s policy was thus the 'hardship' caused to ratepayers – nowhere did he consider the 'hardship' that would be caused to public transport as a consequence of his judgement.

He also permitted himself some characteristically reactionary remarks. For instance, challenging the G.L.C. Labour group's argument that they were merely carrying out a manifesto commitment supported by voters, he declared that 'A manifesto issued by a political party . . . is not to be taken as gospel . . . Very few of the electorate read it in full.' Besides the point that this was not the issue, he was confusing the difference between the small print in a manifesto and the dominant plank of it. For few if any voters could have been ignorant about the fares cut. It had been drawn up over a period of two years of consultation and was the main campaign issue. Instead, Lord Denning was indulging in his regular pastime of airing his own political prejudices.

His extraordinary conclusion stretched to the limits the elasticity of judicial discretion. The actions of the G.L.C., he maintained, 'went beyond their statutory powers and are null and void'. The legal basis for such a statement was not really argued through, and Lord Denning made sure that he had it both ways by saying: 'Even if they were within their statutory powers, they were distorted by giving undue weight to the manifesto and by the arbitrary and unfair nature of the decision.' In other words *he* felt the fares cut was 'unfair', *he* felt the G.L.C.'s powers had been exceeded. It was his personal opinion that he was relying upon rather than something enshrined in statute. The accompanying two judgements by Lord Justice Oliver and Lord Justice Watkins were more closely argued but ultimately just as dependent upon political opinion. They, however, had the advantage not possessed by elected political representatives of being able to dress up their political prejudices in judicial language and thereby claim a higher mandate for them.

In brief, then, the burden of the legal case against the G.L.C. was that the authority owed a duty to ratepayers to charge as much as possible for fares but no more; that the supplementary rate was unreasonable; that the G.L.C. had not fairly balanced the interests of ratepayers against those of the travelling public; and that the Labour councillors had given undue weight to their manifesto commitment to cut fares in the light of changed circumstances brought about by withdrawal of the government block grant.

The device used by Lord Denning and his colleagues was really the one to which Lewis Carroll through Humpty Dumpty had alluded – to make words mean just what judges choose them to mean.

Thus, under Section 1 of the Transport (London) Act 1969, the G.L.C. has the duty to provide an 'integrated, efficient, and economic' transport system. The judges seized on the term 'economic' and defined it in a particular, narrow (and political) way to mean 'businesslike' and 'profitable'. That is to say they interpreted it to mean 'commercial' rather than to interpret it in a broader fashion which would have paid regard to the economic consequences on the whole transport and social infrastructure of the city, if public transport continued to decline and was replaced by private vehicles. Thus, they challenged the right of the G.L.C. to subsidize fares, although they also fudged the extent to which subsidy might be possible. In practice London Transport fares had been subsidized ever since the 1969 Act, though much less so than other capital cities in the industrialized world.

But inspection of the parliamentary debates which preceded the passing of the 1969 Act makes it clear that Parliament at least intended the G.L.C. to have the power to determine policy over such matters as the level of subsidy. Moving the second reading of the Bill on 17 December 1968, the Minister of Transport, Richard Marsh, spoke of the role of the G.L.C. in relation to the London Transport Executive. He said the Bill gave the G.L.C. the right to determine policy and to take the consequent financial responsibility:

This is very important, because if the council wishes the executive to do something that will cause it to fall short of its financial targets, it will itself have to take financial responsibility for it. The council might wish, for example, the executive to run a series of services at a loss for social or planning reasons. It might wish to keep fares down at a time when costs are rising and there is no scope for economies. It is free to do so. But it has to bear the cost.

During the Committee stage of the Bill on 17 March 1969, Mr Marsh said that a democratically elected local authority should have the power to use rates 'in a particular way for the benefit of its electors'. It should have 'the right to say, "we will use our rates in this particular direction not as a social service but because the economic cost to us in London – to industry and to the public – would be much higher if we did not use our funds this way".' In other words, the elected government of the day had pre-empted any Denning-type argument about the nature of 'economic' in the Act. The language used seems so straightforward that even an Appeal Court judge could have understood it. But that did not stop their lordships.

As a footnote to the parliamentary debate over the Bill it is also interesting to contrast Mrs Thatcher's delight in 1981 as prime minister at Lord Denning's judgement, with her statement as the then frontbench spokesperson on transport welcoming the government intention to allow for subsidy from the rates. She was joined by Michael Heseltine, who argued that 'it would be better to subsidize those uneconomic services from the rates than to put up the fares for all the travellers'. Times change.

On 17 December 1981, moving with unusual haste, the law lords unanimously upheld the Court of Appeal. They repeated what can only be construed as a narrowly capitalist interpretation of the law. The term in the Act 'integrated, efficient and economic transport facilities' meant that services should be run on a 'cost effective basis', argued Lord Wilberforce. Lord Scarman said that the burden on ratepayers should be avoided or diminished as much as possible. Again, their judgements were riddled with politically subjective remarks: instead of leaving duly elected politicians to determine political decisions, they happily abrogated this right to themselves. 'The Law Lords appear to have indulged in a legalistic play on words without regard for the social consequences,' commented the *Guardian*.

The G.L.C. leader, Ken Livingstone, aptly related the judgement to the failure of the Secretary for the Environment, Michael Heseltine, to secure tough new powers curbing still more the financial autonomy of local councils:

In a sense the Law Lords have saved Heseltine because he can't get through the legislation he wants to get control over councils, but the Law Lords' judgement makes it unnecessary, because it shifts the whole balance of every decision in local government, massively, against expenditure ... the Law Lords have affirmed ... that our primary duty is to the relationship like that between directors of a company and shareholders. It is to make the least expenditure and the best profit: services are secondary.[71]

These quickly proved prophetic words. Not only was the Labour G.L.C. forced completely to abandon its cheap fares policy (doubling them from 21 March 1982, although eight months later obtaining legal advice allowing for a 25 per cent cut on the new rates), but councils elsewhere in the country were forced to abandon or cut down on their subsidies too. As each council wrestled with the problem, it was clear that the basis of the legal judgements was ambiguous. It was not clear by *how* much a council could legally subsidize any more, with conflicting advice from various eminent lawyers. Greater Manchester Council, for example, put its fares up by 15 per cent, while South Yorkshire County Council at one stage received legal advice that their fares (which had been frozen since 1975) would have to be raised by a mind-boggling 1,270 per cent to remain within the law as newly defined.

In the event, South Yorkshire's low fares were reprieved after a High Court ruling on 17 February that metropolitan authorities *outside* London could have cheap fares subsidized by the rates. While it came as a welcome and unexpected relief to these authorities, the ruling merely underlined the topsy-turvy state of the law and the way in which the judiciary held sway over elected representatives. Giving judgement that the Labour-controlled Merseyside County Council's decision to cut bus fares by 10 per cent and levy a 6p supplementary rate was lawful, Mr Justice Woolf relied on a rather thin basis for differentiating between the 1969 Act governing London Transport and the Transport Act 1968 which applies generally through the country. He noted, for instance, that whereas the London Act imposed a duty to provide 'integrated, efficient and economic transport facilities', the 1968 Act does not include the word 'economic' in its list of objectives. This he gave as one of the reasons why the financial constraints in London were more stringent than elsewhere. Although it *favoured* cheap fares, this judgement showed (as conversely did the one *against* the G.L.C.) just how much scope was found for legal nit-picking in matters of public policy. The absurdity of a position where two Transport Acts passed within a year of each other under the same Labour government (and doubtless the work of the same parliamentary draftsmen) could be interpreted in opposite ways underlined the hazards of allowing the judiciary to be final arbiters over political decisions. Just to compound matters, the same Judge, Mr Justice Woolf, had ruled a few weeks previously against a supplementary rate levied by West Midlands County Council to subsidize a 25 per cent cut in public transport fares, and the council was forced to put up fares by 70 per cent (for technical reasons, however, this ruling had less status than his ruling in the Merseyside case).

Soon the law lords' decision over the G.L.C. was reverberating beyond transport policy. In his judgement, Lord Diplock had emphasized the concept of 'fiduciary duty' when he argued that knowingly relinquishing central government grant was clearly 'a thriftless use of moneys obtained by the G.L.C. from ratepayers . . . It was thus a breach of the fiduciary duty owed by the G.L.C. to the ratepayers.' The concept of 'fiduciary duty' went back to the judgement given in 1923 against Poplar Council, where the Appeal Court declared that councillors were in a 'fiduciary position' to *every* ratepayer and not just those who had elected them. 'A councillor is not entitled to be unduly generous at the expense of those on whose behalf he is a trustee,' said the judges.[72]

In the wake of this judgement, the Department of the Environment (D.o.E.) produced a special legal opinion advising councillors of their duty to ratepayers and the legal position of councils which exceeded their spending targets set by central government. It contained an implicit warning that to exceed these targets would be to run a real risk of acting unlawfully, with councillors being vulnerable to being individually surcharged. As the *Guardian* explained following a D.o.E. briefing:

Mr Heseltine is now relying strongly on councillors' fear of the implications of this judgement to keep local authority spending within his targets. This could make up for his two failures to get tougher legislation through Parliament to do the job. Mr Heseltine is aware that council officials will tend to put a cautious interpretation on fiduciary duty and that councillors may feel obliged to sacrifice spending ambitions when faced with the threat of court action.[73]

Indeed at the very time this D.o.E. advice was being circulated, the Labour-controlled Inner London Education Authority voted to avoid a legal confrontation by adopting an economy budget of £795 million for the year 1982/3 which was 1 per cent lower in real terms than its then existing expenditure. An alternative, which would have maintained existing services and incurred £11 million extra spending towards fulfilling Labour's additional manifesto commitments, was defeated after legal advice that court action would be likely if a larger budget were accepted.

It is clear from the opinion given to the I.L.E.A. by counsel just how much of a legal straitjacket had been placed on local councils by the law lords.[74] The opinion considered different budgetary options as if they were purely and simply *legal* matters, rather than *political* and *social* questions. Various lumps of money were bandied about in the opinion, regardless of their consequences for the educational services the authority was charged with providing. The term 'reasonable' was used as if it were not itself ambiguous. In practice, a budget increase became 'reasonable' if lawyers said so – and even they could not be sure, given the uncertain state of the law. A similar dilemma had faced the G.L.C. councillors when they tried to fulfil their election manifesto commitment to freeze council rent levels. Labour felt that tenants had suffered disproportionately high rent increases under the previous Tory administration, and a freeze was a way of redressing the situation. But the policy had to be abandoned in the face of legal advice insisting that the councillors would be acting 'illegally' and would themselves be surcharged for millions of pounds of revenue notionally 'lost' by a freeze. The judges had given lawyers a pistol to hold to the heads of councillors – and more to the point, Labour councillors. For it was the threat perceived by the Tory government and the judiciary of radical Labour councils determined to defend public services which necessitated the intervention of the courts.

·THE CITIZEN AND THE LAW·

'The great majority of the population,' reported the organization Justice in 1977, 'is ignorant not only of what the law is, but of how it works.'[75] Rights mean very little if they are based on ignorance, and there is a sense in which the judiciary by its very secretiveness shuts out access by the ordinary citizen. The inadequacies of legal services have been well documented,[76] but it is necessary to be clear about the *political* consequences of the manner in which the contemporary legal system operates. Its effect is to the advantage of certain, mostly more powerful and well-off, sections of the community, and to the disadvantage of other, mostly powerless and poor, sections. In other words the working of the legal system is inherently biased, if not by design – for in theory all are equal in the eyes of the law – then at least by default.

Here again we see the critical role of judicial discretion at work. For example, a survey published in 1981 of 600 Crown court cases in various parts of the country, selected at random, showed the way in which the courts use their discretion to make defendants pay for legal representation, sometimes even if they have been acquitted. It concluded: 'The situation as it is at the moment means that, although, according to the law, a defendant is not guilty, the judge can override this, subject to no other authority, bound by no rules of procedure, and decide that that same person should nevertheless be punished financially.'[77] In March 1982 the same kind of discretion was exercised when Shell and B.P. were given an unprecedented £33,000 from the legal aid fund to pay the costs of defending an action brought by parents who said that lead in petrol was causing brain damage to their children.

Another study of Crown court cases, by Baldwin and McConville, described the way in which the pressures of 'administrative expediency' induced many defendants who were innocent or who were unlikely to be convicted into pleading guilty.[78] The Senate of the Bar (the controlling body of barristers) tried to stop publication of this study on the questionable grounds that it 'would be directly contrary to the public interest'.[79] (They might more appropriately have said 'the interests of the legal system'.) For its significance lay in stripping away another piece of the veneer of impartial, fair and technical mystique with which the legal system surrounds itself. Baldwin and McConville found that about 1 in 6 defendants were pressured into pleading guilty through a series of what they term 'informal settlements'. The key agency of this is 'plea bargaining', which they define as 'the practice whereby the defendant enters a plea of guilty in return for which he will be given some consideration that results in a sentence concession'.[80] The whole system tends to conspire against defendants in this situation. The web of judge/barrister relationships and prosecutor/defence counsel links is based, the authors show, on discretion and pragmatism primarily geared to providing convenient working and administrative arrangements for *them*, rather than justice for defendants. And although the Court of Appeal in 1978 declared that 'Plea bargaining has no place in the English criminal law',[81] another study confirmed 'the pervasiveness of bargaining in the administration of justice'.[82]

This is not to suggest that all such bargaining is wrong or that it always works against the interests of defendants; doubtless it makes sense sometimes. The real issue is the failure by the judiciary and the legal profession openly to concede that it is rife – indeed that it is an integral part of how the system operates. Perhaps their reluctance is born out of fear of the political reality of British justice being placed under consequent public scrutiny.

The need for such scrutiny was shown when His Honour Judge Pickles made an unusually candid admission of what actually happens during plea bargaining:

Bargains between judges and defendants as to sentence happen every day. It is in the interest of all concerned that they should . . . The practice of Crown Court Judges varies widely. Some see counsel in their rooms whenever they are asked. Some refuse to see counsel at all. One judge . . . told me that he only sees counsel he can trust . . . Some judges send for counsel before the case starts and virtually give directions for 'carving it up' . . . Some judges negotiate more subtly, by sending and receiving messages through their clerks or the court clerks . . . Judges miss life [at the Bar] and day after day see their former colleagues only across the formal courtroom. It is good to have a chat with the lads. How tempting to sit down and sort it all out sensibly, wigs off . . . The tension of open court has gone. The shorthand writer is absent. No press or public. Even the accused – around whose fate it all revolves – is not there . . . In this easy atmosphere [the formal rules] can be overlooked in a genuine effort to find a sensible short-cut, off the record.[83]

One study (of 100 court cases) which focused on the process of mitigation pointed out that since over 80 per cent of those appearing for indictable offences plead guilty, what goes on between the point of conviction and sentence is the experience which the majority of individuals have of the decision-making processes of the courts.[84] It found that judges had extensive discretion in assessing mitigation pleas and imposing sentences.

· THE LEGAL PROFESSION ·

Barristers have probably the best protected closed shop in the country. First of all, theirs is a profession blocked to ordinary young people. The initial hurdle is a university degree, followed by a period as a 'pupil' – at least a year studying under a qualified barrister, for which no grants are normally available and for which, until very recently, the pupil barrister had to pay fees. The next hurdle is finding a place in barristers' chambers; and finally there is the problem of surviving while building up a reputation. The content of legal education is governed through the Inns of Court, controlled by their 'benchers' – senior lawyers who are, in the main, judges. Advancement in the profession is conditional on the approval of this same group of people, and they of course are consulted by the Lord Chancellor's Department on the appointment of judges. The Bar – and thus the judiciary – is virtually hermetically sealed from society outside. Given this, it is hardly surprising to find two political consequences: first, that the legal profession is highly conservative and socially narrow in composition; second, that it can be politically controlled by the legal establishment.

For example, women are badly under-represented within the legal profession. Evidence collected by the Equal Opportunities Commission in 1978 showed that the proportion of women in practice at the Bar was only 8.2 per cent; the proportion of women solicitors with practising certificates was 6.5 per cent (women solicitors actually in practice amount only to about 4.5 per cent); and out of 384 Queen's Counsel, only four were women. Historically, the legal profession

both supported discriminatory laws and practices in society at large, and upheld discrimination in its own ranks. None of the supposed chivalry which men claimed underlay all their actions, was extended towards females endeavouring to join their ranks. To this day, the profession tends to manifest a grudging and uncomfortable tolerance rather than a facilitative welcome to women entrants.[85]

This is just one example of the conservative nature of lawyers as a group. The fact that barristers regulate themselves through the Professional Conduct Committee of the Bar Council means that they are effectively 'a law unto themselves', as one analyst put it.[86] This is especially important in a profession so tightly controlled by its own establishment, with judges' power over barristers in court being supplemented by their influence outside through the Bar. To challenge this power structure, as some radical and black lawyers have tried to do, is to invite ostracism not merely from the hallowed inns of the Temple but thereby from the ability to practise *effectively* in the court. For hostility from judges to individual barristers not only affects the careers of the latter, it affects the justice meted out to their clients as well.

Not that barristers have a particularly good record in representing their clients' interests. While top barristers may be highly competent and those fortunate enough to have access to them are therefore defended well, that is not the case for the vast majority of ordinary people who find themselves in court. One study found that in 96 per cent of uncontested cases and 79 per cent of contested trials in the higher criminal courts, clients saw their barristers for the *first* time on the morning of the trial.[87]

The subservient relationship between clients and their barristers has important political consequences, as Tom Hayden points out:

The law, like politics, is organized around a principle of 'representation' rather than direct participation by the people most affected. The citizen is reduced to being a client. He exercises choice only when he selects a lawyer. The lawyer then takes over as the expert in how best to represent his client's interests. The lawyer speaks for the client not in the particular style of that individual but in a proper and formalized way. Within this ritualized situation, the lawyer's highest obligation is not to the client but to the legal system itself. As a sworn 'officer of the court', the lawyer is obliged to accept the judge as the 'governor of the trial'.[88]

Significantly, he adds that 'when politics and identity are on trial and a client's state of mind is the crime, a lawyer tends to become part of the political confrontation'.

Under this system, and especially in political trials, the defendant becomes the victim, finding that 'justice' consists of the playing out of an elaborate game between two allegedly opposing lawyers, with the judge as umpire. He or she feels like a football being kicked back and forward in between passing references to reports of ancient cases. Against the background of the turgid legalese and Victorian procedure of the courtroom, the case gradually loses all relevance to defendants who sink back, watching their fate played out before them. Courts are a close-knit world of legal etiquette and legal in-jokes. 'Me learned friend this . . . Me learned friend that . . . If you would be so kind as to turn to page 892, Queens Bench Division 1868 . . . Much obliged Me Lord.' (When I defended myself at the Old Bailey in 1972 on a charge of conspiracy I momentarily slipped into the practice of referring to the prosecuting counsel as 'me learned friend', and was instantly rebuked by the judge for my impudence; not being a qualified barrister I was not sufficiently 'learned' to use this cosy terminology.)

One of the specific problems from the defendant's standpoint is what appears to be an unhealthily close relationship between prosecuting and defending counsel, evidence for which has been documented.[89] As spectators at their trials defendants realize that their defence counsel have more in common with the prosecutors than with them. Indeed, they can be seen having a smoke together during an adjournment or chatting intimately together over lunch! In a political trial, what is to the defendant a 'war' seems merely like a game to the barristers, which also means that the latter are very reluctant to press the political cause of a defendant.

Operating within the conservative confines of the legal system, solicitors are similarly constrained, the problem being increased by the political and class bias of solicitors as a profession. A study of housing, for example, has shown that, partly because some 80 per cent of solicitors' work is conveyancing, solicitors tend to identify with the interests of property speculators rather than tenants.[90] In 1968 a study of London solicitors showed that they served rich rather than poor areas. Sixty-nine per cent of London's solicitors were then located in just six out of 118 postal districts. Thirteen postal districts had no firms of solicitors at all, eighteen had just one firm, including the poor East End area of Poplar, and nineteen had just two firms, including the equally deprived area of Bethnal Green. The study also showed that only about twenty of the total number of firms in London dealt with criminal cases on any sort of scale.[91] However, since then the situation has improved substantially through the wider availability of legal aid, the emergence of a more radical breed of solicitors prepared to concentrate on legal aid work, and the setting up of law centres.

The politics of the judiciary thus come through at every level, from the bottom in the differential representation of defendants, to the top in the discretion and at times bias of judges. And how could it be otherwise? For as Lord Scarman has written, 'A fundamental truth . . . is that law and politics cannot, and at the highest level should not, be kept separate.'[92]

Another leading judge, Lord Devlin, acknowledged in 1972 that:

In theory the judiciary is the neutral force between Government and the governed. The judge interprets and applies the law without favour to either . . . British judges have never practised such detachment . . . In the criminal law the judges regard themselves at least as much concerned as the executive with the prosecution of law and order.[93]

But Lord Denning, anxious to maintain the fiction of judicial impartiality and independence from politics, has written in the same public school booklet: 'As a judge I have no party politics whatsoever.' But in the same paragraph he went on, 'These independent schools of ours are a priceless asset to our society. We must never let them become prey to doctrinaire politicians.'[94] What he meant by this of course was the Labour Party's commitment, widely debated at the time he was writing in 1981, to abolish private education. At least, however, Labour had been warned by 'non party political' Lord Denning: he was prepared to do all in *his* power to resist any future plans Labour might have in that direction.

What is more, Lord Denning could say and do this sort of thing safe in the knowledge that he was a member of a well-protected judicial elite. Although there are about 100 men in what may be termed the 'higher judiciary', in practice only thirty of these are the real policy-makers.[95] This small group determines what is the 'public interest' and establishes the broad parameters within which discretion is exercised down in the lower ranks of the judiciary. The evidence also suggests that it is a 'politically cohesive' group – much more so than in many other countries.[96] In Britain today, as in the past, judicial discretion means political power.

5

MAGISTRATES

A magistrates' court is an institution rhetorically
functioning to perpetuate the notion of possible justice in a society
whose total organization is directed at the maintenance
of the capitalist exploitation of labour, production and control.

(Pat Carlen, *Magistrates' Justice*
(Martin Robertson, 1976), p. 98)

Traditionally, most attention is focused on 'big' legal cases at the Old
Bailey and at Crown courts around the country. Journalists are usually
on permanent duty there, and so public debate tends to revolve around
the procedures and attitudes operating at that level of the judicial system.
It is a level where leading judges and top Queen's Counsel perform,
where defendants are invariably represented in court, and where generally
the administration of justice is professional.

But to focus at that level gives no more representative a picture of the
workings of the law in Britain today than attention on the stars of First
Division football gives an idea of what the reality is for lower divisions, let
alone the weekend leagues where most football in Britain is actually played.

Over 90 per cent of all criminal justice is processed through magistrates' courts. They are the places where the day-to-day law operates,
and they thus give some insight into the extent of 'ordinary' political
trials. In bygone days they were known as 'police courts' (a few still have
the name etched into their frontage). Today they could well be called
'class courts', directly reflecting the wider class structure: 'Defendants
tend to be young and working class; magistrates old and middle class.' [1]

· ORIGINS ·

While the title 'Justice of the Peace' is ancient, the office itself is really a
modern one. It dates only from the mid-nineteenth century; before that

'justices' combined political and judicial authority. Sitting as magistrates, they imposed the law on their tenants and inferiors; meeting in Quarter Sessions they issued instructions for the conduct of local affairs in such matters as police, the Poor Law, roads, sanitation and so on. They were also quite capable of performing a politically partisan role. During the Combination Act period, for example, they used their powers repressively, sometimes even acting as *agents provocateurs* when they encouraged their own informers and spies to lead others to form illegal combinations – and then imposed heavy punishment on the offenders.[2] The tension between the emerging working class and magistrates was illustrated in 1823 by the case of one Ryding, who 'deliberately attacked his master with a weapon rather than his fists so as to make his crime too serious to be within the jurisdiction of the magistrates'.[3]

As democratic consciousness grew, more and more functions came to be described as 'political' and were taken away from the justices and put in the hands of elected local authorities. These authorities, and government departments, also acquired the wide new range of functions which the expansion of state activity in the Industrial Revolution brought with it. Only law and order, including control of the police, failed to pass into the hands of elected councils and their full-time officials.

In *towns*, Quarter Sessions were held under the authority of the borough charter; the mayor and the other officers of the corporation were the magistrates, and 'this small and oligarchical group co-opted new members when necessary without further outside interference'.[4] The landmark legislation, the Municipal Reform Act of 1835, separated judicial and legal functions and placed the appointment of justices in the hands of the Lord Chancellor.

In *rural* areas it was not until fifty years later that elected councils took over the magistracy's powers. The County Councils Act of 1888 was a logical outcome of the extension of the franchise to men in rural areas in 1881, as the 1835 municipal reforms had followed from the great Reform Act of 1832.

From these early days, political controversy has surrounded the appointment of magistrates. In the 1880s, complaints that individuals became magistrates as a reward for political service to the Tory Party were 'rife'.[5] In the early part of this century, renewed concern along the same lines eventually led to the setting up of a Royal Commission on the Selection of Justices of the Peace, which reported in 1910. It was 'devised with the main aim of warding off pressure to appoint to the bench

simply as a reward for political service'.[6] It recommended a system of
'advisory committees' which could take local soundings on people suitable
to be magistrates and make recommendations for appointments. In the
first half of the century these advisory committees were convened by the
Lord Lieutenants, themselves mostly members of prominent and wealthy
local families who had military experience. The advisory committees
were eventually given the power to make recommendations directly to
the Lord Chancellor after another Royal Commission had recommended
this in 1948. It had been set up partly in response to further allegations
of political bias in the selection of J.P.s.

· COMPOSITION OF THE BENCH ·

The membership of the advisory committees is a closely guarded secret.
Officially this is to prevent pressure being put on them: in reality such
secrecy conceals the fact that virtually all members of advisory committees are magistrates of long standing. Although the secrecy makes it
difficult to scrutinize the basis upon which J.P.s are selected, broadly
speaking what happens is this: names are suggested to the advisory
committee through various routes (voluntary groups, political parties, or
individuals of some social standing). Then follows a period of investigation of likely candidates on an informal basis: the individuals themselves
may not be interviewed and usually are not aware that discreet inquiries
are proceeding as to their suitability. The next they hear (and it takes
many months) is directly from the Lord Chancellor's office welcoming
them to the fold. Those who have been through this experience find it
distinctly odd.

The magistracy remains strongly dominated by supporters of the
Conservative Party, who tend to nominate the 'right sort' of people –
that is people from their own social and political circles. Their choices
are rarely couched in terms of class or political objection to other candidates, but that is their effect. 'Party interest remains an issue largely
because . . . resentment is caused by the rejection of Labour Party nom-
inations or the obvious presence of too many Tories. In periods of
Labour Government, this can bring quite strong intervention by the
Lord Chancellor in appointments to particular divisions . . . with pressure
on advisory committees to substitute accredited Labour for Tory nom-
inations.'[7]

Labour protests, such as those which led to the creation of the 1948 Royal Commission, have resulted in an oft-noted response – the call that appointments to the bench should be 'non-political'. As in so many other areas of national life, the call to 'keep out politics' means to 'keep out left-of-centre politics' and leave the status quo; an explicitly reactionary call. This is borne out by recent research which closely examined seven benches and a total of 430 magistrates. The sample found that 37 per cent were Conservative and 35 per cent Labour, 8 per cent Liberal and 20 per cent undeclared or non-political, of whom it was concluded that 'this 20 per cent is more likely to include people with right- rather than left-wing sympathies'.[8] But there is ample evidence that the real divide in British politics – between left and right, *including* Labour Party members, manifests itself in the composition of the bench. As the same research found: 'The rejection of left-wingers has also caused a lot of muttering. "Extreme" views of any kind are always regarded by an advisory committee as a disqualification . . . On the other hand, the Labour Party may very well ask, how far removed from the far left do you have to be before your views cease to appear extreme to a predominantly right-wing advisory committee?'[9]

But politics is not the only contentious matter in the composition of magistrates. They are on the whole elderly – 40 per cent of those on advisory committees and 25 per cent of J.P.s are over 65. They are mostly male – just one-third of both groups are women. Working-class people are badly under-represented, and there is an abject absence of individuals from the black community, even in areas where there are relatively large numbers of black people.[10] One study suggested that 'the magistracy is not representative in any real sense of the wider community'.[11] A survey in Coventry, conducted in 1981 by solicitor and law lecturer Michael King, found that of the city's 167 J.P.s only one was a West Indian and two were Indians. Together, they amounted to just 1.8 per cent of the bench, whereas the two communities comprised 7 per cent of the city's population. This encouraged King to conclude: 'The present system of choosing magistrates has in effect created a self perpetuating power group almost totally resistant to change and completely lacking in democratic accountability or control.'[12]

In all there are about 23,000 'lay' magistrates in England and Wales who dispense what is known as 'amateur justice'. But there are also about 50 full-time professionals, known as 'stipendiary magistrates'. They were first appointed in 1792 for the Court of Middlesex, to deal with the corrupt state into which the administration of justice had fallen in London. Such was the opposition to paid justices, who it was feared would become servants of the central state rather than the local community, that the chief metropolitan magistrate had, during the preceding half century, been paid out of Secret Service funds, lest his relationship with the government became known.[13] Stipendiaries now hear all cases in Inner London magistrates' courts and share the work with lay magistrates in other urban areas. They have usually had legal experience, and many have served the state in other legal capacities.

·POLITICS OF MAGISTRATES' COURTS·

The composition of the bench is by no means the whole story in the politics of magistrates' courts. First, they are seen as hostile and alien institutions for many defendants, particularly if, as is likely, they are from working-class backgrounds. Evidence collected by Pat Carlen over a twenty-month period in eight London courts suggested that defendants are in a hopeless position. They rarely hear all that is going on around them, since between them and the bench are usually clerks, solicitors, probation officers, social workers, press reporters and police, all of whom have their own professional language. Many understand 'nothing at all' or 'very little' of the procedure in court. They are given little information, left waiting for hours, and shuffled around from room to room. They are, moreover, *expected* to plead guilty, especially by the police who see a guilty plea as the appropriate response for someone in the position of a defendant. A warrant officer in one of the courts studied claimed that West Indians were 'stubborn' because they did not plead guilty often enough. The point to be stressed about these findings is not that there was some concerted attempt by officialdom to bear down upon defendants – more that for bureaucratic reasons the courts are geared up to process defendants in sausage-machine-like fashion. Carlen describes what she terms a 'professional monopoly' of rules and procedures which produce a situation where 'a defendant in a magistrates' court is, by definition, an incompetent member of society'.[14] Even the most sensitive of members of the bench cannot compensate for the depressing and powerless role ascribed to the accused. Reinforcing it all is the fact that the majority are not legally represented and, even when they are, too many lawyers read their briefs literally minutes before they step into court.

The second factor is the attitude of the bench towards the police. By and large, such evidence as there is suggests that the bench favours the police's version of events rather than that of the defendant.[15] It has been pointed out that 'most magistrates do not come from walks of life where they are likely to see the rough side of policing'.[16] They are therefore intrinsically likely to see the picture through the eyes of the police rather than the accused, particularly since the more experienced they become on the bench the more hardened a view they will take of criminal activity and the unpleasant and dangerous job the police have to do to combat it. In one case where the accused had refused on medical grounds to put their hands on their heads and stand against the wall, during a police search of a hotel bar in Bournemouth in 1972, the magistrate told them: 'You have to do what the police tell you. Everyone has to. If the police told the Prime Minister to do so, he must.'[17]

There is a strongly held view that magistrates' courts today live up to their old name of 'police courts'. One practising solicitor with some seventeen years' experience reported in 1980:

I have actually known cases where the police have reduced the charge from actual bodily harm to assault on police in order to keep it in the magistrates' court because they know full well that if a jury heard such a case justice might actually be done – the defendant acquitted and the police officer disciplined or expelled from the force. 'Justice' in the magistrates' court has become a joke . . . they used to be called and still are police courts.[18]

The same solicitor also argued that the 'majority of magistrates instead of determining guilt or innocence on the basis of "beyond reasonable doubt" determine the matter on the basis that it is for the defence to prove innocence'. And he recalled how one magistrate had said in court in the mid-1970s: 'We never acquit in this court.'

Such a view will square with the experience of those who have followed particularly the more contentious cases. But the more general flow of cases through the courts would probably not be so starkly handled. The Secretary of the Magistrates' Association pointed out in response to the solicitor quoted above that in 1975, where the principal charge was an assault on a constable, magistrates acquitted in 27 per cent of contested cases and juries in 20 per cent. He quoted research saying that these and other statistics 'give the lie to the crude assertion that magistrates are incurably prosecution minded. Since half the defendants who contest their cases in magistrates' courts are acquitted, this notion must now be laid to rest.'[19]

Furthermore, J.P.s have been just as prone to idiosyncratic behaviour as judges, reinforcing again the argument that the operation of the law is vulnerable to prejudice and incompetence, and palpably lacks the consistency and certainty alleged to be one of its main virtues. Back in 1962 a study showed a wide disparity in sentencing by magistrates,[20] and partly as a result of this a new training scheme was instituted for J.P.s from 1966. But in 1980, another survey found wide variations in prison sentencing by magistrates. Dorset county magistrates, for example, were found to have a rate of prison sentencing 50 per cent higher than the national average, the report commenting: 'For every one man sent to prison in Gwent . . . the Dorset magistrates sent four.'[21] Another extraordinary lack of consistency was revealed in 1982 by a survey of punishments imposed by London magistrates on first offenders pleading guilty to possessing cannabis. It found that anything from a conditional discharge to a fine of £75 could be imposed for similar offences. According to the survey, Highgate magistrates were 'quite severe; conditional discharges rare'. By contrast, Marylebone was 'possibly the least severe court in London for cannabis offenders. Conditional discharges not unusual and most fines won't exceed £25 for first offenders.'[22] Moreover, a four-year survey published in 1982 showed wide discrepancies in the granting of legal aid by magistrates. It even revealed differences between neighbouring areas: defendants in Slough, for example, were 28 times more likely to be refused aid than in Reading. In inner London, the court with the highest refusal rate – 26 per cent – was Highbury; interestingly, social workers picketed it in protest in 1979 and in that year the court's refusal rate dropped to 15 per cent, compared with 29 and 42 per cent in 1977 and 1978 respectively.[23]

In the same court at Highbury a stipendiary magistrate told a woman teacher in January 1982 that she 'should expect to be hit' in the course of her career at least six times.[24] The teacher, Suzanne Puttock, had complained of being hit by the parents of a pupil, but the magistrate refused her permission to take out a private summons, telling her she was wasting ratepayers' money. (Later, a case was brought, resulting in the parent being found guilty of assault.)

Another example of magisterial discretion occurred in 1971, when the chairman of Staines Magistrates' Court called a twelve-year-old boy into court where his mother was appearing on a charge of stealing money and asked him: 'Do you know why your mother is up here today?' The magistrate, Mr John Slagg, asked if anyone could support the woman after he had read probation reports. The boy was the only relative in court. 'You look clean and tidy, that's your mother's doing, is it?' he asked the boy. 'Does she look after you well?' The boy answered 'Yes.'[25]

The role of the J.P.s illustrates very well the problem of attempting what may be termed a 'consensus' model of decision-making in a society riddled with class conflict and inequality. One study suggested that 'lay justice is administered by people who in the main are moderate, fair and conscientious: decent people picked for their ability to get on with other decent people'.[26] And if that is the case, who could possibly object to it? But the issue here is not so much to question the sincerity of magistrates. It is to question the political role which, willy nilly, they find themselves playing if they do not *consciously* align themselves with the poor and the powerless in our society. To play a consensus role is to maintain the consensus: the status quo, which is itself a political stance.

· POLITICAL CASES ·

But in political trials J.P.s often do not play a 'neutral' or even a 'fair' or 'moderate' role, and their political prejudices are frequently exposed. (In a slightly different context, I recall how, when coming up for committal in 1975 in my mistaken identity case, my defence was anxious to avoid one particular magistrate in the South West London Court who was known to local solicitors for what they termed his 'racist' views.)

One of the clearest examples of the political role of magistrates has been the use of the ancient power to 'bind over' to keep the peace. It derives from the Justices of the Peace Act 1361, which gives virtually arbitrary powers to magistrates. It can be quite reasonably used in place of a formal prosecution in return for which the police would drop a charge. But it can be and has been used against a defendant *after* his acquittal. It has even been used against *witnesses* attending the court. Here again we see the enormous discretionary power that can be wielded in the legal system.

The 1361 statute was aimed at renegade soldiers marauding around the country after returning from the French wars – hardly appropriate to contemporary conditions. An updated version is the 1952 Magistrates

Court Act. But whereas this stipulates that magistrates should hear formal evidence before making an order, the 1361 Act gives what amounts to unrestricted power. Theoretically, the individual's consent to be bound over has to be obtained. But if such consent is not obtained, the court has the power to impose a prison sentence: consent in these circumstances is somewhat academic, as has been shown in a series of political cases.

Back in 1913, George Lansbury M.P. fell foul of the Act for supporting militancy by suffragettes. So did the trade unionist Tom Mann during the hunger marches in 1932. More recently, Bertrand Russell was imprisoned under the Act in 1961 with other members of the Committee of 100. Vietnam protesters arrested outside the American Embassy in 1965 and 1966 were bound over for a year, effectively barring them from participating in political activity during that time, while in 1969 the pacifist Pat Arrowsmith was jailed for six months for refusing to be bound over following an *entirely peaceful* protest outside a factory supplying equipment for the American army in the Vietnam war. There have been numerous other cases of the arbitrary exercise of such power by magistrates in a manner that can only be described as politically biased. On the other hand, the Act has often been used to discourage 'Peeping Toms' from pestering women and to discourage poison-pen letter writers. It is usually only when the power is used to control political activity that it has been challenged.

· RECENT DEVELOPMENTS ·

The 1977 Criminal Law Act tremendously extended the powers of magistrates. The origins of these provisions of the Act go back to 1973, when Lord Hailsham, the Conservative Lord Chancellor, was seeking ways in which the growing delays between arrest and trial could be reduced, with the apparently laudable aim of reducing the time which people spent in custody. Rejecting the possibility of increasing the number of courts with juries, Lord Hailsham and Robert Carr, the Home Secretary, instead appointed a committee under Lord Justice James. It was charged with investigating the distribution of criminal business between courts – specifically, between Crown courts and magistrates' courts. Having asked this question, Lord Hailsham received the only possible answer. The James Committee reported in November 1975, and recommended that the simplest way of relieving the burden on

Crown courts was to increase the number of offences which could only be tried by magistrates. The proposals were enthusiastically adopted by the Labour government and formed part of the 1977 Act.

The most significant transfer to magistrates' courts concerned public order offences – obstruction of the highway, obstruction of the police, threatening behaviour, assault on the police – which are those normally brought against people arrested on political demonstrations. Arrest on a demonstration is a random matter in many respects, often depending on the tactics which the police choose to employ. But the aftermath of two major confrontations in London – Grunwick in 1977 and the anti-fascist demonstration in Southall during the 1979 election campaign – has sharply highlighted the political role which magistrates can play with their new extended powers.

There were loud complaints that those arrested at Grunwick were being harshly dealt with, particularly by the magistrates' courts at Willesden and Barnet. In the months during which mass picketing took place outside the Grunwick factory, over 500 people were arrested. In the majority of cases, heavy fines and even prison sentences were handed out to first offenders, and in very few cases was evidence for the prosecution given by anyone other than police officers. The cases were heard at first before magistrates at Barnet. The rate of conviction was around 75 to 80 per cent. The police were reported to be surprised: they had only expected convictions to be as high as 55 per cent.

When cases began to be heard at Willesden, the conviction rate went above even that of Barnet. One reason for this was certainly the attitude of the magistrates towards those arrested during the mass pickets, which led them to treat the demonstrators less sympathetically than other defendants. One magistrate, Mrs Dorothy Oakley, was overheard commenting on the Grunwick affair shortly before she sat in judgement on arrested pickets, and the doctor to whom she expressed her opinions later gave a sworn statement:

Mrs Oakley said that she was one of the few magistrates who is not politically involved in this trial; that is, to say, does not support one side or the other. Most of the other magistrates have strong political feelings about the issue, and belong to one or other political parties. Mrs Oakley went on to say that many of those arrested had been tried by stipendiary magistrates. This was very unsatisfactory, she explained, because a stipendiary magistrate does not know local conditions, does not know what has been going on here, and has been giving them all very light sentences. About 40 per cent have got off. 'We shall have to change all that, and they will all get stiffer sentences.' According to the sworn statement, Mrs Oakley added that she had liked trade unions in her youth – she was brought up in a mining town – but that now they had become too powerful. [27]

Mrs Oakley's sentiments are probably quite common; she probably reflected feelings of residents of Willesden who were not aware that the tactic of mass picketing had been chosen as a last resort by the strike committee at Grunwick in the face of an obdurate and politically motivated employer. But that is not the point. Magistrates are supposed to try cases on their merits; to examine the evidence and to decide on the basis of probabilities. This is not what Mrs Oakley was contemplating; because of her knowledge of local circumstances she was planning to convict a greater proportion of defendants than she (wrongly) thought had been convicted by other magistrates.

Many demonstrators fear that, once they are singled out for arrest, a fine – usually steep – is inevitable. This is no doubt in line with the thoughts of the law-and-order brigade – but it is clear that for some magistrates the courts are simply a way of enforcing their political and social views.

Similar complaints arose from court sequels to the anti-fascist demonstration in Southall, West London, on 23 April 1979. The National Front held its annual celebration of St George's day in Southall town hall, in a clear provocation of the area's large Asian community. Despite local efforts to have the meeting cancelled, the local Conservative-controlled council allowed it to go ahead. The N.F. claimed – and the Conservative council agreed – that the meeting was an 'election meeting' connected with the forthcoming general election, and that the Representation of the People Act therefore gave them a right to meet in council premises. Neighbouring Labour-controlled Brent Council, however, had prohibited a similar meeting in their borough on the grounds that National Front meetings are not open to the public, as election meetings must be by law.

Thousands of local people took to the streets to oppose the handful of N.F. supporters meeting in their town. They clashed with an even larger number of police. Police action on that day raised many questions, notably those surrounding the death of the teacher and anti-fascist activist Blair Peach. [28] The 342 people arrested was the largest number on one day since the sit-down protests in central London by the Committee of 100 in 1961.

Those 342 appeared before magistrates at Barnet, which in itself provoked protests from defendants and their lawyers as Barnet is twenty miles from Southall where most of the defendants lived. The decision that the majority of cases arising out of the trial should be heard at Barnet was coupled with the decision that the defendants would appear, not before a bench of lay magistrates, but before stipendiary magistrates who normally work in courts in central London.

Four stipendiaries in particular were the subject of much criticism by lawyers and defendants' organizations. They are a typical sample of those who become stipendiaries. Edmund MacDermott became a stipendiary magistrate in 1972. A qualified barrister since 1935, he had joined the Department of the Director of Public Prosecutions in 1946, serving as Assistant D.P.P. from 1968 until his appointment to the bench. Peter Badge, a solicitor, worked for the Metropolitan Police and became a magistrates' clerk in Marlow in 1967 while still in private practice. As solicitor to the Detention Appeals Tribunal in Northern Ireland between 1973 and 1975, he was responsible for the presentation of the case of the police and the security forces for continued detention without trial. Brian Canham, a barrister since 1955, had served with the Army's legal services in Germany from 1956 to 1963, prosecuting at court martials. Kenneth Cooke was a solicitor and clerk to various magistrates' courts in Lancashire and Yorkshire before becoming a stipendiary magistrate in 1970.

The rate of convictions at Barnet for those arrested at Southall who appeared before the four stipendiaries was 81 per cent. Convictions in magistrates' courts normally average around 52 per cent. By the beginning of November 1979, the four had between them decided 116 cases: there were 21 acquittals; 10 people were jailed, 16 received suspended sentences; fines and costs were levied totalling just over £8,000; and 38 people were bound over to keep the peace.[29]

The choice of these four men to hear the cases arising out of Southall was clearly crucial to the outcome of the cases. In view of the severity of the police action on the day, the sequels in court were seen by the community in Southall as a continuation of a punitive attack by the authorities on those who were protesting against racism: the fines were regarded in much the same manner as the collective punishments levied on colonial villagers who defied British rule by supporting nationalists. **The consequences of the demonstration and the trials had a far greater impact on the Southall community than any change of government, local** or national, could have done. Yet the process by which the four men who were responsible for this were given that authority is not only not a democratic process, it is a secret one. They were appointed to the bench by the Lord Chancellor's office, and that office also selected them for the special courts at Barnet. Sir Brian Robertson, Secretary of Commission in the Lord Chancellor's Office, said, 'It's a question of matching the work to the suitabilities.'[30]

The reaction of the local community to the high level of convictions, following directly on the atrocious police behaviour, was compounded by the lack of coverage of the trials in the media. The silence was broken by a B.B.C. Television 'Open Door' programme on 22 September 1979. Freed from the usual restrictions imposed by the B.B.C. – which operates informal agreements to discuss the contents of programmes involving the police with the force before screening them – the Southall Defence Committee put up a hard-hitting indictment of the police action and of the actions of the magistrates. Following this there was coverage of the complaints of the Southall community in the *Guardian* and the *Observer* and on radio, focusing particularly on the occasion on which Mr Canham bound over two *witnesses* to keep the peace, on the grounds that they had been part of a riotous crowd.

Early in December 1979, almost all of the thirty or so lawyers who had been involved in defending at Barnet magistrates' court signed a petition to the Lord Chancellor protesting at the abnormally high rate of conviction, the excessively severe sentences and the distance between Southall and the court.[31]

Perhaps the most interesting feature of the Southall trials appeared after the publicity. The conviction rate abruptly dropped. Of the four magistrates who followed the controversial stipendiaries, only one, Mr Roger Sanders, had a high conviction rate – 71 per cent. Two, Mr Christopher Burke and Mr David Meier, convicted only in 43 and 44 per cent of cases respectively. Only five jail sentences were handed out.[32]

Kapil Juj, a spokesman for Southall Rights, the organization which had been coordinating the legal defence of the arrested, said: 'The reason for the change is the amount of publicity generated about the case.' In some cases the police did not offer evidence, and Mr Juj said that, in other cases, the magistrates who sat later took more notice of defence evidence.

The lesson – which should bring comfort to all democrats – is that even the political acts of magistrates – centrally appointed and apparently well insulated from popular pressure – are in fact amenable to pressure outside the courts. Like many other institutions of government, courts' decisions can be influenced. And the larger the number of people, the more awkward the fuss they create, the more the authorities are likely to shift, albeit slightly, in the desired direction.

By contrast, the tension that can arise between being a member of the labour movement and acting on the bench was illustrated in two examples connected with the 1980 strike by steelworkers. Ray Davies, a member of their union, the Iron and Steel Trades Confederation, who was also a mid-Glamorgan county councillor, was 'sacked' from being a J.P. over his arrest on a picket line. More subtle pressure was exerted on Labour J.P.s to 'stand down' over cases involving steel pickets in Sheffield. The suggestion apparently came from Tories on their bench who felt that Labour Party members would be susceptible to political bias.[33] (In fact they refused to stand down.)

So magistrates' justice can be a chancy business for the accused, and the manner in which J.P.s exercise their wide powers of discretion in political trials confirms that their role can be far from impartial.

THE JURY

> For more than seven out of the eight centuries during which the judges of
> the common law have administered justice in this country, trial by jury
> ensured that Englishmen got the sort of justice they liked and not the sort
> of justice that the government or lawyers or any body of experts thought
> was good for them.
>
> (Lord Devlin, *Trial by Jury* (Stevens, 1971), pp. 159–60)

Part of the history of political trials is the history of the argument about
the composition of juries – and of charges of rigging them, packing them
and vetting them. In virtually all trials where defendants have had political motives for their actions, the state has attempted to control the
composition of juries, to remove jurors who might sympathize with the
political aims of the defendants and hence who might acquit the political
opponents of those in power.

The 1970s saw a period of political controversy over the role of juries
which continues to this day. The police criticized the whole principle of
trial by jury; jury vetting by the authorities was exposed; and there was
unprecedented investigation and public discussion over how juries reach
their verdicts, later followed by a change in the law to put a stop to such
public debate.

Why should there historically have been such anxiety by the authorities
on the role of juries? For it is hard to envisage how juries could somehow
be organized into a radical or reforming agency. Their selection is usually
described as 'random' – though the randomness of the process has been
open to question – but it is at least haphazard, making it impossible for
any organized radical group to control the composition of a given jury.
And the operation of the rest of the judicial process – the relationship
between police, lawyers, magistrates, judges, state servants and the inherited and opaque rituals of the courts – is a relatively certain barrier
against things going wrong from the standpoint of the authorities. Moreover, those who come before the courts as a result of their political

opinions generally represent a minority at the time, even when their cause – for example, universal suffrage – later triumphs.

At best, a jury represents that part of the legal process which is least controlled by the state and the ruling class.

Judges are part of the state by definition; prosecution lawyers and the police are acting on its behalf.

Defence lawyers can act for their clients only within the rules of the courts, the traditions of their professions and the pressures of following a career. The ultimate sanction – suspension or disbarment – is sometimes used against barristers who break the unwritten rules of conduct in court – although more often barristers who behave in a way of which the judges disapprove can have their fees reduced by court officials. Equally, there is little discussion of the rights and powers of the citizen when he or she is called on to be a juror. The functions of the courts are given even less attention in education syllabuses than those of elected bodies, while systematic research and even journalistic coverage on the functioning of juries has been frowned upon. In these circumstances, the jury system is an unpredictable rather than a positively democratic part of the administration of justice. Yet successive governments have sought to curtail even this uncontrolled part of the judicial apparatus, right down to the present day.

·HISTORY OF THE JURY·

The jury, like Parliament, is an immensely ancient part of the British Constitution. But, like Parliament, reforms in the nineteenth and twentieth centuries – in response to the Industrial Revolution and to the growth of working-class political power – have transformed it into something quite different. Juries first emerged as a way of determining the facts of criminal cases after the Church in the person of Pope Innocent III banned the normal method, direct judgement by God as manifested through trial by ordeal, in 1215.[1] They were drawn from the locality where the trial was conducted and generally were local people – freemen rather than serfs – who had direct knowledge of the circumstances of the alleged offence and the offender.

They were of two kinds, distinguished by their functions. Grand juries drew up bills of indictment which were heard at Quarter Sessions or Assizes. Petty juries gradually evolved into the jury as we know it today: twelve people who hear the facts of a case from witnesses and lawyers and decide on guilt or innocence. Coroner's juries, like grand juries, in theory had powers of investigation and still do.

From the sixteenth century until 1949 petty juries were for many years divided into 'special' and 'common' juries. A hierarchy of property qualifications thus existed: grand juries which investigated crime and framed charges; special juries which were used in serious cases and particularly in the political trials of the eighteenth and nineteenth centuries; and common juries. The grand jury has remained a central part of the U.S. judicial system, where it retains its investigative functions, and has been used at times as an instrument for prying into the activities of left-wing organizations. It was abolished in England and Wales in 1933 after falling into disuse in the late nineteenth century as a result of the professionalization of the judicial system and the police. Special juries eventually disappeared only in 1949; even after their use in political trials declined, there were still cases where they were thought useful.

The selection and powers of juries remained extremely unclear until 1825. The Home Secretary, Sir Robert Peel, was responsible in that year for a Juries Act which repealed no less than eighty-five previous Acts relating to juries, and set new property qualifications which were to be the same throughout the country. At least, this was to be the case in the counties – such uniformity was only achieved for boroughs by the 1922 Juries Act.

Prior to this and in the absence of clear statutory provision, local custom determined the qualification for those to be included in juries. In general, sheriffs kept the lists of those qualified and coroners summoned them to do service. The position on qualification for jury service before 1825 was only slightly less chaotic than the position of the parliamentary franchise before 1832. Under these conditions, rigging and packing of juries could hardly be distinguished from 'normal' selection.

For example, the right of the Crown, when prosecuting, to challenge jurors without giving reasons – the 'pre-emptory challenge' – was abolished by statute in 1305. But to replace this abolished Crown right, a custom arose by which jurors whom the Crown did not like were asked to 'stand by for the Crown'. In practice this amounted to pre-emptory challenge, the right to challenge without giving reasons, which the 1305 Act had explicitly abolished. The jurors 'stood by' in this way would, in *theory*, not be removed from the trial. If for some reason challenges to the panel of potential jurors exhausted the numbers available, these jurors would again be considered by the court, at which point the prosecutor would have to give a reason for his challenge.[2] In *practice* there were always sufficient empanelled men acceptable to the Crown, so that this rarely happened. (Though in the trial of Horne Took in 1794, the Attorney General mistakenly asked all the empanelled potential jurors to stand by. The panel was exhausted and the Attorney, on being asked to give his reasons for the standing by, could find none.) The Crown's right to ask jurors to stand by has survived all reforms of the jury and judicial procedure, so that when the Attorney General Sam Silkin published his guidelines for jury vetting in 1978, the exercise of the prosecution's right to ask a juror to stand by was described as 'analogous to the Defence's right to pre-emptory challenge'.

If exercised to the full, the right to ask jurors to stand by was a powerful Crown asset in controlling membership of the jury. By contrast, the defence right to pre-emptory challenge was limited by successive Acts. For felonies, as the more serious crimes were termed before the 1967 Criminal Justice Act, up to thirty-five pre-emptory challenges were allowed prior to the 1825 Act, when the number was reduced to twenty. It was further reduced to seven by the 1949 Juries Act. This Act introduced a right to seven pre-emptory challenges in cases of misdemeanour, as less serious crimes were then termed. The seven challenges were reduced to three by the 1977 Criminal Law Act.

·CONTROLLING JURIES·

There are numerous historic examples to show how anxious those in power have been to control the political role of juries. During Tudor times there were a number of political trials for sedition and treason. One of these involved the Bishop of Rochester, and the jurors who found him guilty of treason in 1535 said afterwards that their verdict was 'full sore against their conscience', but they had feared 'for the safety of their goods and lives which they were all well assured to lose, in case they acquitted him'.[3]

By contrast, in the seventeenth century no jury could be found to convict Sir John Lilburne, the Levellers' leader. The reason was not because the case against him was weak in either law or evidence. The jurors' attitude was rather a manifestation 'of strong anti-Government feeling among the populace of London at the time'.[4] The uncooperative stance of London juries was also expressed in the acquittal of the Quakers Penn and Mead in a political trial in 1670. They had been charged with taking part in an unlawful assembly, and the judge was so angry at the unwillingness of the jury to bring in a guilty verdict that he imprisoned them for two nights, until his fellow judges decreed that he had no power to do this. Known as the Bushell's case, this is sometimes seen as a triumphant turning point, marking the independence of juries. But in fact the assertiveness of the jurors and the eventual climb-down by the judges only occurred against a background of a strong tide of public opinion, including a House of Commons vote the previous year to limit judicial power. It was cases like this which encouraged the state to 'pack' juries – something which was done quite blatantly by leaders of the propertied classes in trials of poachers and smugglers.

For the right to 'stand by' to be exercised in order to control the jury, the panel had to be well chosen. William Mitchell, under-sheriff at Lewes, wrote to the Duke of Richmond in 1749 concerning a jury which had been picked by him for a trial of six Sussex smugglers: 'I am favoured with your Grace's letter, and have sent enclosed a copy of the jury, which I have made out as well as I can, and have returned a great part of them from out of the West Sussex, that your Grace may be the easier informed about them and if they should not be the proper persons, they may be challenged by the Crown at the assizes.' [5] The resistance of the Sussex smugglers, who had been pursued by all available means by the Duke of Richmond between 1748 and 1750, to the enforcement of the revenue laws stemmed from smuggling's role as the source of income which raised the standard of living of landless agricultural labourers above mere subsistence.

Poachers were treated in a similar fashion. In the early eighteenth century, Sir Robert Walpole made use of his office and political influence to secure for himself and his circle as much material benefit as possible. In particular, his control of the royal forests and their products was an important means of using public office for private profit. This was bitterly resented by labourers and yeomen farmers alike; and they resisted by continuing to poach deer, and to remove timber and turfs from royal forests for fuel. They went about disguised, and were known to the authorities as 'Blacks'. Parliament rushed through the infamous 'Black Act' of May 1723, which, historian E. P. Thompson estimates, created up to 250 new capital offences. It was ruthlessly applied, and the government of the day sought to ensure that arrested poachers were convicted.

Acting on the direct order of Walpole, a Windsor gamekeeper called Baptist Nunn travelled the home counties, bribing under-sheriffs and their clerks to alter the panel of jurors, bribing the jurors themselves, paying the families of Crown witnesses, and arranging for witnesses to attend the Assizes. He was not always successful, for among those arraigned as 'Blacks' were substantial yeomen who were no doubt of some standing and reputation in the area. Many were later acquitted 'against the evidence'.[6]

Later that year the government decided to move trials of Blacks from the county Assizes to London, where they could be heard before the King's Bench with a special jury. Delafaye, Secretary to the Lords Justices, wrote, 'now we may depend on having juries of men of probity and well enclined towards their King's and country's service and interest'.[7] Nevertheless, a special jury acquitted an accused man, John Huntridge, despite the combined efforts of Walpole, his potential ally Viscount Townshend, and the entire administration to convict him under the Black Act.

A study of trials of Wilkite radicals in the late eighteenth century showed that they 'were overtly political', with radical counsel making 'a naked political appeal to jurors'.[8] In 1771 John Wilkes and Frederick Bull, two radical sheriffs of the City of London, produced *A Letter to the Jurors of Great Britain*, arguing in it: 'As the people have a share in legislation, to prevent improper laws being passed; so likewise have they a share in the administration of justice, that these laws may not become engines of oppression.'

In 1817 Jonathon Wooler, editor of the radical paper *Black Dwarf*, was prosecuted for seditious libel for his attacks on the government of the day. This prosecution was just one measure adopted by a government anxious to stifle the rising tide of radical opinion. A clerk of the Treasury Solicitors, who were responsible for the conduct of the prosecution, visited the office of the Secondaries, the court officials then responsible for the drawing up of the jury lists, and tried to persuade them to mark the names of 'good men' on the list.[9]

The incident illuminated the conditions of the time. The jurors whose selection the government of the day was seeking to control were all drawn from the special jury lists: all must have been relatively wealthy, and the community from which they were drawn was small enough for the clerk to know the political opinions of many of them. The charge was politically contentious; and there were those, even among the fraction of the population qualified for jury service by reason of their status in the community, who did not identify with the ruling class of the time. London juries in particular, even the special juries with higher property qualifications, were not safe as far as the Crown was concerned: hence the official efforts to pack the jury by selecting 'good men', and to obtain information so that those who were politically suspected could be asked to 'stand by'.

In the case of William Hone, accused of blasphemous libel, the Master, a lower ranking judge in charge of choosing the jury from the lists compiled by the Secondaries, was observed by Hone's defence lawyers to be going through the jury list, ostensibly letting his pen fall on names at random, while actually calling out other names from the list. Also in Hone's case, the Attorney General had previously sought information from other officials on the political views of the potential jurors. When Hone came to trial, many of the hand-picked jurors failed to appear; a demonstration numbering 20,000 assembled outside the Guildhall in his support and he was acquitted on all the three charges he faced. Of the jurors who were eventually assembled, none were challenged by the Attorney General without reason.

A special committee appointed by the Common Council of the City of London found that of the 485 names listed in the jury book, 226 were not even householders in the city, and thus not qualified to serve. In addition the committee found that several jurors had been called to serve on upwards of 40 (and some on more than 50) of the 114 cases heard before the Court of Kings Bench during the 1817 law terms.[10] The Common Council tightened up its procedures, and the general confusion which made rigging of juries so easy in part disappeared when the Juries Act became law in 1825.

But the practice of government rigging of juries continued. The qualifications introduced by the 1825 Act for jury service outside the City of London were that the person concerned should be male, and should be tenant or owner of a house whose rateable value was £20 (£30 in the counties of Middlesex, when it existed, and London after it came into existence as a county). In the City, the traditional qualification of lands or property worth £100 was continued. This qualification came to mean, as the nineteenth century passed, that juries were confined to the well-to-do, a middle class with increasing class consciousness about property. Although the parliamentary franchise was regulated and extended in 1832, 1867 and 1884, only inflation altered the social composition of the jury, and that very slowly.

But where the Crown faced evident problems, the rigging continued. In Ireland – where the requirements for jury service were, after 1828, identical to those in England and Wales – successive Irish Attorneys General gave instructions ('guidance') to Crown prosecutors. These purported to forbid the standing by of jurors on the basis purely of their religious or political convictions. But they actually resulted in ruling out members of secret societies (meaning in practice political groups) and of 'trade combinations' whenever the defendant was engaged in the same or similar associations. Information about potential jurors was to come from 'any magistrate, chief constable or public officer'. A parliamentary select committee on Irish Jury Laws was told in 1881: '[The police] . . . know everything about the men in a district and their character and they would have no hesitation in giving him [the Crown Solicitor] confidential information to see how the right should be exercised.'[11] In principle this does not differ at all from the practice today. Observers at political trials, even before the codification and publication of the current guidelines for jury vetting, were able to see that the Crown prosecutors were referring to files provided by the police before asking particular jurors to stand by.

Given the continuing agitation against British rule in Ireland through the nineteenth century, it is not surprising that the rigging was directed towards reducing the number of Catholics (and hence nationalist sympathizers) on juries, and such accusations became part of the general current of criticism of British rule.

In England and Wales, the fact that jurors were drawn exclusively from the middle and upper classes meant that examples of vetting in the nineteenth and early twentieth century are hard to find. Certainly, the authorities interfered with jury trials when they felt it necessary; but the social composition of juries meant that the necessity seldom arose. Whereas in the eighteenth century middle-class jurors' interests were often at odds with those of the Crown and its courts, they faced a common threat in the nineteenth century from an emerging working class and so had a unity of purpose, certainly in political trials of trade unionists and reformers.

· THE MODERN PRACTICE ·

When the Attorney General, Sam Silkin, published his guidelines on jury vetting in 1978, the statement which accompanied it said that the practice of vetting jurors in trials concerning official secrets had grown up 'since 1948'. The date is significant, since it coincides with the spread of McCarthyism across the Atlantic, and the agreement between the Western powers to institute security vetting for state employees. There was only one official admission of the use of vetting between 1948 and 1975. Lord Dilhorne admitted that in 1963, when he was Sir Reginald Manningham-Buller and Attorney General in the then Conservative government, he arranged for the jury to be vetted and for a member of the Communist Party to be excluded from it in the trial of George Blake, accused of spying for Russia.

During the 1950s and 1960s, there was considerable agitation for the right to jury service to become co-extensive with the franchise. A departmental committee of inquiry, under Lord Morris of Borth-y-Gest, a High Court judge, was appointed to consider the right of jury service and reported in 1965.[12] It found that on the 1964 electoral register, about 7,150,000 names were marked with the 'J' which designated them as entitled to jury service, which was 22.5 per cent of the 31.77 million people entitled to vote. The committee confirmed what many people had realized: that in confining the right to do jury service to owners or tenants of a house with a rateable value of more than £20, there was a noticeable discrimination against women, who formed only 11 per cent of those entitled to do jury service – that is, although 77 per cent of the electorate as a whole were ineligible, nearly 98 per cent of women were kept off juries. As Lord Devlin said in 1956: 'The jury is not really representative of the nation as a whole. It is predominantly male, middle-aged, middle-minded and middle-class.'[13] Nevertheless, rate revaluations consequent on inflation were increasing the numbers of jurors: 4.7 times as many people were entitled to serve on juries in 1964 as in 1955.

The gradual reduction of the property qualification as the community became more affluent was to draw in wider social classes; but it continued to discriminate against women, who were rarely householders, and young people who, even if they were in professional careers, tended not to become the sole occupiers, owners or tenants of property until in their late twenties or later.

But even the slight broadening of jury membership which had occurred was used as an excuse by the Metropolitan Police Commissioner, then Sir John Waldron, and the Association of Chief Police Officers (A.C.P.O.), to bemoan to the Morris Committee the 'marked deterioration' in the quality of jurors. A.C.P.O. thought that the tendency was most marked in urban juries and that this stemmed from the tendency of the professional classes to move their homes out of the cities into the surrounding countryside.

This was in vain. The Morris Committee recommended in 1965 that the right to jury service should be co-extensive with the franchise, with the continuation of exemptions which had applied to the police, members of the legal profession, and so on. Thus the functioning of the jury was to be changed in a manner more significant than anything which had happened since 1825.

A persistent police campaign met the Morris recommendations, and the police claimed that jurors were likely to be influenced or intimidated by professional criminals. Foremost in the campaign was Mr Robert Mark, Chief Constable of Leicester. In 1965, writing in *Police* journal, he said: 'The criminal trial is less a test of guilt or innocence than a competition . . . a kind of show jumping contest in which the rider for the prosecution must clear every obstacle in order to succeed.'[14] At the time there was a great deal of press reporting and comment on the activities of the Kray gang and similar organizations. Against this general background, in its 1967 Criminal Justice Act, the then Labour government took the unprecedented step of allowing jurors to convict or acquit by a majority of ten to two. Until then, juries had to consider a case until all of them agreed and their verdict was unanimous.

In a commentary on the proposal for majority verdicts published by the National Council for Civil Liberties, barrister Cedric Thornberry wrote that the only available evidence advanced for the change was

offered in a written Parliamentary answer in the House of Commons on the 3rd August. Then it was asserted that three cases of attempted intimidation of jurymen in the Metropolitan area had been reported to the police in 1966. Three cases in many hundreds of jury trials! And these three were cases 'reported to the police' – they were mere allegations. No prosecution took place . . . Reticence became a confession of ignorance on 19th October, when the Home Secretary found himself unable to give any statistics relative to the corruption of jurors in London or anywhere else during any one of the previous ten years.[15]

Basil Wigoder Q.C. pointed out that one corrupted juror would be unlikely to do more than cause a jury to disagree. A new trial would then take place, and the likelihood of a second jury being corrupted was remote, unless arrangements for preserving the integrity of the jury were quite appalling.[16]

So, despite the official explanation of the reason for majority verdicts being 'intimidation of jurors', it is difficult not to conclude that the real reasons were *political* – those given by the police chiefs when they had expressed concern in 1964 at the 'lowering of standards' caused by increasing numbers of working-class people serving on juries.

But whereas the 1967 Criminal Justice Act introduced majority verdicts, legislation on the Morris Committee's recommendations did not occur until the 1972 Criminal Justice Act. From April 1974 this permitted anybody of voting age, subject to certain miscellaneous restrictions, to be a juror, although old age pensioners are excluded (one can be a judge until 75, so it is not clear why such a lower age limit is applied to jurors). The effect of this was to increase the number of potential jurors from about 8 million to 30 million.

·ATTACKS ON JURY TRIALS·

It can hardly have been coincidental that at the time this major change was working its way through, police attacks on trial by jury became increasingly strident. Robert Mark, by now Metropolitan Chief Commissioner, criticized the jury system in his notorious Dimbleby lecture on B.B.C. television in 1973, arguing that acquittal by juries encouraged criminals to go free.[17] Such jury acquittals, he argued, are 'unlikely to mean that the accused is innocent in the true sense of the word'.[18] Logically, on Mark's reasoning, a trial should hardly be necessary: he 'knows' defendants are guilty, which is presumably the basis for his claim that too many guilty go free. He also ignored the fact that the vast majority of indictable cases are tried summarily in magistrates' courts, and that some two-thirds of these involve defendants who plead guilty. Even in Crown courts, 60 per cent plead guilty. Jury trials occur in less than 5 per cent of all indictable cases, and it is obviously likely that these involve cases where there is some doubt. The acquittal rate in higher courts rose from 39 per cent of those pleading not guilty in 1965[19] (before majority verdicts were introduced) to 50 per cent in 1973.[20] It later rose to 60 per cent, but dropped to 56 per cent in 1976.[21] About one-third of all acquittals are directed by the court. Put another way, the picture amounts to this: about 92 per cent of offences are heard in magistrates' courts, and of the remainder only 10 per cent in 1978 involved jury acquittals, i.e. 0.8 per cent of offences. It may be the firm and genuine belief of virtually all police officers that everyone whom they bring to court is guilty. But this can lead to a dangerous contempt on their part for the processes of jury trial, as expressed by Mark in 1975 when he maintained that juries 'are occasionally stupid, prejudiced, barely literate and often incapable of applying the law as public opinion is led to suppose they do'.[22]

By the time he was saying this sort of thing, juries – in keeping with the general change in social attitudes in the early 1970s and against a background of vigorous campaigning by trade unionists and socialists – were less prepared to be deferential and to accept automatically the word of the police. In the more reactionary climate at the turn of the decade this provoked a further spate of attacks on the composition of juries – expressed mainly through justification for jury vetting.

In the end, however, it is impossible to divorce the debate about juries from the political interests at stake. Even Lord Devlin implies as much when he sees a virtue in juries being independent of direct state control:

What makes juries worthwhile is that they see things differently from judges . . . that the function which they filled two centuries ago as a corrective to the corruption and partiality of judges requires essentially the same qualities as the function they perform today as an organ of the disestablishment.[23]

Significantly, while there has been continuous pressure from the police, judges, civil servants and politicians over what they defined as 'bias' inherent in modern, more popularly based juries, attempts by defendants and their lawyers to work within the existing rules in order to remove what they saw as bias or possible bias on the part of the jury have been strenuously resisted. They have either been declared outside the rules of court procedure or have provoked changes to the rules to prevent them from being used again.

In 1963, during an Official Secrets Act trial arising out of a demonstration at the U.S. Air Force base at Wethersfield, Terry Chandler, a supporter of the Committee of 100 who was defending himself, was allowed by the judge to ask jurors to 'stand by' after he had exhausted his seven pre-emptory challenges. When the Crown appealed this, Lord Justice Parker ruled that there was no defence right to 'stand by' jurors.

In 1973, also at the Old Bailey, defence lawyers for eight young people facing charges of conspiracy to cause explosions were allowed by Mr Justice James to ask extensive questions about the political views of jurors. The eight, known as the 'Stoke Newington Eight', were accused of causing explosions at the homes of various prominent people, including Conservative ministers, and at government offices – activities claimed to be associated with the 'Angry Brigade'. All the defendants held left-wing political views, and part of the Crown case was that they had carried out their bombings in support of their political views. Lest they be convicted for their views alone, the defence asked potential jurors a wide range of questions which included whether they were members of the Conservative Party and which newspapers they read. Four of the eight were convicted and four acquitted.

Following the trial, senior members of the judiciary in 1973 issued what is known as a 'practice direction'. This amounts to an instruction, issued by senior judges after consultation with others of their colleagues, as to how judges shall use the large discretion which they have within the law on how trials shall be conducted. Henceforth, such wide-ranging questions were banned. The extent to which defence lawyers may question potential jurors is in practice variable and depends on the judge. Questions about the connections of jurors with institutions concerned in the case are allowed. General questions designed to probe jurors' political opinions are not. The scope here for political discretion is clear.

The justification for defence challenges to jurors' political opinions, race, or occupation is grounded on the traditional constitutional doctrine that the accused are to be tried by their peers. That was not the case in fact until 1974. Before then, the property qualification ensured that defendants were judged by relatively more prosperous sections of the community. Once every adult became entitled to sit on a jury, the question of which section of the community should judge defendants became important. In one important case in 1971, involving nine black people arrested on a demonstration and charged with offences ranging from obstruction to causing an affray, the defence had argued strongly that the jury should be entirely black. Seven pre-emptory challenges for each of nine defendants could go a long way towards ensuring, even from a panel on which black people were under-represented, that the majority of people on the jury were black.

In a sense, this is a departure from the direction in which jury composition was moving throughout the previous 300 years; black jurors are preferred by black defendants because they have a better knowledge of the black community's experience in this country, and particularly of their unsatisfactory treatment at the hands of the police. This is a reversal of the trend by which jurors are supposed to be ignorant both of the facts of the case and of the circumstances of the defendants before they hear the case in court.

A similar move was the attempt by defence lawyers, in trials of building workers arrested during the construction strike of autumn 1972, to challenge jurors in order to ensure that as many jurors as possible were from manual occupations. Here again the defence lawyers were trying to get jurors who were familiar with the experiences of working people, including trade union organization, the motives behind strikes and the way in which they were organized.

All such moves to select juries who could counterpose their own experience to an 'official' view shared by prosecutors and judges alike have been stopped in different ways. The trials of the building workers took place at the end of 1973 – they had not in fact been arrested until February, five months after the offences which they were charged with conspiring to commit were alleged to have occurred. During the law vacation the Conservative Lord Chancellor, Lord Hailsham, ordered that jurors' occupations were to be removed from the lists of the jury panel, supplied to prosecutor and defence lawyers alike, on the basis of which pre-emptory challenges by the defence could be made.[24] This was done after consultation with the Home Secretary, Mr Robert Carr, and the Attorney General, Sir Peter Rawlinson. The Conservative government, of which all three were members, was very worried by the increasingly militant trade-union reaction to its economic policies. Even the official representatives of the legal profession, the Bar Council, were not consulted by the Lord Chancellor. His initiative might also have been connected with the fact that several of the strikers who had been tried before a jury at Mold Crown Court had been acquitted after defence counsel had ensured by challenges that trade unionists were not under-represented on the jury.

· JURIES AND POLITICS ·

In my own trial in August 1972, on a private prosecution for conspiracy to disrupt all-white South African sports tours, the defence team had

discussed beforehand the possible composition of the jury. The case
came to court during a period when race feelings had been inflamed by
racist exploitation of the entry to Britain of numbers of British Asian
refugees from Uganda. The media and groups like the National Front
had been whipping up public emotions,[25] and both my lawyers and I
were extremely concerned that we might face at least some jurors with
racist views. Because of the political character of the trial and the enormous difficulty of countering a conspiracy charge, we had also considered
beforehand the possibility that I would 'sack' my barristers and conduct
my own defence in order to appeal directly to the jury on what amounted
to a political basis (and this in fact happened, at the end of the prosecution
case).

So when it came to those few minutes at the start of the trial when the
jury is empanelled, we anxiously scrutinized each potential juror. For
the most part it was a totally subjective and chancy judgement. We did
object to a number of jurors. But we held our breath when two black
jurors stepped up, one a West Indian, the other an Asian. In fact they
were not challenged by the prosecution, which was obviously to my
advantage. I was eventually acquitted on three of the main conspiracy
counts after a 'hung' jury had failed to agree. On the fourth count,
involving a brief sit-down on a tennis court, the evidence was overwhelming and I was convicted – but then only on a majority verdict of
10 to 2. It doesn't take much imagination to guess who the two were.
Indeed, so far as the verdicts in general were concerned, an analysis of
the trial by the *Sunday Times* journalist, Derek Humphry, confirmed:
'It was evident that Hain had succeeded in going over the heads of the
prosecution and the judge and influencing the majority of the jury with
his political philosophy.'[26] So political trials can sometimes be resisted
by a political appeal to the jury.

Conversely, the operation of political views in court can be a disadvantage, as my second experience of an Old Bailey trial confirmed in 1976,
when I faced a charge of bank theft in a celebrated case of mistaken
identity. The jury took over five hours to reach their verdict of not guilty
and then only on a majority basis, which amazed the legal commentators
and journalists who were convinced of the 'ludicrous' nature of the
charge against me.[27] But a private disclosure by one of the jurors which
reached the defence afterwards revealed that one of their number had
held out in the jury room against the rest of his colleagues, in a manner
which flew in the face of the evidence and suggested he was influenced

more by political and racial prejudice than by the facts before him. (However, lest this is used to criticize the principle of trial by juries, it should be stressed that the judge, Alan King-Hamilton, astonished members of the legal profession by his handling of the case, in particular his extraordinary summing-up which, unusually in trial procedure, had to be challenged half-way through by defence counsel.[28] I would certainly have entrusted my future to the jury rather than the trial judge. Instead, the point to be stressed is that politics can play a key role in the execution of justice.)

But what *does* happen inside a contemporary jury room? Evidence on this is scarce and the authorities wish it to remain so. There was for years a general understanding that, because jurors were not obliged in court to give reasons for their verdicts, they were prohibited from speaking to others about what went on in the jury room even after the trial was over. A notice enjoining secrecy is displayed in every jury room. But the practice has, until now, had no statutory legal basis. In recent years many newspapers, particularly after political trials, have interviewed jurors.

This practice was clearly not to the state's liking, and matters came to a head over the trial of Jeremy Thorpe and three other men for conspiracy to murder. After their acquittal, the *New Statesman* carried an interview with one of the jurors on the reasons for their verdict. It was an interesting article, because it explained why they had acquitted Mr Thorpe of the murder charge. The evidence simply was not strong enough, the juror maintained. Yet he remained convinced that a guilty verdict would have resulted if the charge had, for example, been conspiracy to *intimidate* rather than to *murder*: 'What we were all agreed on was that there was definitely a conspiracy of some sort. They were definitely guilty of something. All of them.'[29] It was clearly of considerable public interest that the basis of the prosecution case was wrongly founded in the eyes of the jury, particularly since throughout the whole sorry episode, going back many years, the authorities had displayed a marked reluctance to investigate allegations of a criminal conspiracy.[30] Was there now some question that the prosecution had been wrongly framed as well?

But if that was the important question raised by the juror's explanation of a verdict which surprised many, it was one which quickly got sidetracked when the state acted to take the *New Statesman* to court for contempt. Clearly, the Attorney General had decided enough was enough: a line had to be drawn somewhere to halt this growing practice of jury disclosure. But the Lord Chief Justice, Lord Widgery, and his fellow judges in the High Court dismissed the case, awarding costs to the defence, Lord Widgery making it clear, however, that while as the law stood the *New Statesman* had committed no offence, that did not mean he approved of the publication of such an article. It was almost an invitation for Parliament to act – which it duly did. During the passage of the Conservative government's Contempt Bill, an amendment was carried in the House of Lords to impose a complete ban on jury disclosure with effect from the autumn of 1981. Secrecy again prevailed over jury decisions: the lid that had been briefly lifted on this crucial area was firmly replaced again.

Academic researchers who have examined the jury system require the assistance of the courts, of police, prosecutors, judges and administrators, for their work. In all cases, therefore, they have refrained from questioning jurors about the verdicts which they have brought in. In effect, there is no trustworthy academic research on how juries think in this country, and journalistic and even anecdotal evidence is probably more reliable than what passes for 'academic research'. The latest such book, by John Baldwin and Michael McConville of Birmingham University, suffers from precisely this defect.[31] Based on a Home Office financed study of 500 'not guilty' pleas in Birmingham Crown Court in 1975–6, it accepts the hierarchy of the administration of justice, and compares jury verdicts with the opinions of 'experts' such as judges and lawyers. It thus misses the vital point that the jury and the defendant are the only amateurs in court, and that the jury's presence is the court's main connection with the normal world outside. The authors found that 36 per cent of jury acquittals and 5 per cent of jury convictions were 'questionable'. They also suggested 'the possibility of racial prejudice by some juries'. But they found that such factors as age, sex or social background of jurors did not affect the outcome of their decisions.

Although the government would evidently rather it were not so, there exists a great deal of evidence from jurors themselves on how juries reach their verdicts. One of the fullest accounts was compiled by *Sunday Times* journalist Peter Gillman.[32] He interviewed members of the juries which decided two trials of black people arising out of a fight at the Carib Club, a popular West Indian dance hall in Cricklewood, London, in October 1974. Gillman's research was directed towards discovering why so few people had been convicted after an incident in which at least 150 police officers had fought with about 500 young black people for over an hour. Twelve policemen were hospitalized. At one trial, lasting 82 days, nine of twelve accused were acquitted, and the jury could not agree about the others. After their second trial, lasting a further 27 days, two of the remaining three were convicted and one acquitted, on the same evidence.

Gillman found that the jurors had, for various reasons, disbelieved police evidence in all twelve cases. But the accused fell into two categories. All those acquitted at the first trial had been arrested as a result of incidents on the stairs of the club, as they were leaving. All claimed that they had been attacked by police who were incensed at earlier attacks on colleagues inside the club's dance hall. The other two were accused of inciting the crowd and joining in attacks on police who had entered the dance hall, the prosecution said, to arrest a suspect.

At the first trial, the jury originally decided by ten to two that one of those accused of attacking police in the dance hall was not guilty. But after considering, and disbelieving, police evidence against those arrested on the club stairs, two of the jurors changed their minds on the first defendant. 'One juror – for acquittal – later said that the two who changed seemed reluctant to see no one punished for the injuries to the police, and unwilling to accept that an 82-day trial, costing £300,000, should have been for nothing,' Gillman reported.

This seems to be a common theme running through the accounts of jurors who have spoken about their experiences. Because someone has actually been brought to court, jurors are usually convinced that they have done something wrong. But unless it is overwhelming for one side or the other, conflicting evidence often leaves considerable doubts in the jury's minds as to whether the accused have done exactly what they are charged with, while jurors are equally certain that they are not as unconnected with the crime as the defence usually maintains. If there were a verdict of 'partly guilty', it would probably be brought in in most cases.

Juries often resolve this by finding some of the accused guilty and some not; the two trials of alleged members of the Angry Brigade were good examples of this – in one trial one of two accused was acquitted, in the other, four of eight. The prosecution often brings 'alternative charges' – lesser charges based on the same set of facts – in the knowledge that a charge of attempted murder, for example, may result in a conviction for causing bodily harm.

Guardian journalist Simon Hoggart, recounting his experience as a juror, quoted a 'middle-aged, Cockney' juror as saying of one accused, 'I reckon she did it, but they haven't proved it, not properly.' These sentiments seemed generally to reflect the feelings of jurors who favoured acquittal.[33]

Journalists' accounts stress the rationality of jurors, not only in assessing the rival versions of the truth put forward by prosecution and defence, but in assessing their own situation as part of a judicial process, their status in relation to the other participants in a trial, and their 'duty' as members of the community. A picture emerges which is far from that of incompetence drawn by senior police officers – although reminiscences of jury service from readers of the *Sun* newspaper in 1973 along the lines 'One juror said, "It's near Christmas – we'll find him not guilty",' should doubtless be taken into account.[34]

When the Criminal Law Bill was introduced by the Labour government in 1977, juries were further circumscribed. The then Minister of State at the Home Office, Alex Lyon, proposed the removal of all rights to pre-emptory challenges by the defence, and the substitution of a right to challenge if 'the balance of the jury was unfair on the grounds of race or sex'.[35] In the end, the Labour government rejected this amendment, and instead accepted a Conservative version which reduced the number of pre-emptory challenges to three. During the debate, in which all those who participated were lawyers, both Mr Ian Percival, then a Tory spokesman on law matters, and later Solicitor General, and Mr Arthur Davidson, then Labour's parliamentary secretary in the Law Officers' Department, agreed that the existing right was 'being abused'. The *New Statesman* commented: 'For abused, read exercised: right-wing politicians never understand the law when it is not on their side.'[36]

The 1977 Criminal Law Act also removed a number of offences away from courts with juries, and allowed them to be tried before magistrates' courts. In addition, it removed the requirement for a coroner to summon a jury in cases of sudden or violent death.

But it has since become clear that at the same time as the Labour government was reducing the right of the defence to challenge jurors, it was regulating, and conniving in, the practice of vetting potential jurors in certain trials on political grounds.

· JURY VETTING ·

Exposure of the current practice of jury vetting involved a process of gradual accumulation of publicly available material into an overwhelming case which first forced official admission, and then official justification, of the practice.

In June 1972, five people went on trial at the Old Bailey accused of conspiring to obtain guns for Saor Eire, said to be a breakaway group from the I.R.A. The case against them collapsed after four days, largely because it was shown that they had been persuaded to obtain the guns by a man who turned out to be an agent provocateur on behalf of the Metropolitan Police Special Branch.[37] But during the trial a police witness mentioned that the jury had been 'vetted'; a check had been made into the political background of potential jurors. The prosecution had, at the beginning of the trial, asked several jurors to 'stand by'.

On his election to Parliament as Labour member for Luton West in February 1974, barrister Brian Sedgemore asked Labour Attorney General Sam Silkin to investigate and to give an assurance that this would not happen again.[38] The Minister of State at the Home Office, Alex Lyon, claimed, 'I am not aware that there is any such practice,' and asked Brian Sedgemore to submit further information.[39] Over a year later, provoked by a further question from Mr Sedgemore, Attorney General Silkin admitted that jury vetting took place. He denied that it was 'the practice of the Crown to object to jurors on the grounds of their political beliefs as such', and added that beliefs were only relevant 'to the extent that depending on the nature of the charge, political views held to an extreme may impair the impartiality of jurors, or give rise to the possibility of improper pressure'.[40]

This acknowledgement of the practice and of government approval of it was buried in a written answer and couched in such terms that little notice was taken of it. Though Mr Silkin said that the Home Secretary would be writing to Mr Sedgemore with details, no such letter ever arrived. What Mr Silkin then concealed, but was later forced to admit, was that 'prior to 1974, a practice had grown up, mainly at the Central Criminal Court, of prosecutors asking the police officer in charge to check police records for information concerning potential jurors'.[41] Such jurors would then be removed by being asked to 'stand by'. Later still, Mr Silkin was more precise about 'prior to 1974', admitting that the practice had gone on 'for at least 30 years – probably for very much longer'.[42]

In 1979 Mr Silkin claimed that he had allowed jury vetting to continue in 1974 because he was faced with the alternative of the total abolition of juries in terrorist trials 'which the authorities were then proposing'.[43] Mr Silkin, who was speaking to a meeting of Labour lawyers at the Labour Party annual conference, did not elaborate on who 'the authorities' were; but they no doubt included senior police officers, the heads of the security services, and civil servants in the Attorney General's Office, the D.P.P.'s Office, and the Home Office. Further evidence on who really exercises political power over such judicial matters suggests that Silkin's 'first impulse was to do away with the whole furtive practice', but that he was 'talked out of it' by his advisers.[44]

In response to Mr Sedgemore's questions, though, there was a flurry of activity in various government departments. Consultation took place between the offices of the Attorney General, the Director of Public Prosecutions, the Lord Chancellor, and the Home Office. But the problem exercising these officials was less to do with substance than with presentation. For, as the Minister of State at the Home Office, Mr Brynmor John, later admitted, 'Guidelines have existed for a number of years. So far as I can trace, they have existed since 1948.'[45] (That year carries a double significance. It was, first of all, the year in which a Juries Act abolished special juries and decreed that all cases would be heard by 'normal' jurors – though all were subject to the property qualification. And it was also the year when the pressure from the United States forced the British government to institute positive vetting for civil servants, ostensibly to remove Communists and Soviet sympathizers, which was used against a broad spectrum of those in the Civil Service holding left-wing opinions.)

· A.B.C. TRIAL ·

As a result, in August 1975 a set of guidelines was produced for the vetting of jurors by the prosecution and drawn to the attention of Crown prosecutors by the Attorney General, and to chief constables by the Home Secretary. But they remained concealed for another three years, until the trial of two journalists, Crispin Aubrey and Duncan Campbell, and a former soldier, John Berry, under the Official Secrets Act at the Old Bailey in September 1978. At the start of the trial, Lord Hutchinson Q.C., Duncan Campbell's defence counsel, learnt from court officials that the prosecution had considered the case sufficiently serious to request a copy of the jury list, the eighty-two people from whom the jury was to be drawn, to vet them for 'loyalty'. In fact the Crown did not object to any of the twelve jurors (later, it turned out, with good reason: the man chosen as the foreman of the jury by its members was a former member of the Army's Special Air Service Regiment, the S.A.S., and three other members of the jury had occupied jobs which required them to sign the Official Secrets Act, that is, to acknowledge that they realized that the Act applied to their work for the government). In the absence of the jury, the defence lawyers raised this point with the judge, Mr Willis. He overruled defence objections and said that the trial should continue. He also, through the clerk of the court, warned journalists that they should not reveal the defence objections. *New Statesman* journalist Christopher Hitchens, however, did reveal the S.A.S. connection on a London Weekend Television programme, and the trial was stopped in bizarre circumstances.[46]

The Crown then applied to have the jury for the second trial vetted. Judge Willis was taken ill during another trial, and the second A.B.C. trial began on 3 October 1978, presided over by Mr Justice Mars-Jones, who allowed the new vetting, despite renewed defence objections. It was, of course, not clear what the vetting process actually was. Concern in the legal profession and the press mounted, and eventually, in response to a request from John Griffith, Professor of Law at London University, the Attorney General published the guidelines, together with an acknowledgement that juries had been vetted in twenty-five cases since their introduction in 1975.[47]

The guidelines allowed the prosecution to make checks on jurors in 'certain exceptional types of case of public importance' where the rules for selecting the jury, and the safeguards against corrupt or biased jurors provided by the majority verdict system, 'may not be sufficient to ensure the proper administration of justice'. The guidelines are very widely drawn: 'It is impossible to define precisely these classes of case, but *broadly speaking* they will be (a) serious offences where strong political motives were involved such as I.R.A. and other terrorist cases and cases under the Official Secrets Act; and (b) serious crimes committed by a member or members of a gang of professional criminals.' (Paragraph 4 of the Guidelines, my italics.) But the sorts of case in which jury vetting takes place are not limited to the examples referred to in the guidelines.

The guidelines specifically allowed the defence in such cases to seek the same information. This was refused by Judges Willis and Mars-Jones in the two A.B.C. trials, while the guidelines were still secret. Once they were published, this was no longer possible. The next publicized case of jury vetting was the 'Persons Unknown' trial in autumn 1979, where six young people, anarchists, were accused of conspiracy to rob and possession of weapons and explosive substances. It showed graphically how the vetting is carried out and the sort of information about jurors which the Crown has available. It showed the sheer impossibility of putting the defence and the prosecution on an equal footing over vetting, but as it is a prosecution weapon anyway, this is not surprising.

· 'PERSONS UNKNOWN' TRIAL ·

The prosecution in the 'Persons Unknown' trial announced in advance that they would be vetting the jury.[48] Permission to do this was given by a judge, Mr Brian Gibbens Q.C., at a hearing in chambers a month before the trial was due to commence. Judge Gibbens also allowed the defence to make its own investigation of the jury panel and even allowed legal aid for them to do so.[49] Later Judge Gibbens confirmed that he did intend the money to be used for private detectives to check jurors on behalf of the defence.[50] Eventually, it became clear that the costs of this would be very large; a private detective costs around £300 a day. So Judge Gibbens ordered that the results of the police check on the jury should be handed to the defence, apparently to reduce costs by avoiding duplication of effort. The Crown agreed to hand over only part of the checks, those with the Criminal Record Office and with 'local C.I.D. officers' in the areas from which the jurors were drawn. Checks with the Special Branch were not given to the defence, although it is clear from the wording of the guidelines that the important evidence is whether a juror is likely to be biased for political reasons and this is much more likely to be found in Special Branch records than elsewhere.[51]

But the information which was handed over to the defence found its way into the press.[52] The *Guardian* reported on 20 September 1979 that of the 93 names on the panel of potential jurors, 19 included the information that one of them lived at an address 'believed to be a squat'; five of those listed had only been the victims of crimes; eight of them had records of minor crime which in four cases were 'spent', and thus protected from disclosure, and in the other four cases were not serious enough to disqualify them from jury service under the 1974 Juries Act. The implication was that these 19 people were vulnerable to being challenged.

The trial judge, Mr Justice Alan King-Hamilton, was furious, describing the publication of the police information as 'an outrageous
breach of confidence'. He ordered that an entirely new panel of jurors
should be vetted for the trial. He also ordered a police inquiry into the
leak, and later criticized the B.B.C. for screening a television programme
on jury vetting, referring the matter to the D.P.P.; after discussions in
the judge's chambers, a modified version of the programme went out as
scheduled. He was concerned that the programme might make jurors in
the case feel uneasy about having been vetted, and implied that public
debate of this kind amounted to a challenge to his ruling that vetting was
lawful. He also suggested that the presence on the programme of the
legal officer of the National Council for Civil Liberties, Harriet Harman,
could be prejudicial, since 'she's much opposed to jury vetting. I believe
she has strong views about it.'[53] In other words, the judge was attempting
to stifle debate about an issue of crucial public concern, using his ill-
defined authority and the device of a referral to the D.P.P. in an open
'try-on' to intimidate the B.B.C. At this time there were renewed protests
on jury vetting from the National Council for Civil Liberties and other
bodies, but the Conservative Attorney General, Sir Michael Havers,
'made it clear that there will be no changes in the guidelines for vetting
potential jurors laid down in 1974'.[54]

The defendants in the case were refused the information on the
vetting of the second jury panel. The one juror from the second panel
asked to 'stand by' by the prosecution turned out to be Mr David
Myddleton, an Old Etonian professor of finance and accounting. His
sole political activity seemed to have been participation in a demonstration
of six people at the Bank of England in 1970, demanding that ordinary
individuals should be entitled to buy gold.[55] It is possible that the
Special Branch confused his right-wing libertarian views on the interference of the government in matters connected with the money supply
with anarchist views, sometimes also described as 'libertarian'. Professor
Myddleton commented: 'I was the only one to be challenged by the
Crown . . . The implication is sinister.'

The 'Persons Unknown' case provoked a furore. Mr Silkin himself
acknowledged there was a need to review the practice of vetting and
there was widespread indignation expressed in the Labour Party, by then
in opposition. As well there might have been, for even more disturbing
was the evidence that informal vetting by police on behalf of the prosecution is far more widespread than even the guidelines allow, going well

beyond overtly political trials. At the trial of twelve prison officers at York in January 1979 (for offences connected with the alleged beating of prisoners after the end of the Hull prison disturbances in August and September 1976), 'the start of the trial was delayed by more than two hours while police took the names of 60 waiting jurors to check against Central Criminal Records'.[56] The Attorney General's office and the Director of Public Prosecutions both said that they had no knowledge of a judge making any similar order. But the decision of Mr Justice Boreham went unchallenged in the courts.

· MORE VETTING ·

It was discovered that, at 'Newport and Northampton, police have been known to give prosecution barristers lists of any jurors with criminal records'.[57] This information covered all offences, in addition to those disqualifying a person from jury service. A barrister who prosecutes at Northampton said that it was 'regularly thrust into his hand' by police, even though he did not ask for it. He added: 'The practice is clearly designed to rig the jury in their favour . . . One officer admitted to me that the list was strictly against the rules.' Superintendent Carter of the Northamptonshire police said: 'It may be that we have misinterpreted the Attorney General's guidelines.' (He can say that again.) The Attorney General's Office claimed that the guidelines were 'intended to put a stop to all that'.[58] If they were, then this comment seems to be the only time when the Attorney General's office have admitted either that vetting does occur beyond cases indicated by the guidelines or that the guidelines were intended to stop it, as opposed to regulating existing practices.

When the whole matter was later raised in Parliament on 25 February 1980, the Attorney General, Sir Michael Havers, said: 'I completely disapprove and thoroughly deprecate what has been happening in North-amptonshire.' And he announced an inquiry – although the fact that his predecessor had apparently also instituted an inquiry when it first came to light in March the previous year suggested some ambiguity in the attitude of the authorities.

Then followed still further developments, illustrating the dubious legal basis of jury vetting and underlining the point that it had been carried out by administrative fiat, without legal authority, let alone prior parliamentary approval. At best the statutory status of jury vetting was confused. First of all the Court of Appeal, presided over by Lord Denning, ruled on 3 March 1980 that it was 'unconstitutional for police authorities to engage in jury vetting'. It was also undesirable, Lord Denning argued: 'So long as a person is eligible for jury service and is not disqualified, I cannot think it is right that, behind his back, the police should go through his records so as to enable him to be asked to "stand by" for the Crown or to be challenged by the defence.'[59]

But the Appeal Court also decided that it had no legal authority to interfere with a Sheffield Crown Court judge who in October 1979 had ordered that a jury could be vetted to try two police officers on a charge of actual bodily harm. Notwithstanding this procedural block on the Appeal Court's powers, Lord Denning also took the opportunity in his judgement to point out that the charge of actual bodily harm 'ranks as a minor one in the catalogue of offences. If there is to be any jury vetting in this case, the door would be open to jury vetting in every case.' Far from being confined to overtly political trials, jury vetting was being sanctioned for ordinary criminal trials, or at least those involving police officers who were able to have their jury vetted by their colleagues. When the case came to court in April 1980, the jury was vetted, resulting in a 'small proportion'[60] of the jury panel being challenged – and the two police officers were acquitted. Presiding over the case, Judge Pickles had previously refused an appeal by the Attorney General not to allow such vetting.

Shortly afterwards, the saga took another turn when the Court of Appeal ruled that jury vetting was after all perfectly lawful, overturning its judgement a few months previously because the case was more specifically directed to the principle involved than the Sheffield police case. In the case of Vincent Mason, the court ruled, the police were not merely entitled but should be encouraged to scrutinize jury panel lists – to see if they contained anyone with prior convictions. As a result of police scrutiny in this case, three jurymen had been asked to stand by, two of whom would not have been eligible because it is a criminal offence to sit on a jury if one has served a sentence of three or more months in the previous ten years; a third had in the past been convicted of burglary and theft. The ruling thus made it 'clear that the prosecution can use not only information that jurymen are technically disqualified but also have criminal convictions which do not amount to disqualification but which suggest unsuitability for the particular case'.[61] This again made a nonsense of the Attorney General's 1975 guidelines limiting jury vetting to extremely serious or politically sensitive cases.

Not surprisingly the Attorney General, Sir Michael Havers, denied that it was his department's policy to authorize vetting simply because defendants were police officers.[62] But the Metropolitan Police have admitted in the past that they 'informally vet juries when policemen are prosecuted'.[63] The practice of vetting juries thus seemed, despite the overt aims as stated in the guidelines and repeated by various Lord Chancellors and Attorneys General, to be part of a concerted continuing effort, by the police and by civil servants in the various departments concerned with the courts, crime and the administration of justice, to ensure that nothing 'went wrong' with important trials.

Further confirmation can be found in the evidence of the Association of Chief Police Officers (A.C.P.O.) to the Royal Commission on Criminal Procedure. A.C.P.O. linked jury vetting with the majority verdict rule, proposing that either juries should be allowed to convict by a majority of only two to one, rather than five to one as at present, or that the police should be allowed greater powers to vet jurors.[64]

· 'RANDOM' JURY SELECTION ·

In any case, the procedure for the selection of juries can be open to easy abuse. Before the right to jury service was made co-extensive with the franchise in 1973, those electors who were entitled to sit as jurors were marked with a 'J' in the electoral registers. These were then made up into a 'jury book' from which the official of each court, normally the chief clerk of the court concerned, chose the jurors 'at random'. Since 1973, and in accordance with practice laid down by the 1974 Juries Act, the electoral register itself is used. The procedure for the selection of jurors in a 'typical' court was described by the Attorney General in 1979:

At the Crown Court in Chester, for example, full-time ushers or clerical staff, under the supervision of the Chief Clerk, undertake the work itself. The electoral registers for the whole of the catchment area for that court are divided into three lists, some part of each parish and ward being included in each of these lists. Summoning then follows a three year cycle, each list being used in sequence. Individual panels of jurors to be summoned for any particular period are compiled by the random selection from the list then in use of one name from each ward or parish of the catchment area, except where the ward or parish is large when two names are selected. [65]

This is *not* random selection. The division of the catchment area is not sufficiently random to guard against any distortion of how social groups in the community are represented on the jury panel, as was shown in the original selection of the jury panel in the 'Bradford Twelve' trial in 1982, which excluded Asians despite the Asian population comprising 10 per cent of Bradford's citizens.

The whole procedure remains somewhat cloudy, however, and it was only under pressure in Parliament that the Attorney General revealed in June 1981 that the Lord Chancellor's Department had approved a new system for jury panel selection 'devised with the assistance of the Royal Statistical Society and it involves the use of random numbers'. [66]

Another example of bias in the selection of panels occurred in November 1978 when two members of the Welsh Language Society were convicted at Carmarthen of conspiring to cause criminal damage to a television transmitter, at a demonstration calling for the establishment of a Welsh-language television channel. It was noted that ten of the twelve jurors listened to the trial on headphones, being unable to understand the defendants, who spoke Welsh throughout. Later, it transpired that eleven of the twelve jurors had English surnames. Tom Ellis M.P. described this as 'a proportion far higher than one would have expected in a Welsh-speaking area'. [67] The chances were estimated at 10,000 to 1 against. A further complaint from Plaid Cymru M.P. Dafydd Elis Thomas elicited the admission from the Home Office that a police officer of 'junior rank' did in fact obtain a copy of the jury list in advance and conducted a limited check which did not affect the composition of the jury. The officer concerned was said to have acted without authority. This is a common excuse on those occasions when police officers are discovered to have acted in a way which embarrasses their superiors.

A major distortion which summoning officials appear deliberately to impose on juries is the number of black people and women called for service. Until 1973, the property qualification ensured that women formed only one-tenth of those selected for jury service. Since the 1973 reform, one might have expected women to out-number men on actual juries. After all, their numbers are roughly equal in the electorate, and women are very under-represented in the jobs, such as police and prison officers, barristers, and so on, which disqualify from jury service, and also in those jobs such as doctors or dentists, which entitle a person to be excused. But Baldwin and McConville found that only one juror in four in the Birmingham trials they covered was a woman. One court official told them that this was because more women than men asked to be excused, because they had to look after young families. This is apparently treated as more important than a man asking to be excused for reasons of his work. But another official admitted that it was the policy of the Birmingham Crown Court to *summon* twice as many men as women, which raises a massive doubt on the randomness of the selection process.[68] This is reinforced by the finding that less than 1 per cent of Birmingham jurors were of Asian or West Indian origin – the proportion in the population is over ten times as large.

·JURORS' RIGHTS AND POWERS·

So the picture emerges of a jury system whose composition is disproportionately influenced by administrative decisions and procedures aimed on the whole at increasing the power of the state over this one independent element in the legal system.

Another part of this process is the role ascribed to jurors. In theory, the jury is all-powerful. It could, for example, intervene after the prosecution case had been completed and throw it out. In practice only judges ever rule that there is no case to hear at that point. But on this and other matters affecting the progress and nature of the trial, juries have potentially enormous powers. Doubtless if they sought to use them, a legally sanctified way would be found to limit such powers.

However, this has not arisen, partly because juries are left in appalling ignorance about their rights. From the moment they are sworn in, they are treated as interlopers, temporarily visiting the temples of justice. While invariably they are treated with great courtesy by judges, there is never any suggestion in the relationship between the two that they have absolute *rights*. Instead, they are virtually there on sufferance. A leading judge, Lord Birkett, once confided: 'I still have the power of dominating juries; they do whatever I wish.'[69]

In March 1982 a black youth, Newton Rose, had his conviction for murder quashed by the Appeal Court because the judge in his case, Judge Edward Clarke, had improperly sent a secret message to the jury that if they did not reach a verdict in a short time he would discharge them. The case resembled the Mackenna case in 1960 where, just after lunch, the trial judge, Mr Justice Stable, told the jury that he had to catch a train for an urgent and important appointment, and that unless they brought in their verdict within ten minutes they would be locked up until the next day; the jury duly brought in a guilty verdict a few minutes later (the Appeal Court quashed the conviction).

However, it is not suggested that juries are actively oppressed and denied dignity or rights. Instead the situation is more complex and the processes which bear down upon jurors more subtle. They arrive in a strange place and one, moreover, with all the elitist trappings of higher authority, where the experts use quaint language and where the protocol is even more quaint, not to say weird. Nobody bothers to *tell* them either exactly what their powers are or what their role is: they just get empanelled and the machinery of the court starts up around them. One juror writing about his experience described it this way:

Jury service is a confusing experience. Jurors are told very little about what is going on. They are kept waiting around without much explanation for hours on end. They get the most cursory explanation of their duties and nobody ever mentions the existence of jury rules. They frequently receive only a partial account of the facts from the evidence and cross-examinations. Too frequently they get a less than adequate interpretation of the law from the judge. [70]

So while their final verdict is decisive – and at that point they have absolute power – their role throughout the critical stages which lead up to the finale is one of subservience: they are spectators rather than participants. They may be expected to play referee at the end but, unlike most referees, they cannot influence the context of events leading up to the climax, to ensure that the whole process is fair. In December 1973 when prison sentences were imposed on two of the pickets involved in the Shrewsbury building workers' strike, the foreman of the jury shouted 'disgraceful' at the judge and walked out of the court. [71] And when the National Council for Civil Liberties produced a special leaflet on jurors' rights, attempts to distribute it to jurors met with mixed fortunes. The foreman in the 1979 Jeremy Thorpe trial ordered a number of copies – but these were confiscated by a petulant Old Bailey usher. [72]

The vast majority of jurors therefore are intimidated. Rather than seeing themselves as the equal of the judge or the clerk of the court, they feel inferior and therefore less powerful. Indeed, the authorities have at times gone to considerable lengths to ensure that this remains the case.

For example, in 1965 a Home Office committee decided to put juries firmly in their place (this at a time, it will be recalled, when the whole principle of jury trial was under attack and shortly before majority verdicts emerged). The committee proposed a pamphlet which expressly avoided telling jurors that they could take notes during proceedings and ask questions whenever they felt like it, explaining:

> It would be unwise to give any positive encouragement to embark upon note-taking. The process of note-taking is one that requires a good deal of experience and skill . . . Rather similar considerations apply to the problem of whether jurors should be told they can ask questions. We think there is some peril in encouraging them to do so . . . it is better if jurors do not intervene too readily, though it can undoubtedly happen that some point that seems to the jury to be important may not have been sufficiently probed, and it would be unfortunate if a jury thought they could never ask a question. Much must be left to the handling of proceedings by the judge. [73]

In other words, 'judge-power' must prevail.

In a number of recent cases where jurors were interviewed afterwards by journalists, for example the Jeremy Thorpe trial, they made it clear that they would have wished to ask more questions or intervene, but felt discouraged from doing so. Some openly expressed their frustration at this role. The initiative of Labour Party and trade union activist Charlotte Atkins, who, when called into court to be empanelled during the height of the jury vetting controversy in 1979, stood up and protested at the practice (and was promptly asked to 'stand by') shows a boldness virtually without precedent. [74]

But a number of jurors in the 'Persons Unknown' case did protest to the Lord Chancellor over remarks made by Judge Alan King-Hamilton. He had bitterly criticized their acquittal of the defendants, saying the jury had been 'remarkably merciful in the face of the evidence', and ordering them to return the next day to hear sentence being passed on another defendant who had pleaded guilty and turned Crown witness.

It is worth quoting at length from their letter to the Lord Chancellor sent on 15 January 1980:

> Sitting on the jury in that case was a long and onerous public service. The trial lasted nearly three months and we had to give up our jobs for that period. Though it was an onerous service, it was one we were willing, as citizens, to

provide. We were, however, appalled and insulted by the remarks of Judge Alan King-Hamilton. Not only did he criticize our verdict, but his remarks cast aspersions on our integrity as jurors and on our intelligence as people. We took our role very seriously and, as our oath obliges us to, considered the case according to the evidence placed before us.

It was, in our view, reprehensible of the judge to criticize us publicly on two occasions. We had no equivalent opportunity to air our views about his remarks. Though he made his remarks in open court in the full knowledge that they would be reported, he told us not to talk to the press.

So there are signs that jurors are becoming less willing to accept a subservient role and, if this tendency progresses, we could well see a fresh controversy breaking out over the principle of trial by jury.

For behind recent criticisms of juries by the police and judges has been not just the political bias we saw earlier against juries more representative of the whole community. Such criticism has included an ingrained conservative desire on the part of the judiciary and the police to retain full control *themselves*.

In 1978 the Association of Chief Police Officers had complained that, prior to 1974, 'juries were predominantly male and middle class, with a responsible outlook and middle class standards ... the Juries Act 1974 completely altered the picture'. A.C.P.O. went on to bemoan the possibility of juries being comprised of people who were 'irresponsible'. Later, one of A.C.P.O.'s leading figures, the Chief Constable of Kent, Barry Pain, complained that crime was on the increase and criminals were 'having their own way', adding: 'One of the areas where they can be stopped is by having impartial, objective juries. And I firmly believe that is necessary. Otherwise you've got to leave it to professional adjudicators ... I see it as the only alternative. In other words you do away with juries.' People who behave 'unreasonably' should be kept off juries, he said.[75]

Speaking on the same television programme, Mr Alan King-Hamilton, by now retired, made it clear that he saw the problem in political terms. Calling for jurors under 25 to be barred, he argued: 'People of that age, particularly students, are inclined to be rebellious and mutinous. One has seen student demonstrations time after time. They grow out of it, but at that age they're anxious to demonstrate that they're against authority and, if you like, the establishment. And if they're on a jury, one way of demonstrating it is, of course, by returning the verdict against the establishment – that is, a verdict of not guilty.' By contrast, Lord Elwyn-Jones, the former Labour Lord Chancellor, expressed a more balanced view on the question that had excited Mr King-Hamilton: 'The younger generation, in particular, is less disposed to accept the word of someone in authority merely because he is in authority. The deferential approach to those in authority has largely gone in our society. I myself, frankly, don't regard that as a disastrous thing at all.'

The battle over jury composition was joined again in 1982, this time over the trial of the 'Thornton Heath Fifteen' – black youngsters charged with riot and murder of a white youth in an area where there had been National Front activity. On the first day, potential jurors thronging the Old Bailey were told to notify the judge if they supported the National Front or felt hostility to black people (one did so). Allowed three challenges per defendant, the defence team used up 37 of its potential 45, resulting in a jury of three Asians, three West Indians and six whites. Then on the second morning, an Asian juror was discharged because she had discovered she was a distant relative of one of the ten black defence barristers. So the whole trial had to start again. There were then challenges to the three white men from the first jury and a further 25 new jurors. The second jury was eventually made up of two Asians, five West Indians and five whites. (Eight of the first jury had survived this second process.)

The affair provoked a recently retired judge, his Honour Gilbert F. Leslie, to complain to *The Times* that pre-emptory challenges should be abolished: '. . . they are usually made because defending counsel thinks that the juror may be intelligent or because the juror is white or a woman,' he wrote.[76] On B.B.C. radio the next day he expanded on this view, saying, 'People wearing ties, people who look intelligent, are being challenged.' The widening of jury eligibility had 'not been a success', he maintained, bemoaning the fact that young jurors do not have 'minds that have been trained'.[77]

In the event, the jury reached guilty verdicts on a large number of the charges, winning fulsome praise from the presiding judge, Mr Justice Farquarson, and even from a leading article in *The Times*.

Later in 1982 the defence in the 'Bradford Twelve' trial challenged the selection of the whole jury panel in a way unprecedented in modern times. Defence counsel argued that the panel had been improperly recruited from the Leeds area, excluding persons from Bradford who were on the electoral register and were qualified to serve. All twelve defendants were young Asians, and the way the jury had been arrayed meant that it contained a disproportionate number of middle-aged and elderly people, with no Asians. The particular catchment areas selected within Leeds had directly resulted both in the absence of Asians and the preponderance of elderly people. Besides this bias, the defence were also concerned that there were no Bradford residents with knowledge of the area, able to weigh the evidence in what was a controversial political trial (discussed fully in Chapter 12). After two days of legal argument, the judge finally agreed to the formation of a new jury panel.

When it came to selecting from this panel, defence barristers made thirty-six challenges against potential jurors, before a jury of seven women, two of whom were black, and five men, including three blacks, was chosen. The judge put four questions agreed between prosecution and defence during this lengthy selection process. He asked whether they or any of their immediate relatives were associated with or sympathetic to groups antagonistic to blacks; whether they were members of the National Front, British Movement or Column 88; whether they had suffered any loss of any kind during civil disturbances in Leeds or Bradford; and whether any member of their immediate family was a serving police officer.

In that way, the defence sought to secure a jury better able to understand the fears and frustrations of Bradford's Asian community, from whom the defendants had been drawn. The importance of this was that the trial revolved around the purpose for which petrol bombs had been made: for self-defence by local Asians fearful of racist attacks (as the defence claimed); or for aggressive assaults on the city centre (as the police maintained). All twelve defendants were acquitted, the jury accepting their self-defence case.

The early summer of 1982 saw another extraordinary twist in the controversy over juries. Lord Denning argued in a new book, *What Next in the Law*, that juries should no longer be selected on a random basis because Britain's population was no longer homogeneous, with the same code of conduct and respect for the law. He wrote:

... the English are no longer a homogeneous race. They are white and black, coloured and brown. They no longer share the same standards of conduct. Some of them come from countries where bribery and graft are accepted as an integral part of life: and where stealing is a virtue so long as you are not found out.

Not surprisingly, this passage by the eighty-three-year-old head of the Appeal Court was roundly condemned as insulting and degrading by the

Society of Black Lawyers. Though he denied being prejudiced he had invited accusations of racism by critics.

But Lord Denning provoked an even more serious furore which ultimately caused him 'prematurely' to announce his resignation from July 1982. In the book he claimed that what he termed a 'packed' jury in the 1980 Bristol riot case failed to convict two among the 'ringleaders' of the riot, because the jury containing five blacks split along racial lines. Actually there was no legally permissible way Lord Denning could have known what went on in the jury room. Airily sweeping this aside, however, he wrote in remarkably forthright terms which defy the whole basis of British justice that the 'ringleaders' got five 'coloured' jurors through exercising their right to pre-emptory challenge, and that 'The evidence against two of the accused was so strong you would think they would be found guilty. But there was a disagreement.'

Outraged at this insinuation, two of the black jurors concerned threatened to issue a writ for libel unless the book was withdrawn and a public apology and damages given. Their solicitor also stated that Lord Denning's account of the case was 'riddled with inaccuracies', a point also confirmed by the *Observer* newspaper. Within a fortnight, Lord Denning was forced to make a humiliating apology, the book was withdrawn, and he brought forward the announcement of his impending retirement.

Bizarre though this episode was, however, Lord Denning's utterances were part of a chorus of attacks on juries from within ruling circles during the same period. These attacks may not have been orchestrated, but the effect was the same: to foster a climate in which the Tory government could move to restrict eligibility for jury service.

There had been calls for the rules to be toughened to bar those who had criminal convictions from sitting on juries, right-wing newspapers such as the *Daily Mail* pouncing eagerly to undermine the principle of trial by jury on a case where a convicted criminal sitting as a juror was spotted by a prison warder on duty in the dock at Coventry Crown Court. In law he was actually disqualified from sitting on a jury because of his long list of convictions, and the trial was halted. At the time there was a lifetime's disqualification from jury service for people given a custodial sentence of five years or more, with anyone who had served a sentence of between three months and five years being disqualified for ten years. This meant that people who had not received prison sentences but who nevertheless had been convicted of serious offences were eligible for jury service. Police spokesmen argued that, as an example, a rapist who had been fined £2,000 could in theory sit the next day as a juror in a rape trial.

Against this background, and with no parliamentary debate, the government tried in June 1982 to slip through a late clause (into an otherwise non-controversial Bill on legal administration) which would have extended jury service disqualification to anyone convicted of an imprisonable offence during the previous ten years. But it was blocked in a procedural manoeuvre by Labour M.P. Robert Kilroy-Silk. It would have banned up to ten million people, among them millions of motorists, and even people convicted of minor offences like carving an initial on a tree. Despite failing to achieve this, however, the government remained determined to pursue it in later legislation.

Meanwhile a related issue had surfaced, with prosecutions for alleged 'jury nobbling' in two Old Bailey trials and dark hints by the Lord Chancellor, Lord Hailsham, that these cases were the tip of an iceberg of jury corruption. In July 1982 new security measures at the Old Bailey were introduced to place jurors out of sight at the back of the court with the stated aim of preventing 'nobbling'. Serious though 'nobbling' is from any point of view, a few allegations were blown up out of all proportion in a systematic attempt to discredit juries. Another part of this was the demand (made in the same month) for the minimum age for jurors to be raised from 18 to 25. This came from John Marriage Q.C., a former chairman of the Criminal Bar Association, who said: 'The 18-year-old is inclined to be anti-authority. He, or she, is basically anti-police . . . I am not impressed by the argument that as they can vote, or die for their country in the Roaring Forties, they should also be allowed to judge their fellow men.'[78] It seemed as if the brief period since 1974 during which the British people truly had been judged by their peers was nearing an end.

· NEW GUIDELINES ·

In 1980 the Attorney General had issued new guidelines on jury vetting in an effort to allay public disquiet which had grown over the previous two years. In future, stated the guidelines, only the Attorney General could authorize vetting and then only in 'certain exceptional types of cases of public importance' – by which was meant national security cases where evidence was heard in camera, or cases involving terrorism.

But like his predecessor, Sam Silkin, Sir Michael Havers provided no statutory basis for his guidelines: they were advisory. That has not in the past stopped local breaches of such advice, for the simple reason that it could not be enforced. Moreover, the courts only a few months previously had declared that they had no power to prevent vetting. As a result they have been criticized as 'an exercise in futility'.[79] Instead of providing statutory protection against jury vetting, the state had merely reinforced the predominant practice of the judiciary by establishing a wide boundary within which there remained considerable scope for discretion and potential manipulation.

For even if such manipulation has been far less blatant than in earlier times, the jury remains a prime political target in the judicial system. For defendants in political trials it may provide the only real hope of securing justice. For the authorities, it is the joker in the pack of a judicial system which is otherwise probably the most secretive and controllable part of the state apparatus. However, for those in power there is a real dilemma over juries: they may be potential rogue animals, returning what, in the eyes of the police, judges or the prosecutors, are 'perverse' verdicts; but they are also a vital source of legitimacy for the legal system. It enhances the credibility of the legal system and the respect for the rule of law to be able to point to the fact that justice for the individual citizen ultimately rests with his or her peers in the privacy of the jury room. For this reason, perhaps, different groups and interests in the state have sometimes disagreed over the role of the jury. Whereas for the police it is a nuisance that they would happily see abandoned, for even conservative judges like Lord Denning the jury should be protected.

The jury system remains a basic safeguard against abuse of power. It may not play the rather romantic role suggested by Lord Devlin, who mistakes its countervailing power against judges for a political independence which in practice is heavily constrained. But it is an important part of individual freedom nonetheless.

Perhaps because it has such importance, there has been a persistent attempt by the authorities to control it, so that it regulates freedom in the way *they* choose. Those in authority, whether they be the Treasury Solicitors of Walpole's day or the Association of Chief Police Officers, have been desperately worried about their inability to do so, even when all available evidence seems to suggest that juries perform their supposed task at least as well, say, as the average government department. Constant, too, is the presumption that obtaining verdicts acceptable to the Crown is the same thing as serving the interests of justice.

In our day the fear of the influence of working people on the judicial system, even in a totally unorganized fashion as atomized individuals, is so great that political abuse of the jury system has been an integral part of the system itself.

CONSPIRACY:
AN AGENT OF GOVERNMENT

What is far more disturbing is the use of the conspiracy weapon
in controversial cases like the trials of Oz and I T, and of Peter Hain and
of the African demonstrators in *Kamara*. It is impossible to prove
that these were political trials in the sense that the defendants were on
trial for their political beliefs; but what can be said with some confidence
is that the offences with which they were charged were all motivated by,
and the result of, their political beliefs. What marks out these quasi-
political cases from the 'ordinary' criminal case is that because of the
tremendous publicity they receive, it is particularly important that justice
should manifestly be seen to be done; but it is precisely in these cases that
judges and juries appear to hand down decisions based on their own ideas
of what is just, or what is good for society – and this role in part is forced
upon them by the nature of the conspiracy charge.

(Robert Hazell, *Conspiracy and Civil Liberties* (Bell, 1974), p. 10)

When Guy Fawkes and his fellow gunpowder plotters were charged with
conspiracy to blow up the Houses of Parliament in 1605, they took their
place in a long tradition directly linking the law of conspiracy to politics.
Since then conspiracy cases have provided some of the clearest examples
of the use of the law to regulate, control and even repress political action.
In the 1970s there were well publicized conspiracy prosecutions of individuals who had acted out of political or social conviction, among them
writers on the 'alternative' newspaper *Oz*, trade unionists in the Shrewsbury building pickets, the 'Angry Brigade' and my own case arising from
the demonstrations against South African sports tours.

These and others provoked considerable disquiet at the use of conspiracy, and the law was eventually reformed under the 1977 Criminal
Law Act. But the charge remains intact and is just as likely to be used
against politically motivated defendants as it has in the past. To understand why, it is instructive to look at the origins of conspiracy.

·ORIGINS·

From the beginning it was a law with a clear political mission. Although it first appeared as a statutory offence, introduced in 1304 to prevent malicious prosecutions, its real political foundations were supplied in the seventeenth century by the Star Chamber which, as one legal authority put it, 'recognized its possibilities as an engine of government and moulded it into a substantive offence of wide scope'.[1] The Star Chamber did this by determining that conspiracy was essentially about an *agreement* to commit an unlawful act, rather than the act itself. It also extended conspiracy to take in all crimes, however trivial they might be.

In retrospect it can be seen that the Star Chamber enabled conspiracy to develop like a 'hydra-headed monster'.[2] Having no clear basis in parliamentary legislation, it was successively extended on a common law basis, that is to say, by judges reinterpreting the law to fit new circumstances. Each new judgement widened the law inexorably, usually reinforcing the heart of conspiracy as the offence of agreeing together to do something unlawful, or to do a lawful act by unlawful means.[3] The logical absurdity of this was illustrated in 1890 in the Whitchurch case, which resulted in the conviction of a woman for conspiring to procure her own abortion – even though it turned out she had not been pregnant! (To compound the felony, an aborted woman had been excluded from liability when Parliament made abortion a crime in 1861.) Very quickly, conspiracy *itself*, or the act of agreeing itself, became the real offence rather than the actual crime.

Prior to this, a judgement in the Starling case of 1663 had widened conspiracy to include an agreement that 'is directed against the public as a whole or against the government'.[4] Here the political purpose of the law was starkly revealed. From the early stages of the rise of industrial capitalism in the seventeenth century, conspiracy began to be used as a device to stop employees organizing against employers, and by the eighteenth century it was clear that, as one legal expert put it, conspiracy laws 'enabled judges to punish by criminal process such conduct as seemed to them socially undesirable, even though the actual deeds committed constituted no crime . . . where the actual deeds were of doubtful criminality, it saved judges from the often embarrassing necessity of having to spell out the crime'.[5] Even a senior judge in the 1970s, Lord Justice Lawton, conceded that, at the end of the eighteenth century and beginning of the nineteenth, 'prosecutions by the Crown for conspiracy were used to stifle criticism and to prevent agitation for religious, social and economic changes'.[6]

Soon the emerging trade union movement found itself under political attack from conspiracy laws. The Tolpuddle Martyrs were charged with what amounted to conspiracy, as the authorities deliberately set out to suppress trade union activity that today would be regarded as entirely unexceptional. Even after the repeal of the Combination Acts (which had made unions illegal), conspiracy was interpreted by judges in scores of cases to make virtually any strike or picket a criminal offence.[7] In 1851 striking tinplate workers were convicted of conspiracy to molest and obstruct their employer, it being found that they had interfered with their employer's 'lawful freedom of action'. In 1867 a group of tailors was convicted of conspiracy for picketing their masters' shops. Even though the judge acknowledged that their action was peaceful, he declared that it amounted to conspiracy to molest because it included 'abusive language or gestures' and was 'calculated to have a deterring effect on the minds of ordinary persons, by exposing them to have their motions watched and to encounter black looks'. In 1871 a group of women were even convicted of conspiracy for saying 'Bah' to blacklegs. A year later gasworkers, who threatened to strike unless a colleague sacked for union activity was reinstated, were convicted of conspiracy and sentenced to twelve months' hard labour because of a judgement arguing that they were guilty of 'unjustifiable annoyance and interference with the masters in the conduct of their business . . . such annoyance and interference as would be likely to have a deterring effect upon masters of ordinary nerve'.

Such cases provoked deep hostility among trade unionists, and Disraeli's government was eventually forced to abolish conspiracy in trade disputes, unless the action taken was itself a crime under the 1875 Conspiracy and Protection of Property Act. But the treatment of trade unionists by the courts prior to this is one of the clearest possible illustrations of the manner in which the ruling class through judges was virtually able to make up the law on conspiracy with the aim of repressing workers. We get no support here for the notion of the law as an objective instrument.

Indeed, notwithstanding the immunity to trade unionists specifically granted under Section 3 of the 1875 Act, they remained very vulnerable to being caught by conspiracy. This was shown by a series of picketing cases in which peacefully persuading others was deemed a 'public nuisance', 'watching and besetting premises' or 'intimidation' of workers; later, mass picketing and 'flying pickets' were also caught by conspiracy. Moreover, workers still remained a target for ill-defined crimes like conspiracy to molest or to induce others to break a contract, if they strayed beyond the strict confines of a trade dispute; even within these confines there was the possibility of conspiracy to commit certain offences.[8]

Meanwhile, the law was being directed at other political targets during this turbulent period of British history. In Ireland, it was used to suppress nationalist movements, and in a series of trials of Fenians, it was often linked to the crimes of treason and sedition. For example, there was the famous trial of Charles Parnell M.P. who, with four others, was charged in 1881 with conspiracy over their campaign to persuade tenants to refuse to pay rent and to take possession of their land if they were faced with eviction. Presiding over the trial, Judge Fitzgerald quite openly admitted that it was 'a political trial', for which conspiracy was eminently suitable.[9] But perhaps because the case was so blatantly political, the jury refused to convict.

After the launching in 1838 of the People's Charter, drawn up by William Lovett, which demanded universal suffrage and democratic accountability, conspiracy charges were used to crush the Chartists. There were a great number of Chartist trials in 1848, the year of revolution throughout Europe, showing how such prosecutions reflected the political threat perceived by the state at particular periods. The same message emerged from a trial in 1892 when six anarchists were charged with conspiracy to cause explosions. The case bore some resemblance to the 'Angry Brigade' and 'Persons Unknown' trials of the 1970s, not least in the hysterical atmosphere of the moment, encouraged then by reports of anarchist activity in Russia and elsewhere in Europe. Initially there was the familiar prosecution allegation of a 'nationwide conspiracy'. In the end, the conspiracy charges were dropped and three of the accused were convicted of possession of explosives and sentenced to ten years in prison. Later it was suggested by a police officer that incriminating evidence against the defendants had been supplied by an *agent provocateur* (something which had previously been alleged by the defence during the trial).[10]

In 1925 conspiracy again starred in a political trial when ten leading members of the Communist Party were prosecuted, conspiracy being linked to sedition and incitement to mutiny. They were jailed for a year. The evidence was highly questionable, based on Party documents, mostly published, and the prosecution made great play of an article in *Workers Weekly* which had urged troops not to act against workers if there were a general strike. But the prosecution was able to exploit the elastic nature of conspiracy to argue that the doctrine of British communism itself amounted to a seditious conspiracy, and indeed the judge directed the jury to that effect. It was a rare example of a twentieth-century sedition trial. Moreover, conspiracy was not in fashion at the time. But as Robert Spicer points out, political trials should be seen in historical contexts: 'Perhaps the trial may best be understood by its results, which were most useful for the government: the leadership of the Communist Party was removed from the political and industrial scene by means of the common law, at a time which was crucial for the preparation of . . . the general strike.'[11]

But this practice of finding a way of making illegal what a judge thought was undesirable has been just one feature of the way conspiracy has been manipulated. Another has been the use of conspiracy to impose greater punishments than would otherwise have been possible if a charge had been brought under the offence itself. For example, in the Shrewsbury building pickets case in 1973, one of those convicted was jailed for three years for conspiracy when the actual offence of intimidation carried a maximum sentence of only three months. The political advantage of such discriminatory sentencing was revealed when the jailed pickets, Denis Warren and Eric Tomlinson, went to appeal in November 1974. Refusing to reduce their sentences, the Court of Appeal made it clear that the severity of the punishment meted out was not related to *their individual* conduct at all. 'On the contrary,' as the *New Law Journal* commented, 'the sentences were held, on appeal, to be justified by the need to deter others engaged in picketing in the context of industrial disputes . . . In other words, they received sentences that were, according to the Court of Appeal, appropriate as a means of stemming a crisis.'

In 1964, the courts extended conspiracy to cover *summary* (i.e. petty) offences; the case concerned contravention of a section of the Road Traffic Act which carried only a small fine, but the judgement enabled a much stiffer sentence to be imposed because the conviction was for conspiracy. In theory the case allowed life imprisonment to be imposed for agreeing, say, to break the speed limit in order to get to a hospital for treatment.

·POLITICS OF CONSPIRACY IN THE 1970s·

The political implications of this became apparent in the 1970s in a flurry of judgements by which conspiracy was used to repress radical dissent. It might be argued that here judges were merely responding to new forms of social, political and industrial unrest, that they were simply applying the established law on conspiracy to circumstances for which all along it was really intended, if only these could have been envisaged in the first place. On this argument, judges are not the political agents they appear to be, but are only exercising their professional duty – they are not 'making' law but 'interpreting it'. But this comforting image of the role of judges unfortunately conflicts with the record. As Geoff Robertson put it:

The common law . . . is constantly being shifted and adapted by judges to meet new situations which are seen as disruptive of civilized society. This process, which undermines the democratic philosophy that all laws must receive the assent of the people's representatives, is sanctioned by the legal tradition that judges only 'declare' what the common law has always been, rather than 'make' new law. But this is a semantic quibble: their 'declaration' of the law necessarily 'extends' the common law, with the effect of proscribing conduct which was not previously thought to be criminal: the result is a new law, as surely as if it had been passed by an overwhelming Parliamentary majority. The doctrine of conspiracy has in recent years proved the most fertile ground for judges and prosecutors to 'discover' that old laws meet new situations. [12]

The point that should be stressed here is not just that conspiracy is a law capable of being 'an engine of government'. It has also been employed as a reactionary tool by judges to by-pass Parliament and to restrict political opposition. In some cases Parliament may well have declined to legislate in an area later pulled in under the rug of conspiracy – so flying in the face of Lord Justice Reid's 1961 dictum that 'Where Parliament fears to tread it is not for the courts to rush in.'

Rush in they have. In the period prior to the 1977 Criminal Law Act, there were some extraordinary judgements, all of them underlining the threat to political action posed by conspiracy charges.

First of all, the law itself was developed to cover new offences, notably that of trespass. A leading criminal law textbook had stated in 1969 that 'an agreement to commit a civil trespass is not indictable'. But within a few years the civil offence of trespass was turned into a criminal act by conspiring to do it. In 1971 some Sierra Leone students protested against their government by occupying its High Commission for a day. They were convicted of conspiracy to trespass and the 1973 Kamara judgement by the House of Lords on the case confirmed that the law on conspiracy did now include civil offences. Lord Hailsham's judgement in Kamara was a classic example of the ubiquitous extension of conspiracy, using the device of 'the public interest', to catch trespass. After Kamara the law became that conspiracy to trespass was a criminal offence when the 'public interest' was at stake or when a 'public domain' had been invaded.

In 1969–70 when I was helping to organize demonstrations against sports apartheid, including invasions of sports fields, it was understood that conspiracy to trespass did not constitute an offence. But, a year later, when I faced a private prosecution, it had been 'discovered' by the judges that this authoritative interpretation of the law was wrong, thus undermining a basic principle of English law, namely that it should not be applied retrospectively. When I came to trial in 1972 the Sierra Leone case had occurred, and my judge was able to rely upon it. Although I was acquitted on three major counts of conspiracy, I was convicted of interrupting play in a Davis Cup tennis match in Bristol by sitting down on the court for a few minutes and distributing leaflets.[13] The actual charge was conspiracy to interfere with the lawful rights of others to watch the game. Judge Bernard Gillis had directed the jury to convict if they found I had interfered with the public's rights by unlawful methods which were 'of substantial public concern – something of importance to citizens who are interested in the maintenance of law and order'. (To digress for a moment, the implications of this are indeed chilling, since protesters would be committing a crime potentially punishable by life imprisonment if they interfered with 'public rights', whatever *that* may mean, using methods which offend supporters of 'law and order', even though the methods themselves are not illegal.) During the trial my lawyers had tried to argue that it was against the public interest that racially constituted South African teams should be playing here in the first place, but the judge would not accept that.

After I was convicted I appealed, and my counsel argued that to run across a tennis court, causing no damage, using no force and interrupting play only for a brief period, was not using 'unlawful means of substantial public concern'. But Lord Justice Roskill had a revealing rejoinder: 'Hain would not have done it had it not been a matter of public concern,' he stated. In its full judgement, the Appeal Court underlined this: 'The whole object of the exercise would not have been achieved if the event had not aroused widespread public interest.' As Geoff Robertson pointedly put it: 'In other words, effective protest *by definition* involves matters of "substantial public concern" because the court equates this with "attracting public attention" which it uncharitably assumes to be the purpose of all protest demonstrations.' [14] Here we see how conspiracy can be used explicitly to stop political dissent. The judges might as well have said in my case: 'We don't like what he was up to, interfering with our enjoyment of cricket, rugby and tennis, and we shall find a way of interpreting the law to stop him doing it.'

· GUILTY UNTIL PROVEN INNOCENT ·

For that purpose the attraction of conspiracy is also that it effectively forces defendants to prove their innocence, thus undermining the classical principle that you are innocent until proven guilty. There are a number of reasons for this. The rules of evidence are much looser, which has proved very useful in conspiracy prosecutions. For instance, it is not usually permissible to allow in evidence statements made by other persons attributing views or actions to a defendant unless they are made either in his presence or with his agreement. This is known as 'hearsay evidence'. But the rules against it have been relaxed in conspiracy cases with devastating effect.

Political activists in particular find it almost impossible to defend themselves against such procedural unfairness, because they have repeatedly found that the distinction between their political *views* and their political *actions* which might have brought the prosecution, is entirely blurred. An innocent or casual expression of support for a political idea may become deadly evidence in court. Similarly, conspiracy cases allow for the introduction of circumstantial evidence which is not normally permitted. The judge in the Angry Brigade trial in 1972 was even able to tell the jury: 'Conspiracy can be effected by a wink or a nod without a word being spoken.' A further handicap for the defendant is the device of being charged with conspiring with 'persons unknown'.

This happened to me in the cricket conspiracy case. I was put in the position of having to call as witnesses various individuals involved in the Stop the Seventy Tour campaign to state that they had not agreed with me before doing a particular act: it was the only way I could *prove* my innocence on those matters. Note here that the prosecution had merely to assert my guilt whereas I had to prove my innocence.

It is an uncanny position to be in. During one campaign speech made to students at Kingston-upon-Thames Polytechnic, I had referred jokingly to having an elderly man up in Manchester who was breeding locusts for demonstrators to let loose on the grass of cricket pitches all over the country. Actually I had never met him and only knew of his activity through a report in the *News of the World*! But my speech was filmed by Granada Television and the programme script was triumphantly produced in court over two years later as a 'conclusive' self-confession of my conspiring with the said gentleman to cause damage to cricket pitches.

Many similar points could be made about trials less overtly political, concerned with public morality. The three main charges here are conspiracy to corrupt public morals, conspiracy to outrage public decency and conspiracy to effect a public mischief. Recent examples have included prosecution of the directors of the underground magazine *IT* in 1972 for carrying advertisements from gay people seeking partners. Another was the prosecution of the editors of *Oz* magazine. In these latter two the defendants' lifestyles and their opinions were effectively on trial rather than their agreement to carry the offending contact advertisements. A police officer in the *Oz* trial admitted that his real objection to the defendants was that 'they attack society and try to change it'.[15]

Also repeated here is the vice of conspiracy charges which enable a charge to be brought by attaching 'conspiracy' in front of something which is not in itself a substantive offence. At the time of the *Oz* and *IT* trials it would not have been possible simply to charge the defendants with 'corrupting public morals', 'outraging public decency' or 'effecting a public mischief'. As conspiracies, however, they became indictable crimes. And it takes little imagination to comprehend the possibilities open to the ruling authorities for clamping down on libertarian views or practices, by using such inherently vague terms as 'public decency', 'public mischief' and 'public morals'.

In 1981, Tom O'Carroll was tried for conspiracy to corrupt public morals. He was secretary of the Paedophile Information Exchange, which had published contact advertisements for adults wanting sexual relations with young children. But understandable public distaste for his activities diverted attention from the fact that conspiracy to corrupt public morals is a highly subjective and political charge; and also that the use of conspiracy enabled the prosecution to mount a case that would have been impossible on the substantive activities themselves which were not actually criminal offences. O'Carroll was convicted and jailed for two years, although his fellow conspirators had been acquitted in a previous trial where the jury had been unable to agree on a verdict against him.

Another conspiracy trial which hit the headlines was that of the Shrewsbury Six. It arose out of the 1972 building strike, where the unions were faced with problems peculiar to the building industry – a low union membership, scattered sites and a large number of self-employed workers. They organized 'flying pickets' to go from site to site, strengthening the strike. Described as a 'political trial' by one analyst,[16] the Shrewsbury case contained many of the familiar characteristics for which conspiracy had become noted: the almost arbitrary selection of a few 'ringleaders'; the blurring of evidence into political views; reliance on inference rather than substantive evidence; and the heavy sentence.

There are many other points which could be made about the iniquities of conspiracy trials, using examples from my own experience and from the experience of many others.[17] Collectively, such iniquities envelop the defendant in what amounts to the *real* conspiracy – one to ensure that justice is not done. No less than an American Supreme Court judge has summed it up well:

When the trial starts, the accused feels the full impact of the conspiracy strategy. Strictly, the prosecution should first establish *prima facie* the conspiracy and identify the conspirators, after which evidence of acts and declarations of each in the course of its execution are admissible against all. But the order of proof of so sprawling a charge is difficult for the judge to control. As a practical matter, the defendant is often confronted with a hodge-podge of acts and statements by others which he may never have authorized or intended or even known about, but which help to persuade the jury of the existence of the conspiracy itself. In other words, a conspiracy often is proved by evidence that is admissible only upon the assumption that the conspiracy existed.[18]

· A POLITICAL WEAPON ·

Against this background, it is easy to see why conspiracy has been such a useful political weapon over the years, not least because, as one leading legal textbook put it, the law 'leaves so much discretion in the hands of the judges that it is hardly too much to say that plausible reasons may be found for declaring it to be a crime to do almost anything which the judges regard as morally wrong or politically or socially dangerous'. An eminent American lawyer, Clarence Darrow, gave an even more graphic description of conspiracy law as 'a worn-out piece of tyranny, this dragnet for compassing the imprisonment and death of men whom the ruling class does not like'.

However, the enthusiastic use of conspiracy charges against political defendants during the 1970s aroused widespread public disquiet. By July 1973 a Working Paper[19] published by the Law Commission recommended severe restrictions on the use of conspiracy (although this did not deter the prosecuting authorities from proceeding regardless). In its final report the commission concluded that conspiracy should be limited to cases where the act is itself a crime.[20] It suggested the abolition of conspiracy to corrupt public morals and to outrage public decency, and it sought to limit the sentences that could be imposed in conspiracy cases. It was a liberal report which ran against the accumulating judgements that had been extending conspiracy almost case by case.

The report's recommendations can be seen against a background of mounting political opposition to conspiracy, with the Trades Union Congress lobbying the government following the widespread outcry from the labour movement at the jailing of the Shrewsbury pickets. Clearly, the state decided that a response was needed, and the Labour government, 'anxious to show its sympathy for the trade unions' demands, implemented the Law Commission's proposals . . . with exemplary speed'.[21] This was done in the 1977 Criminal Law Act under which, for the first time, Parliament introduced a *statutory* offence of conspiracy. It tied up the tangled mess of common law conspiracy, limiting it to agreements to commit a criminal offence and so removing the worst excesses created by Lord Hailsham's Kamara judgement; conspiracy to trespass, for example, was abolished. It regulated sentencing and prevented proceedings for conspiracy to commit summary offences except where the Director of Public Prosecutions gives consent. But these welcome reforms were offset by the retention of conspiracy to corrupt public morals or to outrage public decency.

Trade unionists still remained vulnerable. For instance section 5(2) of the Act allows the offences of conspiracy to defraud to continue to exist as part of the common law, so that 'conspiracy to defraud in furtherance of a trade dispute, even if the defrauding would not be illegal, is an offence'.[22] So shop stewards could conceivably be prosecuted and face sentences of up to life imprisonment even if they have not used methods which are in themselves criminal. (The creation of the statutory criminal offence directed mainly at residential squatters also means that factory occupations or work-ins, previously exempt under the 1875 Act, could be threatened.)

Any illusions about the new law were quickly exposed by the extraordinary 'Persons Unknown' trial during 1979. During this, the prosecution were able to introduce material in traditional conspiracy case fashion, concerning lifestyles, personal opinions and social habits, while other features of the case also harked back to the pre-1977 period. Six anarchists were arrested by the Anti-Terrorist Squad in the summer of 1978 and charged with conspiracy to cause explosions. With the zealous assistance of Fleet Street, the individuals were presented as being part of a 'nationwide conspiracy to overthrow society'. However, diligent investigation by the police failed to uncover the necessary evidence to support the charge of conspiracy to cause explosions (none actually occurred, nor could any evidence of an *agreement* to commit them be found). Within ten months of their arrest, the police were forced to drop the charge, replacing it instead with conspiracy to rob. Again, five of the six defendants were not charged with any *actual* robberies; the sixth turned state witness and played a dubious role in the whole affair. As the trial progressed it emerged that the prosecution was only able to stick its case together under the aegis of a generalized allegation of an 'anarchist' conspiracy of subversion. Eventually the jury acquitted the four defendants (the fifth having jumped bail and disappeared). Much of the case had rested on the confession of the sixth defendant, a gangster. The trial – dubbed 'Persons Unknown' since the defendants were charged with conspiracy with persons known and unknown – came as an uncomfortable jolt to those who felt that the sordid history of conspiracy had been ended with the 1977 Act.

For ultimately conspiracy is too convenient a law for the establishment to relinquish. Focusing as it does on the *agreement* to commit an offence, it is a ready-made dragnet for politics, the very essence of which is also based upon individuals *agreeing* collectively to take action. 'The normal facts of political activity leading to public meetings and demonstrations give wide scope for charges of conspiracy,'[23] one legal expert writes, while another confirms that the same is true of trade unionists: '. . . since industrial action is by nature collective . . . it falls automatically within the mischief of combination.'[24] But conspiracy has not simply been a political weapon in a general sense. It has had very specific ideological targets: trade unionists, socialists, libertarians – those within the progressive political tradition who have dissented from the status quo. As C. H. Rolph put it: '. . . the history of the law of conspiracy is now the history of the class struggle and the regulation of wages'.[25]

This was no more evident than in the *Mogul* case in 1889, where it was determined that an organized drive by a powerful group of tea traders to stamp out competition was not a conspiracy because they had acted 'with the lawful object of protecting and extending their trade and increasing their profits'.[26] Under capitalism some conspiracies are more acceptable than others. The difference today is that judges pretend that the use of conspiracy is 'non-political', whereas in the last century they made no bones about the fact that it resulted in political trials, as for example the judge openly admitted in the trial of the Irish nationalist, Parnell.

TRADE UNIONISM

The historical development of labour law is explicable in terms of
industrial and political conflict. Whether or not one approves
or disapproves of trade unions or regards them as too powerful or not
powerful enough, it would be difficult to deny that labour law's
development has reflected attacks on trade unions and counter-attacks by
unions . . . One of the recurrent themes in this development
has been the tension between two of the organs of the State, Parliament
and the courts. Parliament has proved susceptible to trade union
as well as employer pressure group activities,
whereas the courts often appeared to be hostile to trade unions.

(Roy Lewis, 'The Historical Development of Labour Law',
British Journal of Industrial Relations, Vol. XIV, No. 1 (March 1976), pp. 13–14)

Analysing the strike by workers at Grunwick during 1976–8, the *Financial Times* journalist, Joe Rogaly, argued that the law

now supports most of the legitimate aims of working people . . . Some of it may
be in need of improvement; for example, the Grunwick case has shown that
people who walk out, and are then sacked, cannot easily win compensation from
an unwilling employer or anyone else . . . Taken as a whole, however, industrial
legislation now protects people through most of their working lives.[1]

By contrast, an analysis of Grunwick from the standpoint of the strikers
argued:

The partisan nature of law enforcement is nothing new to the British trade
union movement. The strikers saw their legal rights flouted and rendered
unenforceable by the intransigence of the employer, the hostility of the judiciary
and police and, at best, the reluctance of the Government to do anything about
it. The company camp, on the other hand, could command the full support of
the state to maintain production.[2]

That the first interpretation (from someone by no means hostile to the
Grunwick strikers) could differ so markedly from the second, underlines

that on the question of trade unionism – perhaps more than any other area – political pre-disposition shapes the way we view the role of the law.

And how could it be otherwise? In a capitalist society like Britain, divided on class lines, it is not possible to be neutral about the role of the major organizations of working-class people, the trade unions. You may adopt, as Joe Rogaly does, the notion that the law's function is fairly to balance the conflicting rights of management and worker – while ignoring the basic capitalist relations which in practice, if not in theory, allow management to retain the upper hand regardless. Or you may adopt an alternative perspective which would see the function of the law as being positively to strengthen the hand of workers against those who own and control capital. However, it is not possible to duck the central fact that the British economy is based on conflict between workers and their unions on the one hand, and employers and the system on the other. That is the backdrop against which the law functions. So it is as well to acknowledge from the outset that over trade unions clear choices have to be made which benefit some groups in society to the detriment of others. There is not any way of avoiding this, as the labour lawyer, Lord Wedderburn, emphasizes by pointing out that it is in the nature of court intervention in industrial disputes that it 'cannot be neutral; it will take one side or the other'.[3] A court's judgement will either uphold an employer's claim or will reject it: there is not normally scope for compromise of the kind which invariably emerges from industrial negotiations or arbitration.

It is also as well to be clear that British law inherently favours the rights of the *individual*, rather than the rights of the *collective*. As one expert explains:

> In crude terms, the idea of individual freedom is a middle-class concept which is often in conflict with the fact of working-class advancement through solidarity. The middle class advance as individuals through educational advantage, promotion prospects and so on; the main instrument of working-class advancement is through collective action.[4]

Under the law, he points out, the *individual right* to cross a picket line tends to override the *collective right* to take industrial action. The courts would view someone exercising such an individual right as an 'innocent citizen' deserving of the law's protection rather than as a 'strike breaker' undermining the workers' collective interest. The law also favours the rights of property owners as against workers. Again, as has been shown with reference to picketing:

If management can employ private police on the gates, in the interests of protecting their profits, by for example stopping pilferage, it should be possible to have the gate manned by those interested in protecting the standard of living of the employees, with similar powers. It is too readily assumed ... that the owners of capital should be entitled to more rights than the owners of labour. Property rights are regarded as sacrosanct except when the property concerned is someone's livelihood. [5]

A brief examination of the history of trade unionism supports this view that the law has been a class instrument. 'Trade unions,' conceded a consultative document produced by the Conservative government in 1981, 'came into existence in the nineteenth century despite the law and not under its protection.' [6] That indeed is an understatement: from their beginnings, trade unions were treated with hostility by the courts, since 'many judges regarded trade unionism as a criminal objective'. [7]

Back in 1351 the Statute of Labourers began a tradition under which workers could not legally combine together to advance their interests. Judges in the 1721 Cambridge Tailors case actually ruled that a 'conspiracy to raise wages' was a criminal offence. This was reinforced by the notorious Combination Acts of 1799 and 1800, introduced for reasons which were explicitly political. To be sure, they were designed to quell mounting unrest among workers at that time, but mostly because of the *political* threat which incipient trade unionism was seen to represent. Concerned about the spread of Weavers' Associations in Lancashire, the Home Secretary wrote in 1799:

If nothing injurious to the safety of the government is actually in contemplation, Associations so formed contain within themselves the means of being converted at any time into a most dangerous instrument to disturb the public tranquillity. [8]

The Acts reinforced existing common law, which made almost all trade unionism illegal. Their particular value to the authorities of the day was to stem a potential *collective* threat to public order, the consequences of which could be seen across the Channel in France. Significantly, they were brought in alongside other repressive measures, including attacks on press freedom and imprisonment without trial.

Ironically, however, the Combination Acts had the opposite effect to that intended. Faced with the upheaval of the Industrial Revolution, workers continued to organize regardless; the Combination Acts merely forced them into more clandestine and violent forms of struggle. E. P. Thompson mentions that the Acts 'served only to bring illegal Jacobin and trade union stands closer together',[9] the Webbs described how this constituted 'veiled insurrection',[10] and by 1824 a House of Commons Committee set up to investigate the problem argued that the Combination Acts had helped produce circumstances 'highly dangerous to the peace of the community'. The result was the repeal of the Acts in 1824, and a new era in which only 'peaceful combinations' were supposedly to be permitted. This change occurred therefore, not because trade unionism was regarded as legitimate, but for pure expediency. Within a year another Act had been passed aimed at curbing an upsurge in industrial action. The definition of 'peaceful combinations' was tightened up to exclude the vague notions of 'molesting' or 'obstructing' persons at work.

· THE TOLPUDDLE MARTYRS ·

Nevertheless, trade unions faced numerous legal obstacles and workers were consistently prosecuted. Perhaps the most notorious example of this was the case of the Tolpuddle Martyrs, which is often referred to today but without much appreciation of its enduring significance. For Tolpuddle was not simply an instance of repression and denial of elementary workers' rights. It was also a classic case of the manipulation of the law for partisan political purposes by government and judiciary alike. There can hardly have been a more vivid debunking of the myth of the impartiality of the law and of its servants.

The Martyrs were six farm labourers from the Dorset village of Tolpuddle who were prosecuted in 1834. The then Home Secretary, Lord Melbourne, was personally alarmed at reports of agricultural trade unionism growing throughout the country. He had family connections with Dorset and was soon engaged in correspondence with the presiding magistrate there, James Frampton, and the Lord Lieutenant of the county, Lord Digby, over reports of local labourers organizing. All three used their positions of power to give effect to their strident anti-unionism, and they picked upon the unfortunate Tolpuddle labourers as a test case.

It should be clear from the outset that the labourers had not infringed the law *knowingly*. There was no public notice posted around Dorset informing them that their activities to organize a welfare fund were illegal under a specific named law. On the contrary, the prosecutors themselves were not at all certain which law to invoke, for the simple reason that no obvious offence had been committed. But that trifling obstacle proved no deterrent to Lord Melbourne, who suggested to Magistrate Frampton that he try an Act of 1817 aimed at 'preventing Seditious Meetings and Assemblies', under which any group whose members undertook oaths not required or authorized by law would be regarded as an unlawful combination. So, although trade unions had ceased to be criminal by repeal of the Combination Acts, the wording of the 1817 legislation – brought in for the quite different purpose of clamping down on revolutionary plots – was manipulated to catch trade unionists, and the Tolpuddle farmworkers were arrested under it.

However, still greater legal ingenuity was required when Lord Melbourne discovered that there might after all be a loophole in the 1817 Act under which they were detained.[11] To overcome this, he and his advisers used a classic device in political trials of linking the charge to another Act. The 1797 Mutiny Act, by happy coincidence, contained ambiguous wording that enabled it to be used against groups other than the armed forces for whom it had been specifically enacted. It also had the advantage of allowing for a much heavier sentence – up to seven years' transportation – and Lord Melbourne was determined to see such an exemplary punishment. Despite the absence of any actual evidence of sedition, the labourers were indicted under the 1797 Act which prevented the 'administering or taking of unlawful oaths' for seditious purposes, duly convicted and deported to Australia. During their trial, the judge revealed his own prejudices when he said that if trade unions were allowed to continue, 'they would ruin masters, cause a stagnation in trade and destroy property'.

Defence counsel in the case argued that the indictment could not possibly apply to poor labouring men who had been members of the Tolpuddle Friendly Society, whose purpose was to act as a cooperative savings group to help the men should they fall ill or be unemployed. How, he asked, could a society whose objective was to 'provide against seasons of scarcity and obviate starvation' be considered an illegal combination for 'seditious or mutinous confederacy'? But his plea was in vain. For in her book, *The Tolpuddle Martyrs*, Joyce Marlow explains how they were as good as guilty before the trial began:

It was a beautifully spun web – it was foolproof and it was legal. For as the *Law Magazine* later said, 'It is not with administering an oath not required or authorized by the law, that the Dorsetshire Labourers stood charged, as still seems to be imagined by the leaders of the Unions . . . but with administering an oath not to reveal a combination which administers such oaths.' You may need to read this subtle distinction a few times, but once absorbed, it explains how the indictment was strictly within the letter of the law. Whether it was within the spirit is another matter, as are the reasons which motivated the indictment. [12]

The case provoked widespread anger and protests from trade unionists, with even *The Times* declaring: 'The crimes which called for punishment were not proved – the crime brought home to the prisoners did not justify the sentence.' [13] Tolpuddle, then, had all the ingredients of a straightforward political trial: a government determined to make an example of a group of dissidents; individual law officers quite willing to abuse their own positions; the virtual invention of an offence to sustain a prosecution; and a trial itself which was a charade. The authorities may as well have taken the Martyrs straight from their homes that February morning in 1834 and put them on the next boat to Australia. And while there could hardly be as stark an example as the Tolpuddle case, we find similarities cropping up time and again in the unfolding clash between trade unionism and the law.

· GROWTH OF TRADE UNIONISM ·

Some later legislation, it should be acknowledged, was not entirely hostile to workers. For example, the 1859 Molestation of Workers Act attempted to clarify the 1825 Act on the repeal of the Combination Laws by specifically exempting peaceful picketing in trade disputes over wages and hours from the penalties of 'molesting' or 'obstructing'. But even if Parliament was prepared to ameliorate its attitude, judges still remained implacably hostile. In 1867, the Boilermakers Society was prevented by the courts from suing the treasurer of their Bradford branch for embezzling union funds. Union officials believed that the 1855 Friendly Societies Act gave protection to union funds. But the Lord Chief Justice stated (in the *Hornby v. Close* judgement) that unions were not covered by the Act: even if they were not criminal, they were still illegal, he said, remarking pointedly that unions acted 'in restraint of trade'. This judgement was later reversed by Parliament in the 1871 Trade Union Act which gave unions *immunities* from aspects of the common law.

But it is important to understand that this Act gave unions no *positive* legal rights. Instead they were granted immunity from the criminal or civil consequences of their actions in 'restraining trade'. Egged on by employers, judges were quick to spot the opportunities that remained for curbing trade union power, notably by extending the law on conspiracy in a series of cases involving workers. Even the passing of the 1875 Conspiracy and Protection of Property Act – which among other things gave strikers immunity from the simple crime of conspiracy if they were involved in a trade dispute, and also gave additional protection for peaceful picketing – did not quell the enthusiasm of the judges, whose ingenuity knew no bounds in their anti-union mission.

The 1871 and 1875 Acts were certainly important in legitimizing trade union activity. But the protection they undoubtedly gave was undermined by judge-made law in a series of cases. Judges allowed cases of *civil* conspiracy successfully to be brought against unions, and severely muddied the right to picket in a series of judgements. In one case in 1896, involving the Amalgamated Trade Society of Fancy Leather Workers, an injunction was granted against peaceful pickets, the judges declaring that the 1875 Act really specified only the 'communication of information' and not the exercise of 'peaceful persuasion': a fine distinction perhaps, but not too fine for either the High Court or the Appeal Court.

This trend supporting *civil* actions against unions – the scope for *criminal* prosecutions having been narrowed by Parliament – was confirmed in the famous Taff Vale case in 1901. The judgement here made unions liable for a civil action claiming damages resulting from a strike. It completely undermined the right to strike and to picket, because even if striking and picketing were allowed, the consequences could be heavy fines imposed by the courts; the Amalgamated Society of Railway Servants had to pay £42,000 following the judgement.

Having been thwarted by the judges, trade unionists now turned to political action to secure their rights. Affiliations to the recently formed Labour Representation Committee jumped, and the unions eventually persuaded Parliament to act, the result being the 1906 Trade Disputes Act, which did for civil law what the 1875 Act had done for criminal law. It prohibited legal action against strikers in tort, and provided a widely based immunity from judge-made law for trade union action. [14]

It was an historic Act, entrenching what has been described as an 'abstentionist' legal structure for trade unionism, giving them blanket immunities from civil actions, but still not positive legal rights as such, with collective bargaining remaining the main instrument of workers' advancement rather than statutory regulations. [15]

The Taff Vale case and the subsequent 1906 Act illustrate two significant themes. First, it is not possible to divorce Taff Vale from the political environment at that time. It was a period of turmoil and outright confrontation between the state and the unions. In 1893 alone, striking miners had been shot at Featherstone and gunboats had been anchored in the Humber to threaten striking dockers. The authorities were particularly concerned by the emerging power of unskilled workers' unions. [16]

Second, Taff Vale showed the determination of judges, acting in response to such a political environment, to declare the law as they saw it rather than as Parliament decreed it. Indeed, the 1906 Act had to undo previous judge-made law, Taff Vale included, rather as the 1871 and 1875 legislation had done. This is not necessarily to suggest that by acting in this way judges were flying in the face of the views of the government of the day. On the contrary, they were acting in the interest of the ruling class as they saw it. But within that context they were nevertheless operating *politically* and *independently*. It is little wonder that trade unionists came to feel that they would have to seek justice by political methods rather than from politically hostile courts. Even then, however, judges were able to retaliate when the law lords discovered in the 1909 *Osborne* case that they could stop unions spending money for political purposes, thereby depriving the new Labour Party of funds. Again political pressure was required, eventually resulting in the 1913 Trade Union Act which provided for unions to establish 'political funds' together with the 'contracting out' system.

· RECENT DEVELOPMENTS ·

From then until the 1960s trade unionism grew, with even judges being unable to curb it. During this period there were of course various restrictions placed by Parliament on trade unions – for example, the 1920 Emergency Powers Act giving the government the ability to break strikes in an emergency, and the 1927 Act preventing sympathy strikes, changing 'contracting out' to 'contracting in' for union political funds and stopping civil service unions from affiliating to the Labour Party (the latter Act was repealed in 1945). A High Court judge also decreed that the 1926 General Strike was 'illegal', in circumstances suggesting some collusion with politicians seeking to halt it. But on the whole the legal and political legitimacy of unions was not challenged.

It was only as the post-Second World War boom expired, and the economic decline from which Britain is still suffering began to bite, that the judiciary was again called on to play its role as an opponent of working-class power. Once more judges saw their duty as being to defend their class in its hour of need.

The thorny issue of picketing raised its head in 1960 in the case of *Piddington v. Bates*, where the local police decided that no more than two pickets were allowed to cover one entrance to a printing firm. When a third attempted to join his colleagues he was arrested and charged with obstruction, even though the whole episode was entirely peaceful. Nevertheless the courts supported the police, Lord Parker arguing: 'I think that a police officer, charged with the duty of preserving the Queen's peace, must be left to take such steps as, on the evidence before him, he thinks proper.' Besides being a significant affirmation of the role of police *discretion*, this judgement, together with others, meant that, as one legal expert put it, the right to picket had 'no more substance than the grin of a Cheshire cat'.[17] In one judgement, delivered in 1973, Lord Reid saw the rights of pickets as being equivalent only to those of hitch-hikers: 'One is familiar with persons at the side of the road signalling to a driver requesting him to stop. It is then for the driver to decide whether he will stop or not. That, in my opinion, a picket is entitled to do.' This particular case, *Hunt v. Broome*, was also interesting for the way in which the courts effectively rewrote the section of the 1971 Industrial Relations Act which expressly permitted picketing that was peaceful. For nobody disputed that John Broome, a local trade union official, had acted peacefully when he picketed a building site in Stockport in September 1972.

During the 1970s, judges and police combined to exploit the vague nature of the law and clamp down on picketing. In one case in 1974, a judge even agreed that to shout 'scab' on a picket line would give the police grounds to break it up. The police had argued that pickets gathering in 1973 outside St Thomas's Hospital shouting 'scabs and such names' could constitute 'insulting words' under the 1936 Public Order Act and could have led to a breach of the peace. In his judgement on the case, the Lord Chief Justice, Lord Widgery, made it clear that there was no right to picket as such: the law only conferred immunities in certain restricted circumstances which were invariably open to judicial interpretation.

Back in 1964 judges had again gone on to the offensive with a judgement in the *Rookes v. Barnard* case in which the law lords ruled that unions could be sued for taking industrial action under the obscure tort of intimidation. A further series of judgements followed this, encouraging the use of injunctions against trade unionists and thereby restricting industrial action. In the familiar pattern of events before and after the turn of the century, Parliament was forced to undo the work of the judges: the Labour government brought in the 1965 Trades Dispute Act giving immunity from the civil wrong of intimidation. It is also worth noting that another familiar pattern had by now asserted itself. There was widespread concern at the growth of shop floor power and in particular 'unofficial strikes', and judges clearly saw it as their duty to defend employers against such nefarious activities.

This question of unofficial activity and shop steward influence had exercised the minds of the authorities since the early 1960s. The report of the Donovan Commission devoted considerable attention to it and official anxiety had reached such a pitch by late 1969 that the then Labour government was persuaded to slide into open conflict with its traditional trade union support and issue its ill-fated White Paper, *In Place of Strife*. It was eventually withdrawn under pressure from the unions but re-emerged in a much more confrontationist form in the Conservatives' 1971 Industrial Relations Act, which was:

a comprehensive, restrictive legal code, abolishing overnight the whole foundation of trade union and labour law embodied in the statutes from 1871 to 1906, overtly aimed at curbing trade union action and strikes by means of legal penalties, and at regulating trade union internal affairs by means of a system of state vetting and registering of trade unions and their rule books. [18]

The Act heralded a new and aggressive assault on trade union activity using the full weight of the law. Whereas for the previous hundred years parliamentary legislation had by and large drawn back from the industrial fight, and allowed unions and judges to battle it out, now it was there punching away in the thick of things. The law itself was to be an instrument aimed at rolling back trade union power and advances in working-class bargaining strength. The engineers' leader, Hugh Scanlon, told the 1972 T.U.C. annual conference that the 'courts which are active under the Act are brazenly political'. But the Act proved a failure, for the simple reason that the trade union movement openly defied it. There was a bruising and messy period of conflict, culminating in the downfall of the Conservative government in 1974.

It should be acknowledged, however, that the defeat of this attempt to tackle trade union power was not achieved by polite persuasion or parliamentary lobbying: it was the result of extra-parliamentary action. The political nature of the law required a political response to challenge it. Thus in 1973 the engineering workers' union, the A.U.E.W., directly challenged the authority of the Act and had assets sequestered by the courts. Finally, it threatened a national engineering strike which was only avoided when an anonymous group of businessmen stepped in following a dispute between the courts and the union and paid its costs. The previous year the Act had been reduced to a state of farce when, in a dispute between dockers and container firms, five shop stewards were jailed, precipitating a call from the T.U.C. for a general strike. It was averted only when a previously obscure figure, the official solicitor, intervened and secured their release. The affair once again exposed popular mythology about the lofty majesty of the law and how it is supposed to take its course regardless of lowly political pressures. When the establishment realized the chips were down they found a way of getting the dockers out of jail.

It is worth recalling exactly how this was managed. On 14 June 1972 the National Industrial Relations Court ordered three Transport and General Workers' Union dockers to be imprisoned for contempt of court. They had defied a court order to prevent them blacking certain haulage firms involved in 'containerization', which threatened traditional docks work. With warrants for their arrest due on 16 June, widespread strikes were threatened and a major national crisis loomed. Then, almost out of nowhere, appeared the official solicitor – described as an 'officer of the court' – who requested the Appeal Court to review the sentence of imprisonment imposed on the dockers; it did, and they were released. But the blacking continued, there were further legal proceedings, and on

21 July the National Industrial Relations Court again made an order for imprisonment, this time for five dockers, and again a national economic crisis threatened, with unofficial dock strikes breaking out immediately. Amid protests to the government from the T.U.C. events began to escalate towards a general strike. Once more the official solicitor appeared, and on 26 July the House of Lords considered a related legal case, delivering a judgement 'with almost unprecedented speed'.[19] It gave a pretext for the Industrial Relations Court president, Sir John Donaldson, to release the dockers. He was the very same judge who had said only a month before: 'By their conduct these men are saying they are above the rule of law. No court should ignore such a challenge. To do so would imperil all law and order.' And on 21 July he had said: 'The issue is whether these men are to be allowed to opt out of the rule of law . . . It is a very simple issue but vastly important, for our whole way of life is based upon acceptance of the rule of law.'

Yet just five days later he was able to swallow these strong words and release them, the whole legal manoeuvre arousing 'the strong suspicion of judicial compliance with political expediency'.[20] Another way of putting it would be to say that the courts and the government had simply manipulated the rules and the law to ward off a political crisis. Within a matter of days the protection of 'our whole way of life' had switched to mean something quite different.

The period of 1972–4 proved a trying one for the Tory government and the judiciary, as widespread industrial militancy challenged their right to rule. Miners organized 'flying pickets', including the one at the Saltley coke depot which forced the police to retreat, and the government was finally brought down after the miners' strike of 1973–4. The law had been used as an overt class weapon, particularly through the 1971 Act, and it had lost.

From the time Labour came to power in 1974 until its defeat in 1979, the law and the unions came into contact with each other on two quite different and often conflicting planes. Labour brought in legislation which granted unions unprecedented rights. But simultaneously, the courts and the judges worked away at reducing these in a number of celebrated cases. It can be seen that the judiciary and the establishment in general never really accepted the legitimacy of the new trade union rights granted by Labour.

Labour's legislation was comprehensive. The 1974–6 Trade Union and Labour Relations Act restored to unions the legal immunities swept aside by the 1971 Act. The 1975 Employment Protection Act secured new collective bargaining and job security rights, while the 1974 Health and Safety at Work Act and the 1975 Sex Discrimination Act covered traditionally neglected areas of concern to trade unionists.

All this was welcomed by the labour movement. But although it undoubtedly represented an important advance, its impact on the ground of industrial reality showed again just how tenuous are even statutory trade union rights when up against a hostile employer acting in concert with equally hostile judges. The Grunwick strike proved a salutary reminder of the historic opposition of the judiciary to trade unions.

· GRUNWICK ·

Grunwick centred on the right of workers to join and be represented by a union of their choice. It began during the August heatwave of 1976 when workers, fed up with bad conditions, walked out from the company's film processing laboratory in North West London. Repeated attempts to establish recognition for the union of their choice, A.P.E.X., failed: normal procedures led nowhere against an intransigent employer. Within months a fuse had been lit which began to explode in all directions. Post Office workers seeking to support the strikers by refusing to handle the firm's lifeblood – its mail – soon found themselves up against the law. Picketing of the firm escalated into mass confrontation, with bitter clashes between trade unions and the Special Patrol Group. Grunwick quickly became both the centre of a national controversy and a symbol of the failure of the law to protect the interests of the workers.[21]

They resorted to the arbitration machinery established under the new Employment Protection Act, and the Advisory Conciliation and Arbitration Service (A.C.A.S.) was asked by the union to intervene. It polled the strikers and found them overwhelmingly in favour of joining A.P.E.X. The management, however, had refused A.C.A.S. permission to consult those still working inside the company. And when A.C.A.S. duly recommended that A.P.E.X. be granted recognition, and with it full negotiating rights, Grunwick refused to accept this. The whole ethos of the arbitration procedure which depended upon both parties accepting the outcome had been rejected by the management, which now went to court to get A.C.A.S.'s recommendation declared void. It failed in the High Court, which ruled in favour of A.C.A.S. but this was overturned in Lord Denning's Appeal Court on 29 July 1977.

Meanwhile another official avenue had been pursued. Partly in order to cool an inflamed situation, the government appointed a court of inquiry under Lord Scarman which sat for two months, investigating all aspects of the dispute, and came out broadly in favour of union recognition and in support of A.P.E.X.[22] But again the company remained unmoved, defying also government attempts to persuade it to reach an agreement with A.P.E.X.

By the time Scarman had reported and A.C.A.S. had been bogged down in the Court of Appeal, the strike's momentum had run out. Repeatedly urged not to indulge in mass picketing, not to request blacking of mail from postal workers, and instead to rely on the due procedures of the law and of official arbitration through both A.C.A.S. and the Scarman inquiry, the strike committee found itself deflected and squeezed into sullen submission. It was little wonder that, when she was asked about the lessons of the affair, Mrs Jayaben Desai, the most prominent of the strikers, remarked bitterly: 'Do not put faith in law and procedure. Rely on your own strength.'

The labour movement had erected a legal infrastructure based upon consensus, which when challenged by a recalcitrant employer was found sorely wanting, and dependence upon which actually deflected the strike from the strategy of direct action that alone could have secured victory for the workers. And why? Quite simply because the power of capital, of its police and its judges, ultimately was more decisive than formal arbitration procedures that assumed an identity of interest between labour and capital. At Grunwick, wrote one commentator, 'The gulf remained unbridgeable . . . [because] Britain is still two nations. The class conflict continues.'[23]

·POST OFFICE WORKERS AND THE RIGHT TO STRIKE·

If there were any doubt that the historic hostility of the judiciary towards the labour movement continues today, then it should be dispelled by the curious experience of Post Office workers in 1976–7. Here, as before, an old law was 'reinterpreted' to apply to circumstances for which it was never envisaged in judgements which did not hide their political bias.

Members of the Union of Post Office Workers* had always assumed that they *did* have the right to strike. Indeed, they exercised it during a one-day national strike in 1964 and again during the seven-week strike over pay in 1971. The union even took 'secondary boycott' action against France in 1973 by banning mail and operator phone calls for one week in protest at French nuclear tests in the Pacific. (Back in 1921, there was a U.P.W. boycott of mail to Hungary in protest against the right-wing coup and the subsequent repression of the 'White Terror'.) There were no legal repercussions on any of those occasions, nor during the numerous work-to-rules and overtime bans which occurred from time to time in the Post Office.

It was only in November 1976 when the U.P.W boycotted mail to Grunwick that doubt arose as to whether postal workers could withdraw their labour legally. Attempting to stop the boycott, the ultra-right-wing National Association for Freedom (N.A.F.F.) took out an injunction, alleging that the union was committing a criminal offence by being in breach of the 1953 Post Office Act. But, on the assurance that the company would agree to arbitration, the U.P.W. suspended its action. The issue was not put to the test until the following January, when N.A.F.F. asked the Labour Attorney General to institute an injunction against both the U.P.W. and the Post Office Engineering Union over the quite separate issue of a planned one-week boycott of post and telecommunications to South Africa.

The Attorney General refused, but N.A.F.F. obtained the support of the Appeal Court, presided over by Lord Denning. The issue became clouded by a celebrated clash between Lord Denning and the Attorney General, Sam Silkin, over their respective powers and duties – a conflict eventually resolved in Mr Silkin's favour by the House of Lords in July 1977. The issues here were extremely complex. In brief, the Lords decided that the Attorney General's discretion could not be challenged by the courts and that he could not be bypassed by a private citizen seeking such an injunction.

But the major anomaly affecting posts and telecommunications workers remained. This was that, with Lord Denning's hearty

* renamed Union of Communication Workers on account of the split into the Post Office and British Telecommunications in October 1981.

endorsement, historic sections of Post Office legislation making it a criminal offence to interfere with mail or telecommunications were interpreted to apply to modern forms of industrial action. The relevant clauses in the 1953 Post Office Act go back to 1710, when the General Post Office was established during Queen Anne's reign, and were aimed primarily at footpads and highwaymen. By Section 40 of Chapter X of the 9th Year of Queen Anne it was made an offence wilfully to detain or delay any postal letter or packet. The same wording, 'wilfully detains or delays', was carried through in later legislation and is found in Section 58 of the 1953 Act. The original source for telecommunications is Section 45 of the 1863 Telegraph Act.

It is obvious that these sections were never intended to apply to trade unionists. They were aimed at stopping strictly criminal interference with communications by persons outside or inside the services. Yet their lordships were not deterred. 'Many statutes are not at all clear but those are clear beyond doubt,' said Lord Denning; he was backed up by Lord Justice Ormrod, who stated that the unions were planning 'the plainest breach of the criminal law which it is possible to imagine'.

Here we can see a court flying its political banner quite openly. In time-honoured fashion the judges allowed the law to catch something not in itself criminal and for which it was never framed – a trade union leader planning a boycott surely being different from a robber pilfering the mails or a businessman bribing a postman to delay an urgent letter to a rival company? What is more, the judges could have given quite a different interpretation. The guidance of union lawyers could have been taken. They pointed out that these sections of the law were not only inappropriate but placed Post Office trade unionists in a uniquely anomalous position compared even with other public service workers, such as in the gas, electricity or water industries. These workers have a legal right to strike even though they are also in what may be termed 'essential services'. Yet the dubious logic of making a postman more like a policeman than an electrician in denying him a right to strike proved no obstacle to the courts.

The implications of the Appeal Court judgement – confirmed on that issue as well by the House of Lords – is that all forms of industrial action by postal or telecommunications workers are now potentially illegal. These include stoppages, work-to-rules, overtime bans and refusal to cross an official picket line in a trade dispute, with even some doubt being thrown over a complete close-down of the service because of an all-out strike.[24]

It should be emphasized that the judges consciously chose this particular interpretation of the law rather than an alternative one. Lord Denning attempted to give some kind of metaphysical authority to their choice when he reaffirmed the classic view of the role of judges:

Whenever a new situation arises which has not been considered before, the judges have to say what the law is. In so doing, we do not change the law. We declare it. We consider it on principle: and then pronounce upon it. As the old writers quaintly put it, the law lies 'in the breast of the judges'.

This is a neat way of dodging the issue, for it implies that there is just one possible interpretation of 'what the law is' when this is palpably not the case. Lord Denning's interpretations of the law on various issues have been regularly turned over by the House of Lords. He was often described as an 'independently minded judge' or as 'an original thinker'. Another description, certainly more accurate in his treatment of trade unionism, would be a 'political judge', exercising his political preferences in his interpretations of the law. In short, the Post Office Workers case provides contemporary proof of the absurdity of the notion of 'objective' law applied in some detached and technical fashion.

·POLITICAL CHOICES·

More recent developments have confirmed the consistent antipathy of the courts towards trade union action. In 1977 the Appeal Court prevented the Association of Broadcasting Staff from 'blacking' coverage of the Football Association cup final to South Africa, on the grounds that it was not a 'trade dispute' and therefore not covered by the 1974–6 Trade Union and Labour Relations Acts. Indeed, the Appeal Court in a number of other cases sought so to limit the scope of the meaning of a 'trade dispute' that many forms of secondary boycott or blacking activities came under question.

In 1978 Lord Denning made it clear that he resented particularly that part of this new legislation protecting trade unionists involved in industrial action. In a speech at Birmingham University, he argued that the definition of 'trade disputes' under the 1974 Act was far too wide, and he bemoaned those who spoke of the right to strike as one of the fundamental rights of mankind: 'I would declare at once that there is no such right known to the law, not at any rate when it is used so as to inflict harm on innocent bystanders, or disrupt essential services or to bring the country to a halt. So far as the law is concerned, those who do such things are exercising not a right but a great power, the power to strike.'[25]

The behaviour of Lord Denning's Appeal Court typified the reluctance of the judiciary to accept the pro-union legislation passed by Labour between 1974 and 1976. There is a continuing thread running through the court's attitude to industrial disputes in the late 1970s which suggests that they saw themselves as a bulwark against advances being made by the labour movement, dramatically shown in the extraordinary confrontation between a Labour Attorney General and the Court of Appeal in 1977. Very often it was less dramatic, with judges simply frustrating the spirit of legislation, as was the case over Grunwick for instance.

During Labour's period in power relations with the judiciary were tense to say the least, with the Leader of the House of Commons and effectively deputy prime minister, Michael Foot, at one stage denouncing the role of judges in a speech to the annual conference of the Union of Post Office Workers: 'It does so happen to be the case that if the freedom of the people of this country – and especially the rights of trade unionists – had been left to the good sense and fairmindedness of judges, we would have precious few freedoms in this country.'[26]

The judges may well have seen their function as being to hold the fort for the return of a Conservative government, for when the Tories regained office in 1979 they duly set about restoring the status quo and undermining many key trade union rights established by Labour.

The new Tory approach was at once more tough and more subtle than the unpopular 1971 Act. Under the 1980 Employment Act, for example, picketing was restricted still further, to the point where the only pickets not open to legal challenge would be those attending in small numbers where they themselves work, who keep out of everybody else's way and who, consequently, are virtually impotent.

As important as the Act itself are the associated 'codes of practice'. The one on picketing gives enormous discretion to police officers on the spot.[27] It is also phrased in such a way that, as one labour lawyer put it, 'it is unclear where the law stops and opinion begins ... opinion masquerades as law'.[28] In other words, judges are invited to exercise their political preferences.

The massive discretionary powers granted to the police and the judiciary encouraged even the British Institute of Management to state that the codes are 'seriously open to criticism on grounds of being over-political in parts',[29] while the all-party House of Commons Select Committee called them 'constitutionally undesirable'.[30] Such criticisms were proved to be valid by the health workers' pay dispute in 1982, when the restrictions on 'secondary picketing' imposed by the 1980 Act were deliberately and systematically flouted on a widespread basis. Postmen, coalminers, dockers, train drivers and council workers all joined picket lines outside hospitals. Furthermore, 'sympathy' industrial action by miners, firemen and bus drivers also took place. But despite such clear contraventions of the law, no prosecutions were brought because it was not politically expedient to do so when there was such evident public sympathy for the nurses and fellow health staff taking industrial action. The Labour Editor of the *Sunday Times* aptly commented: 'Ministers, by their inaction, are doing exactly what their critics pre-dicted. If the law is being broken, then injunctions should be served, and justice take its course. If the only reason that the law is being ignored is that politicians find it inconvenient, then the law is not a principle but an expedient, to be used at pragmatic whim.' It was well into the strike that an injunction was served by newspaper employers on Fleet Street electricians' leader Sean Geraghty, resulting in a £350 fine and costs estimated at £10,000.

In tandem with its still tougher successor brought in in 1982, the 1980 Employment Act has quite openly given a political brief to the judiciary to use its power to curb trade union activity. By giving such discretion to the courts and police the Tories have ensured that trials brought under the Acts will be seen by trade unionists at least as 'political'. For we are now in the middle of one of those periods referred to by the labour lawyer, Lord Wedderburn, who explained that

the eras of judicial 'creativity', of new doctrines hostile to trade union interests, have been largely, though not entirely, coterminous with the periods of British social history in which the trade unions have been perceived by middle-class opinion as a threat to the established social order. That was certainly true of the judge-made law of the periods 1961 to 1969, and 1976 to 1979. The lack of such 'creativity' by the courts in the 1930s can similarly be related to the extreme weakness of trade unions in that decade.[31]

And it is this kind of political backdrop to the relationship between law and trade unionism which so many well-meaning commentators refuse to acknowledge. Thus, again, Joe Rogaly may make some valid points when he argues:

... the distinctive feature of British experience that is relevant to the present argument is that for most of our modern industrial history trade union independence has been brought about by carving areas of immunity away from the common law. It is not so much a question of saying 'you have a right to form a union or to go on strike' as, rather, saying 'if you do those things you will not be taken to court for doing them'. This legal tradition is the principal reason why to this day British trade unions prefer to separate their activities from the law, and to exist in a constitutional world of their own ... The sense of history that is characteristic of most union leaders tells them that all that has been achieved in the past has come about in spite of the law, rather than because of it and that therefore this is the way matters can develop from now on, in spite of the recent introduction of laws that positively favour trade unionism. [32]

Aside from the obvious retort to this last sentence that any alleged union honeymoon with the law under Labour was quickly ended by Mrs Thatcher's government, this view fails to acknowledge that the law overwhelmingly reflects the imbalance of power and wealth in Britain. It favours the ruling class at the expense of the working class, employer at the expense of worker. This is most certainly so in cases where there is a challenge to the existing structure of *power* – in other words where trade unionism necessarily leads to a political act – but it is broader than that. A small exchange between a judge and a shop stewards' convenor illustrates the point. It occurred during the dispute in 1981 where 390 engineering workers at the East London firm, Staffa Products Ltd, occupied their factory in protest against the management's decision to close it down, move the plant and create some 300 redundancies. The company sought a court order to evict their workforce but before it was duly granted, convenor Dave Green deplored the use of the courts in a dispute between management and workers. 'We are fighting for our jobs, and we are taking better care of the factory than the bosses did when they were in control,' he maintained. And when asked by the judge about a point in the proceedings, Green replied: 'If there's any law in the land to make management save our jobs, then please apply it.' The judge answered, 'There are none.' To which Green then said, 'Well, make one up.' [33] Perhaps he was conscious of judges' historic facility for 'making up the law'. In any event it was clear which party to the dispute the court was able to assist: those having their *property* rights trespassed upon rather than those having their *job* rights trespassed upon.

The only 'right to work' recently supported by the courts was that enunciated in 1974 by Lord Denning in a closed shop case when a worker was suspended on full pay by his employer because he refused to join the appropriate union, the A.U.E.W. In 1979 and 1980, Lord Denning again asserted the 'right to work' of non-strikers when he ruled against secondary action in strikes by journalists and steelworkers. Thus the burden of Lord Denning's idea of the 'right to work' has fallen more on trade union officials than on employers.

Socialists have from time to time argued for what Peter Townsend recently termed a 'legally enforceable right to work'. [34] During the 1880s and 1890s a 'Right to Work Bill' was drafted by radicals concerned with the mass unemployment of those depression years, and in 1907 Ramsay MacDonald introduced a Bill known as the 'Right to Work' Bill, imposing a duty on public authorities to provide jobs for the unemployed. But the role of the judiciary has simply emphasized the point made by one legal expert that 'in our type of market economy a "right to work" enforceable against the State, would be meaningless . . . [and] would encourage a false consciousness among workers'. [35]

For the history of British trade unionism consists of a regular stream of political trials in which the judiciary has tried to roll back the advances of working-class power.

OFFICIALLY SECRET

This then is the formal outline of mystery-making in British government. At every turn, for reasons of self-importance, political convenience and bureaucratic camouflage, it is made elaborately difficult for the ordinary member of the public to work out precisely how he is being governed. It is a closed system, in which a great deal of trouble is taken to prepare authorized versions of events and direct them through controlled channels. Secrecy and propaganda are two sides of the same coin.

(David Leigh, *Frontiers of Secrecy*
(Junction Books, 1980), pp. 44–5)

If *knowledge* is power, as is often said, then still more *secrecy* is power. And in Britain, official secrecy is a jealously guarded privilege, the authorities having been able to use it to their great advantage. Of all the much-trumpeted virtues of British democracy, openness is not one. Britain remains, albeit in a deceptive way, perhaps the most secretive society in the Western world, with many other countries having freedom of information legislation which the British state has consistently refused to concede.

Instead, it has cloaked itself in a mass of laws, regulations, habit and tradition, some of it covering activity so trivial as to be absurd, but most of it having a clear *political* purpose: to protect the interests of the governors at the expense of the governed. As a recent study argued: 'Britain is about as secretive as a state can be and still qualify as a democracy.'[1] Official secrecy provides one of the clearest examples of an overtly political use of the law and legal institutions. It is 'politically biased' in broadly two ways: first, enabling the interests of those in power to be protected rather than the interests of the ordinary citizen; and second, official secrecy has been used consistently against the left.

·NATIONAL SECURITY·

Criticism of official secrecy invariably produces the ready reply of 'national security', a useful ploy since the critic is immediately disarmed with the accusation of endangering the safety of the nation, 'playing into the hands' of hostile powers abroad and subversive or criminal elements at home. In this way even a mundane or parochial action by a statutory authority can effectively be protected by a sleight of hand that deflects questions into the area of spies, treason and so forth. The Official Secrets Acts have been notorious for this. In reality however, as the M.P. Michael Meacher showed, 'Official secrecy has much more to do with protecting the government of the day from embarrassment than with the nation's security,' and he lists a series of examples covering matters such as consumer goods, health and safety to illustrate this.[2]

But it is not simply bureaucrats who are afforded a comfortable hiding space. The notion of 'national security' has been marshalled for very clear political purposes. Tony Bunyan describes how the Official Secrets Acts have historically been directed *internally*, rather than at some external threat to the country:

> The extent to which the Acts 'deter' agents of foreign countries from continuing their activities is clearly negligible, and the penalties for being caught are accepted as a necessary risk in this kind of work. In internal affairs the very reverse is true: the Acts not only deter mischievous 'leaking of information', but also underpin the traditional secrecy of the workings of the state on the part of the Civil Service. By this means information is so restricted as to guarantee an ill-informed parliament, press and people on the central issues of the day. The Acts also represent a formidable weapon should internal conflict arise within Britain, and the laws could be used most effectively against political opponents of all kinds.[3]

Indeed, since the Second World War, the emphasis of 'national security' work has tended to shift to what the state regards as the 'enemy within'.[4] Alongside this has come an insidious change in the whole idea of what is 'subversive'. Thus, while in the early 1960s Lord Denning described a subversive as someone 'who would contemplate the overthrow of government by unlawful means', by the late 1970s this clear stipulation of *illegality* had dropped by the wayside. In 1975 a Labour Home Office Minister, Lord Harris, said that a subversive included someone who wanted to 'undermine or overthrow parliamentary democracy by political, industrial or violent means'. In 1978 Labour Home Secretary Merlyn Rees saw subversives as 'people I think are causing a problem for the state'.

From the standpoint of the authorities, the threat of such subversion, we should note, comes overwhelmingly from the left – as Tony Benn confirms from his experience as a Cabinet minister: 'The security services, or at least an element within them, regard those who work within the Labour movement, especially its socialist activists, as being a security risk for that reason alone. Conservatives would not be so classified.'[5] This view can be confirmed by examining the pattern of security service work during the past twenty years as the British economy has slumped steadily into crisis. The major targets have been those who have supported a socialist answer to this crisis.

But 'official secrecy' or 'national security' is not simply a pretext for political bias against the left. Along with the judiciary, the security services have been expressing their *own* political objectives. These are likely to be contrary to those of their nominal head if he is a Labour prime minister – even a right-wing one, like Harold Wilson, who said after he had resigned in 1976 that he had not been aware of 'what was happening, fully, in Security', and complained of 'right-wing' factions in MI5 and MI6.[6] The security services have begun to develop their own political ideology. This ideology, while in tune with the capitalist state, is nevertheless independent of it and may also be explained by a desire to protect a growing bureaucracy with its *specific* interests and objectives. As John Bruce Lockhart, an intelligence officer, said in 1973, the security services can provide false information in order to protect their own vested interests, or because that is what they think their political masters would like to hear, or because they wish to cover their own incompetence. In this way, he said, they can develop their own political policies and can plot and manoeuvre for their own ends.[7] So we can see how the twin notions of 'national security' and official secrecy conspire together in a manner that can only be described as 'political'. But how exactly have they been able to do this?

· OFFICIAL SECRETS ACTS ·

First of all they have had the considerable assistance of the Official Secrets Acts. More than adequately analysed elsewhere,[8] the Acts have been one of the clearest examples of the application of the law in a politically discriminatory way and have produced a series of political trials. The Acts prohibit unofficial disclosure of information about the state. Section 1 – known as the 'spying clause' – covers disclosure of information which 'might be directly or indirectly, useful to an enemy'. Section 2 covers supplying or receiving 'official information' about the internal activities of central government. Later clauses are so framed as to give the state the exclusive power to determine what information it considers should be 'prohibited'. There is no real 'objective' definition, capable of independent adjudication by the courts, as to what is or is not an official secret: the criteria are purely political, determined by the government or, to be more precise, the security services.

The foundations of the legislation are to be found in the 1911 Official Secrets Act, which was introduced amid concern about the activities of German spies before the First World War. However, it covered internal government secrecy as well and – appropriately enough in the light of its later history – was rushed through the House of Commons in a mere thirty minutes: something of an all-time record for Parliament with its normally convoluted and time-consuming procedures. There were supplementary updating Acts in 1920 and 1939. The official Franks Committee, set up to examine the working of the Acts, confirmed in its Report in 1972 that it had long been intended to use them as 'a general check against civil service leaks of all kinds', not confined 'to matters connected with the safety of the State'.[9] The sweeping definition of official secrecy under the legislation allowed a former head of MI5, Sir Martin Furnival-Jones, to inform the Franks Committee: 'It is an official secret if it's in an official file.' Senior civil servants today would find little to fault in the attitude of a Permanent Secretary in 1873: 'The unauthorized use of information is the worst fault a civil servant can commit. It is on the same footing as cowardice by a soldier.'[10]

Despite the criticisms of the Acts made by Franks, and their recommendations for reform which included abolition of Section 2, successive governments, both Conservative and Labour (the latter despite manifesto commitments to radical reforms) have made no changes. Tony Bunyan aptly comments:

So in the end the central contradiction appears. The Government sets up a Committee which suggests the state relinquishes its hold over much official information: the Committee reports back to the Government, which then decides what to accept and what to reject.[11]

Labour issued a White Paper in July 1978 recommending half-hearted changes, and the only really serious attempt at reform was made by the Thatcher government in October 1979. But its proposal to amend Section 2 would actually have made it even more oppressive, and was abandoned amid public outcry – and specifically because of the Anthony Blunt affair which broke at the time: he would probably not have been unmasked as a traitor if the new Tory measure had then been law.

The advantages of such a weapon as the Official Secrets Act has been amply demonstrated in a number of prosecutions leading to what can be described as nothing else than 'political trials'. In 1970 the *Sunday Telegraph* was prosecuted, together with Jonathan Aitken (then a journalist and later a Tory M.P.), over publication in the paper of a critical official British report on the Nigerian civil war. This upset the Nigerian government, which had the support of the British in its battle against Biafran rebels, and the British state duly obliged with a prosecution. However, it ended ignominiously with the acquittal of all the defendants. The judge in the case, Mr Justice Caulfield, criticized Section 2 and suggested that it might be 'pensioned off'.[12] The case brought cries for change, following which the Franks Committee was set up.

The menace of the Official Secrets Act as a political law has been more as a *deterrent*, for the few trials that have occurred, like the *Telegraph* one, have been less than successful. Another was the 'A.B.C.' trial, labelled after the surnames of the three defendants, journalists Crispin Aubrey and Duncan Campbell, and John Berry, a former corporal in Signals Intelligence work. They were arrested by Special Branch officers in February 1977 while the two journalists were interviewing Berry about his experiences. They were initially charged under Section 2, which covers the communication or receipt of official information, with Section 1 'espionage charges' being added later. There can have been few more blatant examples of a politically motivated prosecution.[13] The espionage charge was withdrawn after the judge said it was 'oppressive' in the middle of a bizarre Old Bailey trial in 1978, it being evident by then that the motive behind the prosecution was primarily to suppress investigative journalism embarrassing to the security services. The three were eventually convicted under Section 2 and received minor, non-custodial sentences. However, not even the catch-all nature of the section stopped the jury agonizing for several days before reaching a verdict. Even then some of them were so worried about their decision that they took the extraordinary step of going to meet the defendants afterwards and apo-

logizing, explaining that the letter of the law had left them no alternative but to convict. The judge, Mr Justice Mars-Jones, also appeared
less than enthusiastic about the case, as shown by his implicit instruction
to the Attorney General to drop the Section 1 charge, his withdrawal of
another charge and the relatively light sentences he imposed.

It could be argued that while the official secrecy legislation has been
politically biased, judges have acted in a less reactionary way than in other
areas of the law analysed in this book. It is worth stressing, therefore, that it
is not suggested that judges are mere 'puppets', responding to some
imaginary central state conspiracy. On the contrary, one of the themes of
political trials in Britain is that judges have been prepared to act
independently, defining the national interest as *they* see it, acting against
political dissent as *they* define it. Defined in its broadest sense, the state is
not necessarily monolithic, although its various agencies act with broadly
compatible objectives. A major theme to emerge from analysis of political
trials is that these agencies, within that common remit, have their own
interests to defend, their own specific political prejudices to exercise. The
security services are more immediately concerned with official secrecy
than, for example, applying conspiracy charges to quell trade unionism,
for which judges have shown particular enthusiasm. Furthermore, it may
be that the unwillingness of the judges to act entirely predictably in the
Telegraph and A.B.C. trials reflected the absence of a consensus within the
state itself on how the question of official secrecy should be applied.

The independence of the security services is underlined by evidence
that the then Home Secretary, Merlyn Rees, was presented with something of a *fait accompli* over the arrest of the A.B.C. trio. Coming as it
did on top of the furore over 'his' decision to deport the radical journalists, Philip Agee and Mark Hosenball, the news of the arrests apparently provoked Rees to remark: 'My God, what are they trying to do to
me *now*!'[14] (Presumably 'they' meant the security agencies.) While his
almost painful apologisms over the A.B.C. and Agee–Hosenball cases
encouraged critics to cast Rees as the villain of the peace, with hindsight
this missed the central point. His real culpability was his loyal defence of
activities by the secret services about which he had little or no prior
knowledge. In defending them he preserved the constitutional fiction of
ministerial responsibility; a more appropriate response from a 'socialist'
minister might have been to state the truth, namely, that he had not
initiated a political prosecution by one of the state agencies theoretically
under his control.

Other aspects of the A.B.C. case have a significant bearing on our argument. First, the three defendants in practice had to prove their innocence – something which appears to be a characteristic of political trials. The normal 'presumption of innocence' did not apply. Second, official secrecy is at once so widely and so vaguely conceived that, as the Franks Committee explained: 'People are not sure what it means, or how it operates in practice, or what kinds of action involve real risk of prosecution under it.' This both deprives the citizen of the right of knowing what the law is and grants to the state the discretionary power to define what it shall be as the state finds is convenient in any situation. Third, the all-embracing nature of official secrecy and its convenience to the security services is well evidenced by the separate charge faced by Duncan Campbell: that he had 'collected information on defence communications which might, directly or indirectly, be useful to an enemy'. Campbell had compiled material from which he helped write an article entitled 'The Eavesdroppers'. The fact that the article relied upon *entirely public sources* was acknowledged by the prosecution, who nevertheless argued that the real offence was gathering together in one place and interpreting such publicly available information. In other words, so long as ordinary citizens had no understanding of the significance of discrete and superficially unconnected bits of public information, the authorities were content. The offence was to present the information in an intelligible fashion so that its true political implications could be recognized.

At the same time, judges have appeared anxious to clear the decks for the government – or more precisely for the security services – to have legal *carte blanche* in this area. Consider, for example, the 1964 case where members of the Committee of 100 – a militant offshoot of the Campaign for Nuclear Disarmament – were charged with conspiracy to incite others to break Section 1 of the Official Secrets Act. The demonstrators tried to occupy Wethersfield military air base in · a campaign to restore it to civilian use. But the House of Lords argued that the defendants' *intentions* were irrelevant, if the government determined their activities to be prejudicial to the state's interests. 'Those who are responsible for the nation's security must be the sole judges of what the national security requires,' maintained the law lords. Similarly in 1977, when the Court of Appeal rejected journalist Mark Hosenball's appeal against deportation under a Home Office order made on national security grounds, Lord Denning argued: 'When the state is in danger, our own cherished freedoms, and even the rules of natural justice, have to take second place.'

·PARLIAMENT'S ROLE·

With such sweeping and virtually extra-legal powers being granted to the state and its security agencies, the role of Parliament is clearly crucial. If Parliament exercised ultimate sovereignty in this area, then it might be argued that matters were, if not perfect, then at least tolerably satisfactory. Unfortunately, however, M.P.s on the floor of the House of Commons have been more or less impotent.[15] By a ritual annual vote, known colloquially as 'The Secret Vote', Parliament each year grants millions of pounds to the security services (in 1982–3 the figure was £66.5 million) without further scrutiny. The only M.P. with any real idea of the full purpose to which such expenditure is put is the Prime Minister. And when one former P.M., Harold Wilson, wrote about this, he was not particularly enlightening: 'The Prime Minister is occasionally questioned on matters arising out of his [security] responsibilities. His answers may be regarded as uniformly uninformative.'[16]

While it could be retorted that the Prime Minister is ultimately answerable to the House of Commons, that constitutional nicety misses the real point. This is not the place to enter into the debate between theorists of 'Cabinet government' and 'prime ministerial government'. Suffice to say that the Prime Minister enjoys massive power and is protected by official secrecy in exercising it. So the question quickly escalates beyond the specific issue of national security to the whole process of government through which it operates.

We find that this process is saturated with secrecy. The thirty-year rule, collective Cabinet responsibility, the oath Privy Councillors must take, ministerial responsibility – all of these combine to concentrate information and therefore power in the hands of an exclusive few, and notably in the hands of one person: the Prime Minister.[17] To take just one instance, the extraordinary rule enforcing secrecy on which particular ministers are members of particular Cabinet committees enables the Prime Minister to manipulate their composition.

There is, moreover, an extensive list of parliamentary questions which government departments simply will not answer.[18] The implications of this were revealed in 1979 by a former Labour Parliamentary Under-

Secretary to the Department of Health and Social Security, Michael Meacher M.P., who confessed that he had suppressed the dangers of hypothermia on the insistence of his civil servants. Where research known to his D.H.S.S. officials had shown deaths from hypothermia running as high as 35,000 a year, he instead referred in an answer to a parliamentary question to only seventeen people being recorded on death certificates as dying directly from the cause: the truth as far as it went, but certainly not the whole truth.

Ultimately, official secrecy prevents proper discussion of *policy*, for if information is denied it is not possible to evaluate policy options and their implications. A classic example of this was the circle of secrecy thrown around the facts and figures upon which Ramsay MacDonald's 1929–31 Labour government deliberated before embarking upon its programme of cuts. Without the necessary information, those outside the Cabinet were unable to challenge the basis of MacDonald's retrenchment programme which was to prove so fatal to the labour movement. In a poignant analysis of this, Tony Benn suggests that something similar happened in 1976 during Cabinet discussion of the equally fatal cuts imposed by the International Monetary Fund.[19]

At local government level, too, similar constraints apply. For instance, the expansion of facilities at the chemical establishment at Porton Down in 1980 could not be scrutinized, let alone challenged, by Salisbury District Council because the Ministry of Defence instructed the council that all changes there were covered by the Official Secrets Act. Yet these changes included a new processing plant and effluent tanks for nerve and riot control gases.[20]

· CIVIL SERVANTS ·

If, then, official secrecy can deny M.P.s or local councillors the opportunity effectively to exercise the duties entrusted to them by the electorate, the role of civil servants becomes critical. The Fulton Committee on the Civil Service stated unequivocally: '. . . the administrative process is surrounded by too much secrecy'.[21] This enables civil servants to exercise considerable influence in a way that can be illustrated by the example of the official jargon they use for classifying different levels of secrecy into (a) Restricted; (b) Confidential; (c) Secret; (d) Top Secret. As David Leigh aptly remarks:

These words have no objective meaning; one could tune the semantics another way and grade documents (a) secret; (b) very secret; (c) very, very secret; (d) earth-shatteringly secret. This subjectivity does not prevent Whitehall from attempting definitions, themselves equally meaningless. Thus 'restricted' means material whose leaking would be 'undesirable in the interests of the nation'; 'confidential' means 'prejudicial to the interests of the nation'; 'secret' means 'serious injury to the interests of the nation'; and 'top secret' means 'exceptionally grave damage to the nation'. [22]

Thus we return to who exactly determines the 'interests of the nation'? The Official Secrets Act, as interpreted by judges, says 'the government'. But if that turns out to be 'the Prime Minister', in *practice* it means a small group of civil servants who advise him or her.

Civil servants exercise enormous influence – and all the more so when they are protected by the web of official secrecy. The almost paranoid concern with secrecy is well illustrated by the Civil Service's *Security Handbook*. It goes into minute detail on procedures for maintaining secrecy – and also confirms that tackling internal 'subversion' (not defined) is the modern state's overriding priority. Significantly, the *Handbook* reveals a desire to restrict information which goes well beyond the scope of the Official Secrets Acts:

In every government office there are numerous items of information the disclosure of which would be prejudicial to the interests of private citizens and to the proper conduct of administration. Any dereliction of duty in this respect concerning classified or unclassified information may lead to disciplinary proceedings being taken, whether or not proceedings are being instituted under the Official Secrets Acts . . . So far as it concerns disclosures the subject matter of the information and its importance or lack of importance are of no concern. [23]

The effect of such a restriction was shown in 1980 by the case of Trevor Brown, a senior chemist at Aldermaston Atomic Weapons Research Establishment. He publicly voiced his concern about health and safety standards there, and although he only revealed information already publicly available, he was severely reprimanded, ultimately resigning his job.[24] His inability to question practices in the Establishment restricted his ability to represent local residents as he was also a local Councillor in the area.*

Consequently, as we probe deeper into the mire of official secrecy, we

* In 1982 this case was due to go before the European Human Rights Court.

find that it becomes progressively more a political and partisan tool for the state, its officials and its agencies. By executive decision, virtually anything can be deemed 'officially secret', and the law can be invoked to sanctify such decisions.

· THE JUDICIARY ·

Furthermore, the judicial process is itself surrounded by intense secrecy. While it may appear that justice is *seen* to be done – court hearings are after all mostly open to the public and the press – in practice the crucial decisions are taken behind closed doors. First and foremost, juries deliberate in secret – and in 1981 under the Contempt of Court Act the law was tightened up to prevent disclosure of jury discussions. This followed the Jeremy Thorpe trial, after which an enlightening interview with several jurors was published in the *New Statesman*, raising fundamental questions about the approach of the prosecution. The Attorney General instituted proceedings against the *New Statesman* which, though unsuccessful, paved the way for the 1981 restrictions. However, the state's enthusiasm for a prosecution in this case contrasted markedly with the blind eye turned to disclosure by the *Guardian* of a juror's criticism of allegations of planted evidence made against the police by the defence in the 1974 I.R.A. trial over the Winchester bombings. At least until 1981, the judiciary appeared to have one rule on juror whistle-blowing that favoured the establishment, and another for an establishment figure and those who mounted an inadequately framed prosecution against him. Indeed the very *obscurity* of the law and procedure governing juries has meant that jurors have consistently been unaware of their potentially extensive powers, and the public too have been unclear about their role. Coupled with the secrecy surrounding juries, this has provided considerable scope for political discretion.

So too have the many other secret aspects of the legal process. We have no real means of finding out about the critical decisions that may be made as part of a prosecution. Why is a defendant charged with one offence rather than another? Indeed, what criteria do the police and prosecuting counsel use in deciding whether to proceed in a case where the evidence is finely balanced?

As I well recall in my own case of mistaken identity – when I was prosecuted in 1975 with theft from a bank near my Putney home – it was impossible to find out why the police had charged me *solely* on the basis of assertions by two twelve-year-old schoolboys. They had unsuccessfully chased the thief and were walking back when I parked alongside them on my way to do some shopping. Quite apart from the bizarre situation of a public figure doing a bank snatch in his own neighbourhood, running off, and obligingly returning to appear alongside his erstwhile pursuers so that they could take his car number and report him to the police, the boys' evidence proved notoriously unreliable when tested in court. Yet, try as the defence could, we could never get the police to discuss, still less disclose, the reasons for bringing the charge. The critical issues of police *procedure* in the early hours – which set in motion a sequence of events leading inexorably to the Old Bailey – could not be raised, let alone challenged. Why? Because attempts to do so were simply stone-walled.

Secrecy protected the police in this instance as it protects judges and lawyers all the way along the judicial line. Plea bargaining, deals between defence and prosecution, the choice of a judge – these are just a few of the matters the public are prevented from scrutinizing. As a result there is wide scope for political discretion and political bias to be exercised: if it were not for the protective cloak of official secrecy, such discretion and bias could be debated and if needs be criticized.

A further factor preventing this is the use of the law of contempt, specifically to curb media coverage. What it is and is not permissible to report is notoriously vague, and the courts have been able to play on this to intimidate investigative journalism or legitimate press coverage. The very vagueness of the notion of contempt places enormous power and discretion in the hands of judges. It hangs over journalists like a sword of Damocles and makes a mockery of the notion of the law as a technical and impartial process.[25]

A further example was the political trial of Harriet Harman, the legal officer of the National Council for Civil Liberties. In February 1982 the law lords ruled that she had committed contempt of court while acting in 1980 as solicitor to Michael Williams in his action against the Home Office for damages arising out of his detention in the special isolation cell known as a 'control unit'. She forced a large number of Home Office documents to be read out in open court in a legal hearing during the trial. After the case, she showed some of the documents to a *Guardian* reporter to enable him to write a feature article about the history of the controversial control units, showing how ministers came to the view that the units were being used in ways that had not been intended, and how they were eventually abandoned. For this, she was found guilty of serious contempt, even though the documents later appeared in the official transcript of the case which could be inspected by any member of the public and even photocopied in the House of Lords record office. The motive for the prosecution of Harriet Harman, suggested one M.P. afterwards,[26] was a vindictive attempt by the Home Office to 'bankrupt' the N.C.C.L., which was landed with legal costs of £25,000.

That the Home Office was pursuing her out of political malice is confirmed by the fact that she had acted no differently from generations of lawyers before her. The well-known solicitor, Lord Goodman, and Lord Hutchinson Q.C., gave evidence for Harriet Harman to demonstrate that lawyers often showed documents to journalists. For example, during the Jeremy Thorpe trial journalists had been invited to a special room to inspect the prosecution's exhibits, including letters of his, obtained by search warrant. The inescapable conclusion is that the Home Office wished to attack the N.C.C.L. because of the organization's consistent and successful record of criticizing Home Office policies and activities. There may also have been a desire to discredit N.C.C.L. lawyers, who have frequently acted in controversial cases embarrassing to officialdom. In this instance, the documents passed to journalists by Harriet Harman were particularly sensitive, including high-level Civil Service memoranda and minutes of ministerial meetings – all revealing a shabby story which the Home Office was anxious should not become public.

A similar determination by the courts to defend official confidentiality was shown in the 1980 case where an employee of the British Steel Corporation leaked to Granada Television documents which showed up B.S.C.'s management in an unfavourable light during the steelworkers' strike. In the Court of Appeal, Lord Denning stated that Granada had not acted 'with a due sense of responsibility' in using the documents, and the law lords upheld the ruling, instructing Granada to name the B.S.C. employee who had acted as their source. In another case in 1981, the Court of Appeal upheld the granting of an injunction against Thames Television. The judgement concerned the planned use by a Thames programme producer of confidential information from a drug company on a controversial drug used for pregnancy testing. Lord Justice Shaw ruled against public disclosure of this information, partly on the grounds that it amounted to what he described as 'the mercenary betrayal of business confidences'.[27]

Inevitably, the secrecy at work here favours the establishment. It has a conservative effect on the media – an effect in turn reinforced by cautious lawyers' advice given to the press.[28]

Once again, therefore, we return to the central problem of *discretion* and the way in which its true role is guarded by official secrecy. Commenting on this, a senior judge, Lord Devlin, points out that the danger of the system of protecting public information 'is that it installs as the judges of what ought to be revealed men whose interest it is to conceal'.[29] The role of discretion is also evident in the way government consistently breaches the Official Secrets Acts by 'leaking' information which happens to suit it. Here we find official secrecy exposed for the charade it is. Government ministers and their civil servants regularly give out information to the press on an unattributable basis. This is legitimate, since it serves the interests of the state, and it is called 'briefing'. By contrast, unauthorized distribution of information is known pejoratively as 'leaking': a classic example occurred in 1976 when Frank Field, then director of the Child Poverty Action Group, was given a set of Cabinet minutes detailing the Labour Cabinet's attempts to renege on a commitment to introduce child benefit. While 'briefing' goes on all the time (indeed is institutionalized in the parliamentary 'lobby' system), the full weight of official secrecy sanctions descends when 'leaking' take place. As a former prime minister, James Callaghan, told the Franks Committee: 'You know the difference between leaking and briefing: leaking is what you do, and briefing is what I do.'

That apparently jocular remark underlines a consistent theme of this chapter: namely that official secrecy facilitates one law for the state and another for those outside it. The result is both a method of manipulating public opinion and a means of defending the *political* interests of those in power.[30]

That essential point is clearly shown by comparing cases where official secrets prosecutions have been mounted – the A.B.C. trial for instance – with cases where a clear breach of the law has occurred with the state turning a blind eye. A good example of the latter happened during the 1930s when Winston Churchill was sent hundreds of secret documents (in blatant breach of the Official Secrets Act) by civil servants supporting his opposition to appeasement of the Nazis. Who is to say that, with the benefit of historical hindsight, the A.B.C. defendants were not acting with motives as noble as Churchill's informers? Whatever the answer to that question, however, the fact remains that Churchill's 'spies' got clean away with breaking the law. It would, of course, have been politically impossible to have prosecuted them – but that merely reinforces the argument developed in this chapter: that official secrecy in its many forms is a political tool of the government and the security services, with the judiciary by and large willing accomplices.

Moreover, in modern times they are invariably accomplices in a *particular* political mission. There is little 'impartiality' about the use of official secrecy. Compare, for instance, the treatment of the A.B.C. defendants with the tolerance shown by the state to the *Daily Express* journalist, Chapman Pincher, who in his many newspaper articles and books has broken the Acts literally hundreds of times. As *State Research* say, 'The lesson is clear: Pincher's stories . . . by and large, serve the interests of the state and its officials while those of radical journalists whom the state cannot control risk arrest, trial and imprisonment.'[31]

10

LESSONS FROM
THE NORTH OF IRELAND

All Northern Ireland courts and the N.I. judiciary are completely
independent of Government control . . . and they are an integral part of
the legal system in the U.K. The courts play a fundamental role
in the protection of human rights in N.I. . . . . No one is imprisoned for
his political beliefs, and there are no political prisoners in N.I.

(Northern Ireland Office, *Protecting Human Rights in Northern Ireland*,
Belfast, February 1979)

The view expressed above typifies the British government's insistence
that the legal system is 'above' the conflict in the North of Ireland.
Contained within this view are two propositions, although they blur into
each other. First of all, it is asserted that the legal system is 'independent'
of direct government control, with a comforting reminder that it is in any
case an 'integral' part of that covering the whole of the U.K. Second, it
is emphatically denied that the basis for prosecution or punishment is
political.

Now while the first proposition on judicial independence can be qualified by reference to the rest of the argument in the book, the second one
raises a separate issue which should not be obscured by the usual official
attempt to merge the two, namely, the basis of the conflict in Northern
Ireland. For the plain fact is that the *motivation* for the criminal acts
committed is *political*, reflecting the political basis of the conflict in the
society.

Northern Ireland therefore provides an opportunity to examine the
role of the law in a situation of extreme conflict – and one which while
uniquely poisoned by violence is legally part of the United Kingdom.
Consequently, in addition to the specific insights from the Northern
Ireland experience itself, the interest lies in the effect it has already had
on the mainland, and the potential effect if political circumstances deteriorated severely in Britain.

·BACKGROUND·

Divided between about one million Protestants and half a million Catholics, Northern Ireland has always been a sectarian state. Ever since it was partitioned from the rest of Ireland in 1921, discrimination against the minority community has been institutionalized, with the Protestants using their political majority to suppress Catholic aspirations and human rights. Effectively the law provided a cover for this, and thus the legal system directly reflected the sectarian politics of the society. The law either turned a blind eye to, or actually sanctified, discrimination in housing, employment, education and gerrymandering of local government boundaries. Protestants dominated the judiciary, also controlling the police and its paramilitary offshoot, the 'B Specials'.

Underpinning this sectarianism was a battery of repressive legal powers. These were seen as being necessary by both loyalists and successive British governments in order to control political opposition from a Catholic community which had never accepted the undemocratic imposition of the border. The Special Powers Act of 1922 was the most notorious example of such legislation. It contained powers to intern indefinitely without charge or trial, to ban organizations, and included the following sweeping section:

> If any person does any act of such a nature as to be calculated to be prejudicial to the preservation of the peace or the maintenance of order in Northern Ireland and not specifically provided for in the regulations, he shall be deemed to be guilty of an offence against the regulations.

Under the Act and its associated measures, the Catholic community was subject to arbitrary arrest and harassment by the forces of the Orange state supported by Britain.

It was hardly surprising, therefore, that the pressure for change built up, exploding in 1968 as the minority demanded its civil rights in an unprecedented series of protests. The situation quickly deteriorated as the civil rights movement was attacked by the police and loyalist vigilantes. By the summer of 1969 Catholics were being burned out of their homes, and the British Army moved in to keep the peace. Very soon, however, the army was engaged in hostilities with the Catholic community and, specifically, the republican movement.

During the 1970s, Britain became increasingly firmly entrenched in the North, with the Army permanently on the streets, and a series of political convulsions saw direct rule from London being introduced in 1972. With these political changes came changes in the law and its enforcement.

Legally backed sectarianism and discrimination was phased out. But the new political purpose of the law was clear nonetheless. As the British stood firm on the question of the border – thereby aligning themselves politically with the Protestants and against the Catholics – the main aim of the legal system became the imposition of security and the crushing of resistance, specifically that being organized by the Provisional I.R.A. Terrorist outrages by the I.R.A. coupled with harassment and brutality from the British Army contributed to a spiral of political violence in the early 1970s.

However, in order to understand the role of the law in this escalating crisis, it is necessary to emphasize the political policy adopted by Britain. Although successive British governments dabbled in various political initiatives (initially fostering more 'liberal' Ulster Unionists and then encouraging 'power-sharing'), they refused to move towards the only realistic long-term political solution: British withdrawal and reunification of the whole of Ireland. So the cornerstone of British policy had necessarily to be the management of civil conflict and control of political unrest.

The techniques varied. Internment without trial was introduced in 1971. Techniques of torture and interrogation were given official blessing and legal authority.[1] So were methods of riot control and sophisticated new technology which gave the British state an unparalleled ability to repress civil disturbances and invade individual rights.[2]

The law gave little or no protection against abuses of power by the security authorities. The presentation of the crisis as a 'war against terrorism' – a presentation encouraged by the tactics of the I.R.A. – manufactured a *carte blanche* for denials of citizens' rights which would not have been tolerated on the mainland.

The judiciary in the North saw its duty as being to assist the security services and the military in their war against terrorism. One exception was in February 1972, when the Northern Ireland High Court ruled that the actions of the British Army had technically been illegal throughout the period since 1969. However, this little embarrassment was soon overcome with a new Act rushed through Parliament in one day, retrospectively legalizing the Army's presence.

· A SWITCH IN STRATEGY ·

In March 1972 Britain imposed direct rule, and the key role of the law in
a crisis which was by now permanent was to be emphasized in two major
changes in British strategy: the first, in 1973, altered the nature of the
courts, and the second, after 1975, produced a switch from a military-
to a police-based approach.

Amid allegations of jury intimidation, sectarian verdicts by juries, and
frustrated by conventional rules limiting admissibility of confessions,
the authorities moved to ensure a higher conviction rate for offences
designated as terrorist. A Commission[3] under Lord Diplock in 1972
recommended special procedures for Northern Ireland courts, which
were introduced late the following year under the 1973 Northern Ireland
(Emergency Provisions) Act which replaced the Special Powers Act. Juries
were suspended in what came to be known as 'Diplock Courts' and the
rules of evidence relaxed so as to admit confessions from suspects without
the normal need for independent corroborative evidence. Powers of
arrest and questioning were extended, and together these changes tended
to increase the conviction rate.[4] By the late 1970s, over 80 per cent of
the convictions in the Diplock Courts were based upon confessions.[5]

These new powers may have been less overtly and politically repressive
than the old ones, in the sense that they removed from politicians the
arbitrary ability to detain and harass which they had enjoyed under the
now repealed Special Powers Act. But they are stringent nonetheless. In
changing the whole practice of the courts they went further than the old
Act. Suspects were still denied elementary rights, leading to widespread
allegations of mistreatment and brutality. The real significance of the
change was the frontline role given to both the security and the judiciary
in the battle against the republican movement, the politicians being
removed from their previous positions on this frontline. The suspension
of Stormont (the North's Parliament) in 1972 and the collapse of the
power-sharing government in 1974 had in any case removed the basis for
local political mediation.

This whole thrust was accentuated by the policy of so-called 'Ulster-
ization' embarked upon in 1975, after which the Army's role was increasingly superseded by local security forces. Between 1973 and 1982, Army
numbers dropped from 21,000 to 11,000; while over the same period the
combined forces of the Royal Ulster Constabulary, the R.U.C. Reserve

and the Ulster Defence Regiment rose from 14,500 to 19,500. This switch, which included the phasing out of internment by December 1975, resulted in a police- rather than a military-based prosecution strategy, part of which in turn meant a greater reliance on the courts instead of military intelligence for tackling terrorist suspects.[6]

· CRIMINALIZATION OF THE CONFLICT ·

The trend was therefore to what has been termed a 'criminalization' strategy, defined as 'the denial of political recognition of any group or person "outside the law" . . . The idea . . . is that the "rule of law" commands greater respect than the "rule of the military".'[7] Indeed, there is evidence that British politicians and military strategists saw the use of the criminal law as a more effective way of exerting *political* control without the embarrassing presence of the British Army mounting early morning raids and saturating the streets.

But to achieve this, it was necessary to have not just the exceptional laws and regulations which had been part and parcel of the Northern Ireland statelet since its inception. As we saw, the very character of the criminal trial had to be altered to meet the new political burden on the legal system. And far greater powers were given to the police.

This in turn has had two broad effects which go to the heart of the problem of 'political trials' in Britain. The key *political role* given to the courts has directed the focus for political conflict, both its origins and its resolution, firstly on to the whole trial system, and secondly into the police station.

The net result has been enormously to increase the capacity for *discretion* which, given the political function of the Northern Ireland legal system, has 'political' and not simply 'legal' consequences. The suspension of juries and the ensuing extra responsibility on judges, changes in the prosecution system and reliance on confessions from suspects, have all encouraged pre-trial bargaining over pleas and charges. While the scope for discretion is obvious here, there has been an additional factor at work. This is that such informal activity has had to be compatible with the smooth functioning of the legal system as a bureaucracy. The shift in emphasis to the pre-trial situation has meant that the whole process of legal bargaining has had to dovetail into the bureaucratic aims of the judiciary. Clearly, of course, these aims have to coincide with the political task given to the legal system in the North. But they also contain the 'independent' element that always characterizes a bureaucracy with its own partisan interests to defend. In this way, the courts may be 'independent' of direct government control as the Northern Ireland Office would have us believe. But not only have they been given an overtly political job to perform, the very procedures introduced enabling them to perform it have increased their independence from democratic accountability.

Similarly with the police, where increased powers of arrest and questioning together with the enhanced new status of confessions has meant that the real decision on guilt or innocence has been shifted from the court to the police station.

So we begin with a criminalization strategy adopted as a more efficient method of political control and we end up giving more power to the judiciary and the police in ways which increase their independence from public accountability and scrutiny. Moreover, the fact that the defendants for whom this system has been designed are acting out of political motives, whether or not the British state chooses to acknowledge it, has meant that the exercise of such discretion has had unavoidable political connotations, as we saw when the 'H-block' hunger strike broke out in 1980–81, with republican prisoners demanding 'political status'.

·IMPACT ON THE BRITISH MAINLAND·

Much of this could be explained away by sceptics as being the product of an 'exceptional' situation dominated by political violence, requiring 'exceptional' laws and having no really direct bearing on England, Wales or Scotland. But there are two general grounds for disputing that simplistic view. First of all, Northern Ireland is legally part of the United Kingdom. 'Exceptional' or not, what is done there is done under U.K. law and by U.K. government decision. If, therefore, the legal system has been 'politicized' in a specific way, this must be taken account of in any survey of the operation of British law. Second, we need to establish what has been the impact on legal procedures and police behaviour, back on the mainland.

For the conflict in the North of Ireland does affect U.K. politics as a whole. Historically, Northern Ireland has been a running sore on British politics. Today, it affects political priorities – for example, military and public spending in the North could be said to be at the expense of public projects in Britain's strife-torn inner cities.

More specifically, however, there is clear evidence of techniques adopted in the North being used in Britain where circumstances have required this. Prior to the 1829 Metropolitan Police Act, Peel had used Ireland as 'a guinea pig' for his new ideology of policing. As one expert shows: 'Their success there in putting down peasant disturbances guaranteed the application of a similar if somewhat less severe form of policing in London.'[8] While the British Special Branch, formed in 1883 to tackle bombings in London by a group of militant Irish republicans known as the Fenians, subsequently had its role widened, its numbers increasing dramatically in the crisis period of the 1960s and 1970s. Dubbed Britain's 'political police', its function has altered from its Irish origins to become one of collecting intelligence and maintaining control over *domestic* political dissidents.[9]

The cross-flow of policing experience was highlighted by close links established by Robert Mark with security services in the North, and by the appointment from 1 January 1980 of Sir Kenneth Newman, until then Chief Constable of the R.U.C., as Commandant of the Police Staff College in Hampshire. In March 1982 Newman was appointed to Britain's top police post as Metropolitan Police Commissioner, the *Sunday Times* reporting at the time: 'The R.U.C. is increasingly seen as the model of what Britain's Metropolitan and other big-city forces will have to become.' Back in August 1976 Newman had told the *Irish Times* that he saw Northern Ireland as a 'laboratory situation' in which many of the problems facing the British police could be examined: 'I did have it very much in mind that British police forces would be faced with, might well be faced with, similar problems in the years ahead,' he explained.

It is also worth noting that the suspension of jury trials for scheduled offences in Northern Ireland was accompanied by a rising tempo of attacks on the right to trial by jury in Britain. Although these attacks were made for the different reasons described in Chapter 6, the principle involved was logically the same as that applying in Northern Ireland: namely, juries were seen as an obstruction to the efficient execution of the law. Furthermore, the questions of increased powers given to the R.U.C. and the extent to which the legal system has been 'bureaucratized' were central to the debate around the Royal Commission on Criminal Procedure which reported in 1981.

The ubiquitous spread of computerized intelligence gathering in Britain was pioneered in Northern Ireland, while the fact that methods of riot control used on the streets of Belfast and Derry were later used in British cities in the summer of 1981 has tended to support the validity of the argument that Northern Ireland has acted 'as the first major testing ground for the technology of political control'.[10] Following these riots, a Home Office report placed in the library of the House of Commons in October 1981 – but which became public only when its existence was revealed in the *Guardian* the following February – proved just how extensively the Irish experience was being applied. It showed that most large metropolitan police forces had trained special riot squads, equipping them with C.S. gas and even plastic bullets. Other equipment supplied included reinforced vans and modified N.A.T.O. glass-fibre helmets as used by the Army in the North. 'Pig squirt' water cannons – mounted on adapted armoured carriers used in Northern Ireland – are now also available for police use, although the Home Office Report prudently recommended that any such vehicle used by the police 'should clearly have as conventional an appearance as possible, and should, therefore, be painted in a colour usually used by the force, for example blue'.[11] Early in 1982, the Home Secretary confirmed to Parliament that 1,000 C.S. gas canisters and 3,000 plastic bullets had been supplied to police in England and Wales.[12] The willingness of the authorities to sanction use of plastic bullets was despite conclusive evidence on their danger, with deaths and blindness as well as serious injuries having occurred to innocent civilians in the North.[13] Although these are seen as 'last resort' weapons by the Home Office and the police, their introduction shows how new threats to social order can quickly sweep aside traditional policing sentiments and methods.

· PREVENTION OF TERRORISM ACT ·

But the starkest example is the Prevention of Terrorism Act, brought in after I.R.A. bombings against civilian targets in Britain had escalated to the atrocity when bombs exploded in two Birmingham pubs, killing 21 people and injuring over 160 others. That occurred on 21 November 1974 and, exactly eight days later, the Prevention of Terrorism (Temporary Provisions) Act came into being, taking only seventeen hours to pass through Parliament and with not a single vote against it.

A piece of legislation which the then Home Secretary, Roy Jenkins, conceded was 'draconian', it was updated in 1976, giving Britain a taste of the kind of law that had applied in Northern Ireland for over fifty years. The police were given arbitrary and almost unprecedented powers of arrest and detention of persons suspected of having any connection with terrorism. The Act enabled organizations to be banned, and gave the Home Office power to exclude from Britain people deemed to have links with terrorists, *completely by-passing* normal judicial checks and procedures. The ability to detain suspects for up to seven days without being charged, coupled with the denial of conventional rights of *habeas corpus* and of a court hearing or an appeal, has meant that the P.T.A. 'represented one of the biggest attacks that there had been during peace time on the rights and freedoms of the people of Britain'.[14]

It is a law which has affected not simply its main political targets – republican activists and sympathizers – but also ordinary citizens who have been detained without cause, harassed, or issued with exclusion orders. The powers under the Act force citizens to prove their innocence, particularly when facing an exclusion order. As a National Council for Civil Liberties study shows, the individual:

is offered the almost impossible task of persuading the Home Secretary and his advisers that the accusations against him – of which he knows nothing – are unfounded. The attitude amongst supporters of the Acts seems to be that this shift in the burden of proof is unimportant – after all, 'innocent people have nothing to fear'. The reality is that for 'innocent' one should read 'non-Irish, not involved or interested in Irish politics, does not live, work or mix socially with Irish people, does not read literature concerning Ireland, does not belong to a political party or any other body which might be critical of British Government policy in Ireland'.[15]

According to a former chairman of the Federation of Irish Societies in Britain, the Act has 'terrified the ordinary Irish people in this country'.[16] While the N.C.C.L. study shows how, for Irish people generally, and for political opponents of the state in particular, the Act has created 'a system of internal exile' (the phrase being borrowed from that describing the position of Soviet dissidents).

The powers to proscribe political groups and to ban Irish demonstrations have inevitably restricted normal peaceful political activity, the temptation it offers being acknowledged in a *Police Review* pamphlet (which carried an introduction by the Tory Home Secretary, William

Whitelaw). The pamphlet's author, a police training officer, wrote: 'A much simpler action to prevent any of our present troubles would be to declare the National Front, the Socialist Workers' Party *or whatever party is causing trouble* to be a proscribed organization' under the P.T.A. (my italics).[17]

In its first seven years, the number of those arrested under the P.T.A. who were actually charged with offences under the Act was under 2 per cent, with those charged with other offences arising out of terrorism being about 5 per cent.[18] These revealing statistics underline the view that the authorities already had fully adequate powers to deal with the problem and that its real purpose was as a political tool.

There is no evidence that the Act has in any way curbed terrorist activity in Britain which ebbed and flowed for other reasons, determined by the state of the conflict in the North regardless of the new legal constraints. Rather, the Act's principal purpose has in practice, even if not by design, been to control and sometimes suppress what on virtually any other political question would have been regarded as legitimate activity.

Given then that it has not fulfilled the purpose for which it was allegedly introduced, we need to understand the political context in which it has operated. At the beginning, the P.T.A. faced hardly any opposition, its critics being almost entirely confined to left-wing or civil liberty groups who could be politically marginalized. Its expressly 'draconian' provisions were no obstacle, because of public outcry, not to say hysteria, over the I.R.A.'s bombing campaign. It was justified as an 'exceptional' Act to deal with an 'exceptional' situation. But that is precisely the rationale used for the many other 'exceptional' laws and procedures implemented in Northern Ireland. In short, the P.T.A. is a no-holds-barred political law to deal with the spilling over into Britain of the political conflict in Ireland. As the *Guardian* put it in a review of the Act in 1980, 'Anybody who advocates the political option in Ireland which the established parties all turn away from – the reunification of the country – is likely to be regarded by police as a potential terrorist and hauled in for questioning under the Act.'[19]

· INCITEMENT TO DISAFFECTION ·

The impact of the conflict in the North on British politics was also illustrated by a series of political trials in the period 1973-5 when people urging British withdrawal were prosecuted for 'incitement to disaffection'. The cases pinpointed a number of by now familiar features of political trials: the thin dividing line between voicing radical opinions and falling foul of the criminal law; the role of political discretion by prosecutors; the use of conspiracy charges; and the revival of old laws.

Incitement to disaffection trials had occurred periodically through the twentieth century, when radical activists and trade unionists appealed to soldiers not to repress their activities. For example, in 1912 a number of syndicalists were prosecuted amid mounting industrial unrest and a miners' strike involving about a million workers. Syndicalists were very active in this agitation and their newspaper, The Syndicalist, published an 'Open Letter to British Soldiers' urging them not to shoot strikers if ordered to do so, and a number of their leading activists were prosecuted under the Incitement to Mutiny Act 1797.[20] In the 1920s a number of Communists were also tried during further outbreaks of industrial instability and trade union agitation. The activities of the National Unemployed Workers' Movement were of particular concern to the authorities, and in the middle of a protest campaign focused around a hunger march on London in 1932, the N.U.W.M.'s leader, Wal Hannington, was arrested and later convicted under the Police Act 1919. In a speech to a rally of 150,000 in Trafalgar Square he had reminded the police that they were drawn from the working class: 'We ask the police to understand that what we are marching for is in their interests as well as the interests of the unemployed ... Let the working class in uniform and out of uniform stand together.'[21] The following year, 1933, four South Wales miners (and members of the Communist Party) were prosecuted for inciting soldiers to defect.

Such activity, coupled with mounting alarm among the military and police authorities at discontent and indiscipline in the police and the Army, formed the background to the introduction of the Incitement to Disaffection Act in 1934. There was paranoia about the 'communist menace' and British intelligence chiefs had been anxiously pressing for an updated law, with MI5 lobbying repeatedly for such an Act.[22] When it came into force, the New Statesman aptly commented that a prosecution under it would result in 'what is by its very nature a political trial'.[23] But apart from a relatively minor case in 1937, the first trials under the Act did not come until 1972 – amid official anxiety about the conflict in Northern Ireland.

In May 1972 an anarchist, Michael Tobin, was imprisoned under the Act for two years at Maidstone for distributing pamphlets urging British soldiers to defect and side with the I.R.A. But four months previously, Joseph Durkin, who admitted drafting these same pamphlets, had been acquitted on a similar charge at Liverpool Crown Court, the disparity in the verdicts suggesting that Durkin had been more successful than Tobin in the style of his political appeal to the jury.

In 1973 a group of pacifists formed the British Withdrawal from Northern Ireland Campaign (B.W.N.I.C.), their main tactic being to provide information to soldiers on how to leave the Army. In August 1973 the long-standing peace activist, Pat Arrowsmith, was arrested in Colchester for distributing the B.W.N.I.C. leaflet 'Some Information for British Soldiers'. She was charged with insulting behaviour under the 1936 Public Order Act and told that an application had been made to the Director of Public Prosecutions for his necessary consent to bring a charge under the Incitement to Disaffection Act. He declined, and in the event Ms Arrowsmith was acquitted of the insulting behaviour offence.

The D.P.P. had exercised his discretion, hoping not to inflame a delicate political situation, and the B.W.N.I.C. campaigners took his failure to proceed as a green light to continue leafleting. But only a week after her acquittal, Pat Arrowsmith was again arrested for distributing the leaflet at Army quarters at Warminster. This time a charge of breach of the peace was coupled with incitement to disaffection. At her week-long Old Bailey trial in May 1974, none of the members of armed forces called as prosecution witnesses said they had been at all influenced by the leaflet. But it was the *political threat* of seducing soldiers to defect which was sufficient to secure a conviction, as the presiding judge made clear to the jury. Pat Arrowsmith was sentenced to eighteen months' imprisonment.

This political trial merely increased the tempo of activity by B.W.N.I.C. supporters, using a carefully revised leaflet entitled 'Some Information for *Discontented* Soldiers' which emphasized an intention not to seduce soldiers from their duty but to aid those who had already decided to leave the Army. This proved too much. Mindful perhaps that in the five years since the British Army had been in the North, 787 soldiers had deserted and not returned, the authorities moved systematically to 'crush' the campaign.[24] With the agreement of Labour's Attorney General, Sam Silkin, the D.P.P. charged fourteen B.W.N.I.C.

supporters with conspiracy to contravene the 1934 Act. The linking of the two charges underlined the political nature of the trial.

But perhaps because of this, the state came badly unstuck when the case reached the Old Bailey late in 1975. Lasting 51 days and costing over £250,000, it resulted in the jury acquitting all the defendants. Once again, there was no direct evidence that the leaflets had had any effect. Instead, the powers under the Act were being used to prevent pacifists from putting forward their beliefs on the grounds that pacifist literature by definition might make a soldier change his mind about continuing in his job. In court, the defendants were able to demonstrate this and – surrounded by an energetic defence campaign – succeeded in convincing the jury that they were victims of political persecution; one of the jurors later said that on retiring to discuss their verdict they had decided 'within ten minutes' to acquit, staying out for an hour and forty minutes mainly to give an impression of solemn consideration of the progress of the ten-week trial; many jurors appeared to have made up their minds early on in the proceedings that they would not convict.

During the trial, the D.P.P. and the Special Branch had received another setback when a Manchester stipendiary magistrate used his discretion to throw out an incitement case against another B.W.N.I.C. activist, Alix Otten, in November 1975. He described the offending 'Discontented Soldiers' leaflet as 'hardly seductive – it contains some very good advice . . . eminently sensible', and implied that the prosecuting authorities were unreasonably expecting him to make a committal for trial.[25]

So the state's attempt to 'crush' the B.W.N.I.C. campaigners did not succeed. Indeed, it brought the 1934 Incitement to Disaffection Act into disrepute – although the authorities doubtless noted that the tempo of 'disaffection' activity subsequently subsided, the energies of the campaign having been necessarily diverted into defending those on trial.

·FUTURE IMPLICATIONS FOR BRITAIN·

So far as the future is concerned, it would be a mistake to be too sanguine about the lessons for Britain from the experience of Northern Ireland. We have already seen the way that legislation and procedures adopted in the North have infected the mainland. But an additional lesson is to be found in use of the law and its agencies for the management and control of social and political unrest. It has to be remembered that Northern Ireland, if not a conventional liberal-democratic society, has at least the trappings of liberal democracy. It is not a fascist state and those whose rhetoric suggests otherwise miss the real point, namely, that state powers exercised through a judicial system explicitly politicized for the task can be a very effective means of controlling political resistance. The 'criminalization strategy' has been particularly adroit, not in any sense as a way of 'solving' the crisis but of keeping it within manageable bounds.

And it should be emphasized that this has been attempted not simply with an iron fist. The other side of the same coin of social control has been the use of the law to reform the previously blatant and universal pattern of sectarian discrimination in the North. Additionally:

The huge expansion in the criminal justice industry since 1969 and the increased commitment under direct rule to non-sectarian recruitment to official posts in the Department of Public Prosecutions and the Courts Service, now provides a major source of employment for better-educated Catholics. There has been a corresponding increase in the readiness of middle-class Catholics to accept the legitimacy of the state. [26]

So this mixture of 'repression' and 'reform' has the same objective of managing political unrest by firmly stamping out serious resistance on the one hand, and on the other removing some embarrassing sectarian anomalies and co-opting potentially dissident elements needed for the smooth functioning of the state.[27]

It would not take a great leap of imagination to envisage political circumstances in Britain which could see some of this experience from the North transported across the Irish Sea and put into practice here. In the absence of a radical socialist government, it is likely that unemployment in Britain will remain above 3,000,000 for the foreseeable future, with an increasingly embittered section of youth hitting out against a system unable to provide them with even the basics of modern life. Such economic circumstances would be accompanied by a continued erosion of public services and further decline of inner cities, with the inevitable stress and strain which that will mean. Added to which will be the race factor, already a potent ingredient in the social strife which spread through the streets of Brixton, Southall, Liverpool, Manchester and elsewhere in 1981.

It is interesting to recall the thinking in official circles well before this, back in the early 1970s. A Conservative M.P., John Biggs Davison, told a military seminar on 4 April 1973:

What happened at Aldershot, what happened at the Old Bailey, reminds us that what happens in Londonderry is very relevant to what can happen in London, and if we lose in Belfast we may have to fight in Brixton or Birmingham. Just as Spain in the thirties was a rehearsal for a wider European conflict, so perhaps what is happening in Northern Ireland is a rehearsal for urban guerrilla war more widely in Europe, and particularly in Great Britain. *

He went on to advocate that the security forces be given new responsibilities to deal with a serious increase in political and social dislocation and unrest. These were not the casual utterances of a known right-wing politician, but reflected a conventional wisdom developing in the armed forces as well. In 1971 Brigadier Frank Kitson had published a book called *Low Intensity Operations*, in which he discussed the role of the state and the Army in conditions of serious economic crisis in Britain. Of particular interest are Kitson's views on the role of the law, in political circumstances not yet warranting outright repression of resistance or social strife.[28] He considers two approaches, the first of which stresses the use of the law as 'just another weapon in the government's arsenal, in which case it becomes little more than a propaganda cover for the disposal of unwanted members of the public'. (That would presumably include the Prevention of Terrorism Act introduced three years after his book was published, since its operation fits to a tee Kitson's description.) His second approach is for the law to 'remain impartial', to be administered 'without any direction from the government', which, he argues, is not only 'morally right' but also 'expedient', since 'it is more compatible with the government's aim of maintaining the allegiance of the population'.

The additional significance of Kitson's argument goes beyond his distinction between overt and covert uses of the law to control dissent. For by discussing the problem in these terms he makes it crystal clear that the law is not some impartial, technical instrument, but a political instrument to be adapted to particular political requirements. In March 1980, he was appointed deputy Commander-in-Chief of U.K. Land Forces, his superior at the time being another counter-insurgency expert, General Sir Timothy Creasey, who had served previously as the General Officer Commanding in Northern Ireland.

* The Army barracks at Aldershot, and the Old Bailey, were the scene of I.R.A. bomb explosions.

But the situation Kitson foresaw should not be interpreted as being confined to dramatic and perhaps unlikely conditions of economic collapse and hyper-inflation. A more credible scenario would be the emergence of what has been described as the 'strong state' in Britain. [29] We are experiencing an insidious growth of state power, as expressed in the strengthening of the security forces, computerized collection of intelligence, sophisticated techniques made possible by new technology – and above all a tightening of the law, with judges showing an enthusiasm for political trials and for exercising their own political preferences. The experience of Northern Ireland suggests that the law and its agencies could increasingly assume a similar frontline role in mainland Britain.

PUBLIC ORDER

> ... when a situation of internal 'crisis' develops, the police become
> preoccupied with their order-maintenance function and become involved
> in vital encounters with the public over highly emotive, sensitive issues,
> such as industrial relations and counter-subversion ... It is in such areas
> that they are presented as the first line of defence of authority
> against challenge; it is in such areas, when public order is challenged, that
> they become most visible as the symbolic and the actual representatives
> of the state.
>
> (Tom Bowden, *Beyond the Limits of the Law*
> (Penguin, 1978), p. 221)

The maintenance of public order is one of the clearest examples of the
political use of the law. Ultimately upon it rests the legitimacy of
government and the stability of the state, and how public order is
enforced in practice is often the crucial yardstick by which a society is
judged and the extent of freedom in it measured. In Britain the law has
consistently been applied in a discretionary manner to suit the political
requirements of the moment.

Precisely because of its obvious sensitivity and strategic value to the
authorities, public order has had to be enforced with a certain subtlety:
sometimes the iron fist has been applied, sometimes the velvet glove.
The criteria for this have included the need to carry the support of
public opinion which in turn has produced a requirement to influence
public opinion. Thus the history of public order in Britain – at least
since the early nineteenth century – is a mixture of both restraint and
force, underpinned by an attempt to mobilize political support for whichever tactics are deemed by the agencies of the state to be appropriate at
any particular time. Pragmatism has been the watchword, and it obscures
the real political factors at work to pretend either that public order is
enforced in a technical, impartial manner or that it is applied in a uniformly repressive fashion. Sir Robert Mark gave an insight into how

sophisticated police strategy could be when he said: 'The real art of policing a free society is to win by appearing to lose.' [1]

From the outset the British police were a public-order police. Indeed, the problem of public order has historically been the most serious one with which the police have had to grapple. And the fact that the British bobby has (deservedly) gained the reputation for being the 'best in the world' is in no small part due to the ingenuity of the British state: 'The British genius was to make this police force, clearly taking sides in a class struggle, appear to be an independent, non-partisan agency simply enforcing the law,' writes Bowden, pointing out also that 'It is a political illusion that has been increasingly difficult to sustain during more recent class confrontations in Britain.' [2]

However, it is also these very modern confrontations which have been presented in such a way as, first, to reinforce the mythology of the impartiality of the police and the law; and, second, to suggest that society is somehow 'threatened' in an unprecedented way by recent public disorder. In the 1970s, media and popular frenzy reached a pitch over police clashes with strikers and demonstrators. Yet historically such clashes have occurred regularly, and it is important to recognize this to appreciate the true character of the law on public order and the political trials it inevitably spawns.

· BACKGROUND ·

Despite the fact that the Association of Chief Police Officers argued in 1977 for increased powers on the grounds that 'the police can no longer prevent public disorder on the streets', this, as E. P. Thompson notes, 'was so much unhistorical humbug . . . In a broad secular view there has never been a time when public disorder in the streets has been less.' [3] Prior to the founding of formal police forces in the 1830s, the Army had been used to counter internal dissent and public disorder. [4] Often it acted brutally, resulting in casualties which make contemporary police clashes with rioters or demonstrators look like tea parties. For example, in 1780 the Gordon riots which inflamed London for nearly a week were suppressed by troops on the orders of King George III. Over 400 people were killed or wounded during the disturbances, and twenty-five of the rioters were subsequently executed. In 1819 there was the 'Peterloo Massacre', when a crowd of 80,000 people in Manchester, attending a peaceful assembly calling for parliamentary reform, was dispersed by a cavalry charge of Army officers: 11 people were killed and 400 wounded. In 1831, a demonstration in Bristol in favour of reform degenerated into a riot in which at least 50 rioters were killed and many hundreds wounded. Afterwards, four rioters were hanged and over 70 imprisoned or sentenced to transportation. Throughout the nineteenth and into the early twentieth century clashes between demonstrators or workers and the police or the Army saw further deaths, and casualties on a massive scale by today's standards. Dissent and protest encountering resistance from the authorities was a major feature of the struggle to win reform. As one historian aptly remarked: 'Sundry "un-English" things have in reality been very English indeed.'[5]

But it was partly the outcry produced by such incidents as Peterloo that encouraged the state to look for a more acceptable agency than the Army for enforcing public order. Hence the formation of the police – which at the time was greeted with protests against 'Peel's Bloody Gang'.[6] True to their mission at birth, the police proceeded to act against demonstrators and against strikers with whom 'confrontations were bloody and brutal affairs'.[7]

The establishment of police forces throughout the country unquestionably gave increased security to ordinary people on an *individual* basis. But when the working class acted *collectively* to secure basic rights, the political function of the police was starkly revealed. Moreover, the public order laws gave to the authorities a virtual *carte blanche* to act as they wished to suppress dissent. It is interesting to note that there was little need felt then by the ruling class to dress up the operations of the law with any pretence of impartiality. For instance, a detailed study of riots and public order in the Black Country in 1835–60 records how the police acted against the working class, because:

power lay with the Lord Lieutenant and the J.P.s who, collectively in Quarter Sessions, were the local legislative, administrative and judicial authorities for the whole country; in Petty Sessions they dispensed local and summary justice for their districts; they had influence over the county police force through the Quarter Sessions and through the Chief Constable, whom they appointed. They could command bodies of police, troops and special constables in times of emergency; and in the Black Country, a large number of the J.P.s were themselves large coal and iron masters, the largest employers and the most powerful economic forces in the region; they could exercise this power to protect their own interests and property through the normal forces of law and order. [8]

Public order laws were thus class laws, and acted as such in the absence both of democratic political institutions and of a strong labour movement that could have exerted a countervailing power which the law would have had to acknowledge.

·CRISIS POLITICS·

But as the basis for parliamentary democracy began to be established through struggle, the use of public order laws ebbed and flowed with periods of 'crisis politics'. During times of economic recession, when the trade unions asserted themselves, or when political dissent multiplied, the law on public order was wheeled out and its powers enforced by the police and judiciary alike. Among the more notable incidents in the twentieth century were strikes and riots at Tonypandy in 1910, and Liverpool in both 1911 and 1919. The police went on strike themselves in 1918 and 1919, offering the apparent prospect of some unity with working-class movements and, not surprisingly, inviting the accusation from the Prime Minister, Lloyd George, that Britain was 'near to Bolshevism'. The use of the armed forces in these disputes and the manner of their intervention confirmed that, as in the previous century, public order legislation gave the British state effectively untrammelled powers to control disturbances. Later, in a further period of economic crisis in the 1930s, public order powers were used against the National Unemployed Workers' Movement, and against both the British Union of Fascists and its opponents.

So the time from the turn of the century to the 1930s was marked by continuous public order prosecutions, particularly against working-class groups, and it is no coincidence that it was also a time of recurring economic crisis. Significantly, however, certain challenges to public order were exempt from the general clampdown. Between 1912 and 1914, those leading resistance against Ulster being absorbed into an independent Ireland were never prosecuted – despite the fact that their activities could easily have been caught within the ambit of public order controls and even conspiracy or sedition laws. The fact that the main spokesmen for this resistance were upper-class figures with close links into the British armed forces was perhaps just a little relevant: 'Quite clearly this was a revolt of Gentlemen and was not to be viewed in the same way as actions of the political militants of the Left.'[9]

So the law could not only be applied to control political unrest, it could also be applied in a discriminatory way. This was very evident in the authorities' handling in the 1930s of the clashes between Mosley's British Union of Fascists and anti-racists. Faced with policing these clashes, the police did not act 'neutrally' and nor did the Home Office. In a way that foreshadowed conflict between racist or Nazi organizations and their opponents in the 1970s, the police tended to act against the interests of left-wing groups and to side with the fascists. 'Jewish organizations bitterly contrasted police laggardliness in prosecuting anti-semitic attacks with the police enthusiasm for protecting the "democratic" rights of the fascists against demonstrators.'[10] While at least one historian has claimed that this interpretation of police behaviour is 'left-wing mythology',[11] the fact remains that the police had a choice and ended up protecting the interests of fascists rather than anti-fascists. The authoritative history of the fascist movement of that time shows this conclusively.[12] It is also interesting to note that whereas there was extensive surveillance of the National Unemployed Workers' Movement, including a Special Branch informer right at its centre, there was no equivalent infiltration of the fascists. Nor did the police use the same kind of aggressive and at times brutal tactics against fascist demonstrators as they did against unemployed marchers. The most notorious example was the unwillingness of the police to intervene when Mosley's stewards beat up hecklers at the 1934 fascist rally in Olympia. It appeared there was one law for the fascists and one for anti-fascists – at least until 1936 when the Public Order Act was introduced to control the activities of the British Union of Fascists.

· POLICING THE MODERN CRISIS ·

From that time we jump to the 1970s to look for comparable public order problems – again a period of economic crisis. Action had been taken to control agitation by nuclear disarmers in the early 1960s, and the growing tide of political radicalism in the late 1960s – including demonstrations against the Vietnam War and student occupations – had met with its fair share of police resistance. But the public order clamp-down accelerated dramatically through the 1970s, with clashes between the police and trade unionists, anti-racists or left-wing activists. The deaths of student Kevin Gately in 1974 at the Red Lion Square demonstration against the National Front, and of teacher Blair Peach in 1979 at the Southall demonstration against the National Front, were the first such fatalities at the hands of the police for about fifty years.

As they had done in previous periods of unrest, in the 1970s the police moved increasingly into the role of controlling public order.[13] They also began joint manoeuvres and cooperation with the Army, drawing on military experience of riot equipment and techniques, many of which had been developed in Northern Ireland. But this was less with a view to accustoming the public to a possible intervention by the armed forces in the public order arena, than to developing the capacity of the police to act in a quasi-military way should that prove necessary. As Bowden puts it:

If then what we are witnessing is, as seems likely, the passing of the heyday of the military in politics, we might well be entering upon a new and menacing phase in which the police, through low-intensity or low-profile control opera-tions, are intervening more and more to affect the daily business of politics, either at the behest of, or in opposition to, incumbent regimes.[14]

Certainly the police have acquired an array of military-type hardware which fits uneasily with the image of the 'bobby on the beat', conforming more to the 'technology of political control'.[15]

Meanwhile, the 1970s saw the structure of the police altered to accom-modate new sections which were manifestations of a 'politicized and para-military' model of policing.[16] The introduction of the Special Patrol Group, the Diplomatic Protection Group and the Bomb Squad all re-flected this shift. The fact that they coincided with acts of terrorism should not obscure the reality that the control of public order represented a greater challenge for the state than isolated terrorist outrages. For ex-ample, the picket of the Saltley coke depot in February 1972, when the police were powerless against determined miners, and the use of 'flying pickets' during the 1972 and 1974 miners' strikes, shook the authorities far more than I.R.A. bombers. There is evidence that Saltley was a watershed for the state. Special 'anti-picket squads' were established by the police, and from then onwards policing of public order grew increas-ingly tough.[17] And why? Quite simply because the interests of the ruling class were being challenged as they had been the previous century when the forces of law and order also showed an enthusiasm for putting down dissent, armed with the full 'majesty of the law'.

Equally, however, this has been done in a 'balanced' way. With few exceptions, the police have not waded in indiscriminately against political dissidents or urban rioters. They *have* been constrained by public opinion and by political opposition. They may have come close to running riot themselves – for example in Southall in 1979 or in Brixton in 1981. But on the whole they have behaved more circumspectly – itself a political recognition of the political constraints within which their public order role is situated.

Increasingly, as the 1980s came in, the police were being asked to control the social consequences of unemployment and public expenditure cuts. With Thatcherism accelerating a long-term decline of British capitalism, the police were thrust into a key role in a political conflict. As Tony Benn argued of the Conservative government's Industry Bill in Parliament on 6 November 1979:

... if industrial policy follows this course the next instrument of the Cabinet will be the Special Patrol Group as the problems created by deindustrialization come to be presented to the public in terms of law and order ... I warn the right hon. gentlemen [Sir Keith Joseph, Secretary of State for Industry] that if the industrial policy he follows leads to ... social tension the Special Patrol Group will not be a substitute for the National Enterprise Board as a way of dealing with it. This policy will lead to an inevitable attack on our democratic freedoms.

In the light of that, it is interesting to note just how rapid had been the change in climate governing public order. Just ten years earlier, in 1969–70, mass demonstrations had occurred during the rugby tour by an all-white South African side. Each of the twenty-five matches saw protests, including disruptions of play and clashes with the police. Some of these clashes were violent – for example at Swansea in November 1969, where the police joined rugby 'vigilantes' in an attack on anti-apartheid demonstrators inside the ground, provoking widespread disquiet.[18] Certainly, the police response was considerably tougher than in the early 1960s during protests by nuclear disarmers. Nevertheless, hundreds of demonstrators who invaded pitches and interrupted games were *not* prosecuted. Their names were merely noted and they were evicted from the ground. While they were not treated with kid gloves, on the whole they escaped both police maltreatment and prosecution for the many public order offences with which they could have been charged – a breach of the peace being just one. Yet when another South African rugby side toured in 1979–80, even though the demonstrators were smaller in number and their campaign less militant than that of the Stop the Seventy Tour Committee, they were dealt with relatively more severely. Firstly, they faced 'saturation policing' – a bigger, tougher and more organized police response which was less tolerant of their right to protest. Secondly, they faced certain prosecution if they managed to get through police lines and on to the field.

Similarly, workers' occupations in the early 1970s (the one at Upper Clyde Shipbuilders being perhaps the best known) were to all intents and purposes ignored by the police and the legal system, whereas quite a different response faced workers at the occupations in 1981 at Laurence Scotts in Manchester and Staffa in London's East End. In the latter case, the police moved in during the early hours of a November Saturday morning, evicted the strikers, and stood guard while equipment needed by the owners was moved out. Shortly afterwards, at Laurence Scotts, a joint helicopter operation between the police and managers lifted out goods and equipment, helping to undermine the strikers.

The crucial point about comparing these different responses ten years apart is that to all intents and purposes *the law was unchanged*. It was simply applied in a different way, the police being able to find the appropriate powers they needed to fulfil the political tasks required of them. So what exactly is the law on public order that gives such flexibility to the state and its agencies?

· PUBLIC ORDER LAWS ·

There are a number of laws the authorities could call upon, most of them having been passed in particular periods of political and economic crisis. They go back to such period pieces as the 1797 Incitement to Mutiny and Unlawful Oaths Act; the 1817 Seditious Meetings Act; the 1886 Riot Damages Act; and the 1908 Public Meeting Act (which was used against the suffragettes). The main one is the 1936 Public Order Act. Together they give extremely broad, not to say sweeping, powers, the principal characteristic of which is the *discretion* they grant to police and prosecutors. Indeed public order, more than any other area of the law, gives such wide discretionary powers to the police that, should they choose to exercise them to the full, almost all rights of public assembly would in practice disappear. More to the point, the police 'can choose either to under-enforce or to over-enforce the law almost as they see fit'.[19] In this they are guided less by the technical letter of the law than by the pressure upon them caused by any given public disorder, together with what public opinion will stand for. But *they* are the ones who make the judgement (which is a political one) as to how they will use their powers.

The conventional wisdom that there is a basic right to protest peacefully under English law is not supported by experience – notwithstanding that assertion by successive judges. In 1975 Lord Denning, for example, quoted with approval a judgement 150 years previously affirming 'the undoubted right of Englishmen to assemble together for the purpose of deliberating upon public grievances'.[20] But in practice there is no such 'positive' right, only a 'negative' right: 'The law does not say: "You can do that"; it says "You cannot do this", which means you can do everything else except that which it says you cannot do.'[21] And whereas Lord Scarman has tried to bridge the gap between these two positions by arguing that 'The right [to demonstrate] of course exists, subject only to limits required by the need for good order and the passage of traffic',[22] he merely sidesteps the central issue, begging the question as to what is meant by such phrases as 'good order': presumably, what the police want them to mean. Patricia Hewitt summarizes the reality: 'the freedom to demonstrate is at the mercy of arbitrary decisions by the police and the executive, often unchallengeable in the courts ... when the police decide it is *not* to be exercised, the freedom to demonstrate is revealed to be an illusion'.[23]

There are many other laws capable of being applied to enforce public order, including obstruction of a public highway and a variety of local government laws. Then there is the Justices of the Peace Act 1361, which gives magistrates the power to bind people over to keep the peace, even if they have committed no offence. In some cases, this power has actually been used against *witnesses* to cases brought against demonstrators. Failure to comply with a binding over can result in imprisonment, as, for example, happened to eleven women protesting against nuclear weapons at Greenham Common in 1982. Nevertheless, the police and the Home Office want still more powers. In 1980 a consultative government Green Paper and a House of Commons committee report proposed new restrictions on public assemblies and demonstrations by giving the police still greater powers to control them,[24] while new legislative controls were promised by Mrs Thatcher's government.

·ELASTIC POWERS·

On closer inspection it is hard to see why the police should bother with pressing for tighter controls, since in two key respects – the way public laws are *defined*, and the *operational independence* secured by the police – their powers are so elastic as to be capable of being stretched to envelop almost every eventuality. Phrases like 'unlawful assembly', 'breach of the peace', 'shouting insulting slogans', 'obstruction', are incapable of technical definition. They are notoriously vague, allowing for widely different interpretations on the part of those applying them, and so loosely specified that the precise manner of their application can depend almost on the whim of an individual police officer. It is therefore often impossible for those contemplating taking action to be certain whether they might commit an illegal act. Even if they are not charged, they may still have broken the law; even if they are charged and acquitted they may have committed an offence which would have produced a conviction in different circumstances or in a different court. In other words, it is the political context which may give rise to an offence rather than the technical definition of the law that is the determining factor.

How, for example, is even the best-intentioned police officer to make a sensible judgement about whether or not a slogan is 'insulting'? One South African rugby player, giving evidence against me in my 1972 trial for conspiracy over the Stop the Seventy Tour campaign, claimed that protesters chanting 'Paint them black and send them back' was insulting to *him*! (Mind you, it was intended to be.)

More specifically still, the mood of individual police officers or their political attitudes may be critical. I have participated in demonstrations where an even-tempered police officer will exercise his discretion in a radically different manner from one with a more aggressive temperament or perhaps a political chip on his shoulder.

Nor have attempts by senior law lords to define insulting behaviour been very convincing. Giving judgement in 1973 in a case where the anti-apartheid activist Dennis Brutus had interrupted a tennis match at Wimbledon, Lord Reid said that 'an ordinary sensible man knows an insult when he sees or hears it'.[25] But this simply sidesteps the problem, since *interpretation* on the ground, not the letter of the law, remains the governing factor. Viscount Dilhorne, in his judgement in the same case, hardly clarified matters when he observed:

Behaviour which evidences a disrespect or contempt for the rights of others does not of itself establish that the behaviour was threatening, abusive or insulting. Such behaviour may be very annoying to those who see it and cause resentment and protests but it does not suffice to show that the behaviour was annoying and did annoy, for a person can be guilty of annoying behaviour without that behaviour being insulting. [26]

Similarly, the leading legal textbook on public order shows how varied is the application of the offence of 'threatening behaviour', even catching practical joking on occasion, for example youths on a camp site who in 1966 made a noise and disturbed campers in the middle of the night.[27]

The absence of clarity or certainty in public order law is well illustrated by my experience in trying to disrupt a tennis match between white South Africa and Britain at Bristol in July 1969. Four of us ran on to the court during the game and sat down. After refusing to leave we were carried off by police officers, the whole incident being perfectly peaceful and lasting perhaps five minutes. We were then detained at a local police station for four hours, while the police questioned and finger-printed us and decided what, if any, charges to bring. In the end they let us go with a mild warning. But three years later (when a private prosecution had been brought against me by a right-wing group with South African support), I was convicted at the Old Bailey for what amounted to conspiracy to trespass over the self-same disruption, receiving a £200 fine which was way above that merited by the particular 'offence' itself. Just to add to the confusion, conspiracy to trespass had not been 'interpreted' by judges as a criminal charge at the time of the protest – it only became so several years later after the *Kamara* ruling by the House of Lords.

However, this is not necessarily to argue for a more rigid and technical application of the law. Clearly, the role of discretion can be of benefit to all concerned. The political climate would become intolerably oppressive, and the legal system would grind to a halt, if each individual who had technically committed an offence were to be prosecuted. The element of flexibility and pragmatism built into our law is a double-edged sword: it can give the legal system a sensible and human face, but it can also open a door to political bias which allows a coach and horses to be driven through the notion of judicial impartiality.

The power to ban demonstrations under the 1936 Public Order Act gave rise to another contentious area. Brought in to deal primarily with fascist marches in the 1930s, bans were applied to the annual May Day march in 1940 – prohibiting it for the first time since 1889. In 1949 and 1950, bans were again applied to fascist marches, catching the May Day march as well.

In London the Commissioner of Police has the power to order a ban, with the Home Secretary's consent. Outside London a chief constable must obtain the agreement of the local council, again subject to the consent of the Home Secretary. Although the Public Order Act expressly permits bans of 'all or any class of processions', since the late 1970s the authorities have adopted the practice of 'blanket bans'. They could have interpreted their powers differently, as occurred in 1961 when the Committee of 100 was alone prevented from organizing demonstrations; or in 1976 when protests in support of an I.R.A. hunger striker were specifically banned. But instead, bans have been applied for particular periods in particular areas, to catch *all* public processions and not just the National Front marches that gave rise to the fresh use of this power. One such ban on a National Front demonstration in the spring of 1981 caught the Campaign for Nuclear Disarmament and anti-vivisectionists, among others. In one ten-month period, March 1981 to January 1982, thirty bans were imposed in England and Wales, ranging from two and a half days in three areas of London, to forty-three days in Liverpool following the summer rioting in the city.

These bans have unquestionably undermined the campaigning ability of racist and Nazi organizations. But the blanket way in which they have been applied has also undermined the civil liberties of perfectly innocent citizens. Lord Scarman's Report on the Brixton Disorders in 1981 acknowledged this unsatisfactory state of affairs. He argued that the existing provisions of the Public Order Act could in fact be applied more selectively against marches likely to stir up racial hatred, and suggested as well that the law could well be amended to allow a *specific* march to be banned if public disorder was inevitable.[28]

In any event, the bans issue underlines the scope for political discretion and produces anomalies which make a nonsense of the concept of impartial law. For example, in Chislehurst, a May Queen procession which indisputably was covered by a general ban in 1981 was nevertheless allowed to continue, 'apparently because local officers found it impossible to believe that such an innocuous event could be prohibited!'[29]

·OPERATIONAL DISCRETION·

Precisely because public order powers are so diffuse and sweeping, they encourage what has been termed 'police vigilantism' – that is the tendency for the police to take the law into their own hands and apply it as they see fit.[30] The fuzzy nature of the law is a virtual invitation to this, especially when the police are under pressure, their personal tolerance strained to breaking point and their resources stretched, as has occurred repeatedly in the modern period of clashes from the late 1960s onwards.

In evidence to a House of Commons committee, both the Metropolitan police chief, Sir David McNee, and the Association of Chief Police Officers stressed the nuisance and disruption of day-to-day life caused by *peaceful* processions.[31] The language they used made it abundantly clear that, as A.C.P.O. said, the police do not perceive such events as 'part of the normal process of daily life'. That is to say, political demonstrations were inherently 'abnormal' and 'self-indulgent', the police chiefs stressing also the 'substantial' financial cost and the 'havoc' caused to the 'normal' life of business people and city centre shoppers.

The police would be nothing if not human if they did not express irritation at the inconvenience they are caused by political demonstrations: everybody likes a quiet life. And we can sympathize with the police's exasperation at being caught 'in the middle'. As the Police Federation Chairman, James Jardine, argued: 'Why should one group of crackpot extremists for the sake of publicity and to stir up racial tension, be able to issue what is virtually an invitation to other groups of crackpots to a public punch-up, with the police starting and ending as Aunt Sallies?'[32] But their objective is a fundamentally *political* one, for they do not criticize the 'disruption' caused to the community by events like football matches which occur far more often than major demonstrations.

The danger is that police attitudes may become even more reactionary, as their traditional image of restraint wears thin under the pressures caused by economic crisis. A booklet produced by the magazine of the Police Federation quotes one officer's solution to the problem of disorder – 'All you have to do is spray them – spray them with machine guns' – while one speaker at the 1979 Federation annual conference warned that people attending demonstrations should expect to get hurt and 'shouldn't come whining'.[33]

A further factor in the public order arena encouraging the police to adopt a hostile political role is the development of what has been described in the U.S.A. as a 'police-industrial complex' having its own influence on police practice. Analogous to the 'military-industrial complex', its influence rose in America after the end of the Vietnam War, as technological expertise and resources went into producing equipment and techniques for social control rather than for military purposes. Hence the experimentation with riot control technology such as 'photic drivers', 'squawk boxes' using infra-sound to disorientate demonstrators, 'instant banana' which makes roads slippery and 'instant mud' which has the reverse effect.[34] If industrialists based in Britain, utilizing experience from Northern Ireland, decided that such products could assist the police, marketing pressures could well help to shift the emphasis of police public order practice in that direction.

· THE LUXULYAN CASE ·

But if we draw back for a moment from such futuristic speculation, and look at police discretionary power today, a recent example of the role of the Devon and Cornwall police underlines the vulnerability of both the police and the law to political pressure. In May 1981 protesters peacefully occupied the site of a planned nuclear power station in Luxulyan, Cornwall, and the Central Electricity Generating Board requested the region's Chief Constable, John Alderson, to clear their property so that survey work could begin. Mr Alderson refused to do so, because he felt that the protesters were not breaking any criminal law. As important, he argued that to remove them forcibly would badly damage relations with the local community.

The whole issue turned on the interpretation of a classically fuzzy area of the law. Thus, while there was no doubt that the police had the right to arrest the protesters without a warrant if there was an actual or threatened breach of the peace – and that they also had the power to disperse an unlawful assembly – the police argued that there was no likelihood of a breach of the peace. The local Chief Inspector stated in an affadavit: 'There is no reason whatsoever for the police to suspect or have any grounds to believe that a breach of the peace is anticipated; the demonstrators are acting in a very passive manner and in no way are they committing a breach of the peace.' He had previously told his chiefs: 'I do not feel we should act as agents for the C.E.G.B. and our relationship with the local community should remain untarnished.'

We might pause to note that, by the standards applied generally across the country, this is an extraordinarily sympathetic attitude for a police force to take, and while it was doubtless influenced by local circumstances it cannot have been a coincidence that the most articulate advocate of 'community policing', John Alderson, was the region's Chief Constable. One somehow cannot imagine James Anderton, for example, behaving with such tolerance (some might say subservience) to demonstrators.

Faced with instransigence from both protesters and police, the C.E.G.B. sought the help of the courts, and a sequence of events followed which, though it might well fit comfortably within the British legal tradition of pragmatism at all costs, also illustrated just how much room for manoeuvre the law on public order does allow, should political circumstances require it.

Lord Denning, presiding over the Court of Appeal on 20 October 1981, drew back from acceding to the C.E.G.B.'s request to *order* the Devon and Cornwall police forcibly to clear the site. Instead he expressed the 'hope' that the Chief Constable would do this. But on the letter of the law, he was quite emphatic: 'By wilfully obstructing the operations of the board they are deliberately breaking the law. The arm of the law is long enough to reach them despite their attempts to avoid it . . . If I were wrong on this point, it would give a licence to every passive resister in the land. He would be able to cock a snook at the law as these groups have done. Public works of the greatest national importance could be held up indefinitely. This cannot be. The rule of law must prevail.'

For Lord Denning, a breach of peace was threatened quite simply because such an occupation might provoke the C.E.G.B. into forcibly removing the protesters. In other words, the potential offence lay in the response of the owner of the property to trespassers, not to any initiative by the protesters themselves, who everybody agreed were acting with commendable passivity throughout. This ingenious 'interpretation' provides yet another example of the way public law enables judges to declare that it means almost whatever they want it to. Lord Denning's two fellow judges were less emphatic than he, but broadly supported the judgement that the protesters were legally in the wrong.

As the legal correspondent of the *Guardian* put it: 'Strictly, therefore, the Chief Constable could still insist that he does not wish to intervene. But this would be unwise since continuing inaction would amount to defiance of the clearly expressed views of the three Appeal Court judges. They may not have the power to order him to act but their view that he should do so is tantamount to a command.'[35]

In the end, Mr Alderson was not required to exercise any force. 'Good sense' prevailed and, magnanimously, the protesters left of their own accord, apparently believing they had made their point. 'The Chief Constable has been put in an impossible situation and we have therefore decided to withdraw voluntarily,' they said. A confrontation was avoided in a display of proverbial British compromise, with Mr Alderson's unusual position being entirely vindicated. He had avoided community hostility being directed at the police, and yet ultimately the dominant interest of the C.E.G.B. had prevailed (Luxulyan remained a prime site for a new nuclear power station). While it would be fascinating to speculate on the consequences for public order if all chief constables acted as he did in similar situations, the Luxulyan case is one of the clearest examples of the way the law can be bent to fit the particular political constraints of the moment.

For dissidents, the message of Luxulyan and Saltley is, paradoxically, the same: if you can manage to secure enough political support for your cause, the forces of law and order will have to find a way out of the situation rather than risk humiliation.

· CONTRASTS IN PUBLIC ORDER ENFORCEMENT ·

The key political role played by discretionary power in public order is shown by a series of cases upon which the law impinged in a disarmingly partisan manner. The lesson of these cases is that the decision *not to* apply the law is as politically significant as the decision *to* apply it. It is too frequently assumed that the workings of a power structure – in this case the judiciary and the police – are to be observed in decisions positively and openly taken, whereas the failure to apply the law is itself a positive act, even though it may not receive our attention. 'Non-decisions', in short, are just as important as 'decisions'.[36]

Consider, first, the more trivial cases. A young woman called Erica Roe gets carried away at a rugby match in January 1982 and 'streaks' across the field baring her breasts to all and sundry. She gets treated with the utmost leniency and becomes a 'page three' media star overnight. The fact that no charges are preferred against her is not because she committed no offence. Clearly she did – as convictions of the men who have streaked across various sporting fields can testify. The law just turned a blind eye to her case because, far from behaving 'indecently' (as the men *self-evidently* were), she as a woman was for once exploiting the rabid sexism of our culture which – fed on a diet of bare bosoms – regarded another pair as harmless fun. The 'non-decision' to prosecute her was, if not determined by explicitly political criteria, certainly influenced by prevailing social mores.

Much the same factors are at work when villagers parade through their streets, disrupting traffic and blocking roads with tractors, in protest against juggernauts thundering through. Clearly guilty of obstructing the highway, they have nevertheless rarely if ever been prosecuted. Similarly, mothers with babies in prams disrupting traffic by walking to and fro across roads in support of their demand for a zebra crossing are very rarely arrested. And why? Simply because public sympathy for their cause would make it imprudent for the authorities to prosecute, and they are not threatening any dominant interests in a manner which requires the intervention of the law. So the political *context* in which an illegal act is committed can be a critical factor in determining whether or not the law is invoked. Certainly, few trade unionists or anti-racist protesters could expect such leniency, as the record of the 1970s shows.

'To put the treatment of protesters in context,' writes Patricia Hewitt, 'one only has to think of the complete freedom accorded to the crowds which throng the footpaths to watch the Lord Mayor's show, or to stand outside Buckingham Palace, or to see the procession of a royal wedding or a state visit. The obstruction to the pavement is considerable, the delays and inconvenience to other people at least as great as that which the police condemn when caused by marches, but no arrest is ever made for obstruction.'[37]

A remarkably frank admission of the way political expediency can rule the day in public order enforcement came in December 1982 when women protesters attempted physically to block entrances to the Greenham Common cruise missile base. Assistant Chief Constable Wyn Jones said that although hundreds of women had committed arrestable offences, they were not 'vindictive or malicious' people, so no arrests were made: 'They were demonstrating because of their deeply held political convictions. I do not think the circumstances justify the full sanctions of the criminal law,' he said.[38] (No doubt these 'circumstances' included likely public controversy resulting from arrests of hundreds of women.)

· SQUATTING ·

In general, the political manipulation of the law on public order rests on the actions of police officers. But judges can play a critical role too, as shown by their treatment of the squatters' movement which grew in the late 1960s and early 1970s as large numbers of homeless people became increasingly frustrated by even greater numbers of empty properties owned either by councils or property developers. The law on trespass was not clear then, and in itself trespass was not a criminal offence. Even to prove a civil wrong, it generally had to be shown that the owner had suffered damage to the property as a result of a squat. Initially, therefore, squatters moved into empty houses almost with impunity. Then followed a series of battles as bailiffs tried to evict them, notably in Redbridge on the fringes of East London.

But as property owners, both private and public, escalated their resistance to squatters, they found the law, even if rather convoluted, to be on their side in the end. As Professor Griffith shows,[39] the judges effectively re-wrote the rules in a series of judgements against squatters, which were 'illogical' in the strict terms of the law as it then stood (it was subsequently reformed in 1977 under the Criminal Law Act). He shows how, in a number of complex cases involving squatters, not just the law but legal procedures and regulations were interpreted in a biased way by judges:

These decisions show a remarkable consistency of approach . . . [they] . . . consistently lead to decisions which favour owners and disfavour occupiers. It is disingenuous of the courts to pretend that they are bound to follow the course they have chosen to follow, and the tears shed for the homeless . . . add insult to injury. What the courts should be seeking is to hold an even balance in interpretation. Yet every procedural defect is excused when it is the fault of the owners and every provision is interpreted strictly against the occupiers.[40]

One of the squatters' organizers, Ron Bailey, records the extent of manipulation of the law that occurred in these cases, as squatters desperately sought successive legal loopholes and judges quickly closed them up with fresh 'interpretations' to defend the interests of property against the needs of people. In one case, the London Borough of Southwark had 400 empty properties which the council *did not intend to use*, and still the courts found against squatters' families who had been quite prepared to

enter into some agreement with the council for temporary occupation
rights.[41]

·PICKETING·

Similar favouritism towards the owners of property can be seen in the
treatment by the law of the thorny question of picketing. We saw in
Chapter 8 how judges successively interpreted the law throughout the
latter stages of the last century and into modern times in order to restrict
the rights of trade unionists. The ambiguous nature of the law in picketing has permitted enormous discretion to be wielded by police on the
ground, invariably against strikers and their supporters. As Greater
Manchester's police chief, James Anderton, conceded, picketing 'is an
enormously subjective area. It requires the greatest discretion.'[42] The
fact is that it is numbers that count in the way the law on picketing is
enforced, as the miners' picket at the Saltley coke depot in 1972 showed:
the police there were powerless to resist the massed ranks of miners
supported by 'flying pickets'. The police's initial insistence that the
pickets be restricted to just twelve was simply ignored, and the miners
won the ensuing bruising confrontation by sheer force of numbers.[43]

On the other hand, in an isolated industrial dispute, with the workers
small in numbers and less able to call on solidarity support from fellow
trade unionists, the police in practice restrict pickets as they see fit. The
police have always been able to demand a restriction of numbers. But the
Code of Practice under the 1980 Employment Act encourages this by
giving them the right to restrict to six pickets; and they can and do
determine where pickets may position themselves as well. In short, the
police can determine whether or not the picket is effective. Their role
can be critical in the workers winning or losing a strike. Anybody who
has been on an industrial picket line knows that police power rather than
the letter of the law or an official code is the critical factor. And successive legal judgements have ensured that this remains the case.[44] As
one labour lawyer has argued: 'The only indisputably lawful pickets . . .
are those who attend in small numbers . . . and keep out of everyone's
way.'[45]

Outside the industrial arena, the law on picketing has been no less
vulnerable to political manipulation. In 1975 local people picketed the
offices of the North London estate agents, Prebbles. It was a decidedly

docile picket: the picketers had full police permission, and consisted of only between four and eight people who stood about on the pavement in front of the Prebbles office for several hours on Saturday mornings, holding placards. But when Prebbles took out an interim injunction against the demonstrators, it was granted by the Court of Appeal. The significance of the case was not just that peaceful pickets were suppressed. It was the use of the device of the *injunction*. The demonstrators were never actually prosecuted for a specific offence – such a recourse to civil law by Prebbles could have taken two years to get to court. Instead they were granted an interim injunction, theoretically pending a full court hearing. But, naturally, Prebbles saw no reason to proceed further. They had secured their objective by halting the momentum of the protesters, who were responding to strong feelings at the time over Prebbles' housing activities – feelings that would have been difficult to revive years later after the case had reached court.

The conclusion must therefore be that the law on public order is political law *par excellence*, designed and enforced to exercise political control, and applied in a discretionary way according to the prevailing balance of political forces. If these forces are more powerful than the agencies of the state (as in Saltley for instance), then the law can be flouted with impunity. If prudence dictates that it is not applied at all (as in cases of the zebra-crossing parents), then the police will ignore the letter and apply instead the spirit of the law. But if the state is confident of being able to enforce public order then it does so, assisted by police manipulation of their powers and judicial manipulation of the law itself. The unwritten motto of the British establishment appears to be: 'Protest all you like lads and lasses – so long as you are ineffective. But if you are effective and if you threaten our interests we have ways of making you stop your troublesome activities.' Or, as Lord Chief Justice Hewart said in more refined, legal prose in 1936: 'English law does not recognize any special right of public meeting either for a political or any other purpose. The right of assembly . . . is nothing more than a view taken by the courts.'

RACISM

The experience of blacks at the hands of Britain's police and courts has now reached the stage at which sections of the community see any trial involving a group of black defendants as a political trial.

(*New Society*, 29 October 1981)

In November 1980 Errol Madden, a young, educationally subnormal black man, was charged with theft of his own property. He had been shopping and had bought a toy car when he was arrested, taken to Battersea police station, threatened and intimidated into signing an untrue confession on the basis of which he was then prosecuted for shoplifting. Fortunately, it later emerged that all along a receipt for the toy was sitting in the bag he was carrying at the time.

The fuss created led to an investigation by the Police Complaints Board, who censured the officers involved and described the case as an 'extraordinary mistake'.[1] Mistake it certainly was. But the evidence suggests that the general circumstances of the case, even if not the detail, were far from 'extraordinary'. Whatever their rights in theory, black people are in practice treated as second-class citizens by society in general and the legal system and the police in particular. From their standpoint the law is a politically hostile force.

The law has played a key role in the regulation of race relations and the control of black people throughout the post-war era during which the black community emerged as a significant part of the British population.

· IMMIGRATION LAWS ·

By the 1970s it was widely agreed that successful racial integration in Britain would depend on keeping numbers of (black) immigrants to a minimum. The consensus on this now spans all the major political parties and is certainly the official orthodoxy, as is evident in the views espoused by the Home Office, the police and judges. Yet just twenty years before, the consensus was quite the reverse: for an 'open door' policy. So how is this abrupt and complete turn-around to be explained?

We need to go back to the central force in post-war migration patterns: the economy. And in doing so we shall see that – contrary to mainstream presentation of the question – it is not possible to explain the position of blacks in Britain today and their relationship to the law except by reference to the economic foundations of immigration. The way black people are treated by immigration policies is one side of the coin: their treatment as domestic citizens is the other. But it is the *same* coin. In 1975 Robert Moore chronicled the 'sad story' of the slide down to successively racist immigration laws, showing how they connect up with community relations:

It is not the story of the development of 'immigration control' that the authorities would have us believe. It is the story of the erosion of the rights of countless citizens and the erection of the immigration colour bar. Ten years ago we discussed the black man as the welcome stranger to our midst and talked about ways to help him 'integrate'. Today the black man is a public enemy, lurking in every cross-Channel lorry, landing by night on southern beaches or at Heathrow with forged papers; he is the 'alien wedge' and we discuss how to keep him out and how to get rid of those already here.[2]

In the post-war years of economic expansion over 11 million migrant workers moved into Europe's industrial north-west, around $2\frac{1}{2}$ million of whom came to Britain.[3] They were required by European capitalism to fill mainly the unskilled or semi-skilled jobs created by the boom. Thus British companies recruited in the West Indies and in the Indian sub-continent where in any case colonial ties remained. For the state the advantage was considerable: in 1970 it was estimated that 'the import of "ready made" workers amounts to a saving, for the country of immigration, of between £8,000 and £16,000 per migrant worker' in terms of the 'social cost' of education, feeding, clothing and housing before working age.[4]

The pattern of such immigration during the 'stop-go' period of the 1950s directly reflected the state of the economy: up in 'boom' years, down in 'trough' years.[5] But if such immigration benefited British capitalists and certain other sections of society, the burden was carried by those least able to bear it. Thus immigrants won *economic* acceptance because of a shortage of workers, but *social* ostracism because of a shortage of public provision, housing in particular. This was a recipe for conflict and tension, with black and white workers prevented 'from coming to a common consciousness of class by intruding that other consciousness of race. It prevents, in other words, the horizontal conflict of classes through the vertical integration of race . . . To put it crudely, the economic profit from immigration had gone to capital, the social cost had gone to labour, but the resulting conflict between the two had been mediated by a common ideology of racism.'[6]

By the mid-1950s, racial attacks were increasing, fascists began to recruit and Mosley's forces re-grouped. In August 1958 there were race riots in Nottingham and then in Notting Hill. On top of this, Britain was looking to the European Economic Community as the captive markets of the empire disappeared. These pressures, coupled with a passing of the growth years of post-war reconstruction, led to a demand to control the supply of black immigration. In 1962 the Commonwealth Immigration Act was passed, in what was to prove the first step down a slippery slope of racist immigration laws: 'Racialism was no longer a matter of free enterprise; it was nationalized. If labour from the "coloured" Commonwealth and colonies was still needed, its intake and deployment was going to be regulated not by the market forces of discrimination but by the regulatory instruments of the state itself.'[7] Within a year the British West Indian Association was complaining of increasing 'police brutality' stemming from the passing of the Act and, shortly after that, West Indian activists produced a critical report on police behaviour entitled *Nigger Hunting in England*.[8]

In 1965 the then Labour government introduced another restriction on black immigration, refining still further the basis for entry to possession of an employment voucher. In 1968 an Act specifically to stop the entry of Kenya Asians was introduced by Labour. The Conservatives then went one better with the 1971 Immigration Act, which was even more blatantly racist: before it came into force in January 1973, Commonwealth immigrants were black settlers; now they became mere migrant workers. While government apologists argued that the intention was simply to institutionalize discrimination against foreign labour, 'because the labour happened to be black, it ended up institutionalizing racism instead'.[9] By the early 1970s unemployment was rising inexorably and so black labour became surplus to the economy's requirements. As economic crisis closed in, the debate quickly shifted from controlling immigration to proposals for repatriation – with Enoch Powell fanning the flames of public prejudice, the media doing much the same, and growing activity by racist and Nazi groups like the National Front. By January 1978 the Conservative leader, soon to be Prime Minister, Margaret Thatcher, had given official approval to the language of the gutter racist by calling for an end to black immigration, for otherwise 'this country might be swamped by people with a different culture'. Press and broadcasting services took up the 'swamping' theme and an all-party House of Commons committee recommended further immigration curbs and also controls on black people already in Britain. The 1981 British Nationality Act introduced by the Tories (but previewed in a Labour Green Paper in 1978) finally confirmed that second- (or third-) class citizenship for blacks had been legally sanctified.

So the history of immigration control laws has also been about controlling the domestic black population. We can see this clearly in the impact of the administrative law spawned by the Acts, much of it delegating enormous powers of discretion to civil servants, police officers and the judiciary. Quite simply, the law actively encouraged state officials to behave in a racist manner.

On entering Britain, the black person's first encounter with racist officialdom is likely to be immigration or customs officials. Handed the task by successive Parliaments of enforcing immigration restrictions, they have had a notorious record. As one ex-immigration officer explained: 'The job was simply keeping out black immigrants.' And, disturbingly, he confirmed the attitudes of those empowered to enforce the law: 'The politics of the vast majority of immigration officers are right-wing. Most are quite honest about this . . . there is such support for the views of Enoch Powell.'[10] Black immigrants frequently found themselves plunged into a nightmare world of interrogation, detention and, for women, forced virginity tests. The onus is usually on the individuals to prove their entitlement to entry, even when they are British subjects returning from a holiday.[11]

The scope for bias, prejudice and the exercise of arbitrary power by state officials has been enormous because of racist immigration controls. What is more, the law – coupled with the political lead now given by Thatcherism – has created a climate in which not just state officials on the front line of immigration control, but those operating welfare, health services, employment exchanges and education, have been given the authority to insist on identity checks or inspection of passports before granting services to black citizens which in law should be theirs by right. The specific linking of welfare benefits to immigrant status for the first time in the 1980 Social Security Act has brought widespread abuse and the formation of a campaign group called 'No Pass Laws Here'.[12] In 1982 it was confirmed that hospitals would check patients' race before admitting them for treatment under the National Health Service. Ostensibly introduced as part of a new government scheme to charge overseas visitors for use of the health service, it represented yet another obstacle to equal treatment and another basis of harassment and denial of rights for black Britons.

This has occurred partly because of the deliberate drive against 'illegal' immigrants from the early 1970s onwards. Police were given the power and encouraged to go on 'fishing expeditions', resulting in widespread harassment and intimidation of black residents.[13] Police have also raided work places employing blacks. In 1980, nearly 1,000 alleged illegal immigrants were rooted out and deported. The pernicious effect has been to sharpen the insecurity and fear of a black community that is already visible and able to be targeted as is no other group simply by virtue of its blackness. What is more, individuals who may only have been 'illegal' on some technicality, and who by right should be entitled to reside here, have been caught.

Thus the cumulative effect of immigration laws and the political climate has been to give to the police and public servants a virtual licence to harass – and to encourage them to exercise it. What is more, the courts have *extended* the exercise of such discretionary powers. Describing court decisions right up to the House of Lords in July 1980, Patricia Hewitt shows[14] that successive judgements have created a situation where the police can arrest a suspected illegal immigrant without a warrant, and detain without charge and without trial for an indefinite period. Normal rights of *habeas corpus* are effectively suspended, and there is no right of appeal to the courts against an *administrative* order to deport the person suspected of being an illegal immigrant. Significantly, although he was nominally in charge of this system as Labour Home Secretary between 1976 and 1979, Merlyn Rees appears not to have comprehended until very late in the day what he had allowed his officials to get up to. In his bumbling way, he confessed to the House of Commons after the general election in 1979: 'I found . . . that someone can be locked up for a long period, purely by administrative order . . . I was beginning to question that,' he said plaintively.[15]

About time too. For, as Patricia Hewitt explains:

It is now possible for someone who came here as a child, who was given permission to settle here and who has known no other home to be picked out by the Home Office years later, on the suspicion that he is not, in fact, the child of the man who claimed to be his father and that his passport was therefore obtained through deception . . . Under the name of administrative removal, the Home Office and the courts have already created and sanctioned a system of repatriation.[16]

The scope for judicial abuse was illustrated by the case of a British-born West Indian teenager found guilty of stealing, who in March 1982 was ordered by Judge John Clay to leave the country and stay away for five years. A typical custodial sentence for the offence might have been up to two years in Borstal, but the judge made his order after learning that the boy and his mother were planning a four-week holiday in Jamaica. In so doing the judge effectively made up a new power and a new punishment under the law – what amounted to backdoor repatriation. Actually, the courts have no power to deport: they can only recommend a deportation to the Home Secretary. The case provoked strong protests to the Lord Chancellor, with the Shadow Home Secretary, Roy Hattersley, pointing out: 'It is clear this policy would only ever be applied to blacks.' However, this pressure did pay off when, several months later, the Court of Appeal quashed the sentence and instead imposed a conditional discharge.

· A BLACK 'UNDERCLASS' ·

Part of the effect of immigration controls and the arbitrary powers they contain has been the 'criminalization' of the black community. Asians in particular are vulnerable to being identified as potential illegal immigrants and are thereby the targets of suspicion and harassment: '. . . immigration control is not just a way of keeping people out. It is also becoming a very powerful way of harassing the community that is here and attempting to undermine the legitimacy of its right to be here,' explained the General Secretary of the Joint Council for the Welfare of Immigrants.[17]

In this way, immigration controls have created an atmosphere in which blacks can be subject to regular surveillance, stopping and searching.

Even if day-to-day life for most ordinary black citizens is remote from
the high profile and overtly political trials described later on in this
chapter, they still experience what can be regarded as a regular series of
street political trials. They are challenged, scrutinized and sometimes
intimidated purely and simply because of law enforcement directed at
them for a clear political reason: they are on trial because they are
black.

The other way in which the black community is 'criminalized' has to
do with their position as an 'underclass', for the most part below the
conventional 'white' class structure. Trapped in a circle of joblessness,
bad housing, inadequate education and welfare provision – and above all
politically powerless – the black community is both economically
deprived and economically exploited. Congregated mostly in run-down
inner city areas, blacks face the classic slide into crime caused by de-
privation. The Scarman Report provided official acknowledgement of
this link between an 'impoverished' environment and the drift into crime,
particularly of young blacks among whom unemployment could be anything above 50 per cent.[18] A study of the politics of 'mugging' (a crime
popularly associated with young blacks) illustrates the pattern of events
which lead to blacks being 'criminalized' as a community:

The first step into the twilight zone of crime comes through sporadic
pilfering: pinching off open stalls or from supermarkets. The second is the lure
of the bigger take – pickpocketing, snatching from a shopping basket, lifting a
wallet ... A certain amount of drifting 'uptown' begins, and the activity ...
requires more social organization, a more stable network. Life comes to depend
more and more on these successes. A fraction of the class is being *criminalized*
... the numbers now forced to survive in these ways on the margin of legal life
are increasing, directly in line with the numbers unemployed ... crime ...
promises to become a regular occupation, a *substitute job*.[19]

The analysis does not condone 'mugging' (or any other crime for
that matter). Nor should there be any excuse for violent attacks or
robbery by anybody – and any fancy politico who seeks to justify such
activity by black youth is not merely morally wrong but politically
confused as well. Nevertheless, historians have begun to distinguish
between 'normal crime', and 'social crime' which is partly a protest
against the status quo by groups excluded from its benefits. As has been
tellingly argued: 'To take the eighteenth-century definition of 'crime'
for granted is to take the eighteenth-century definition of property-right
and class for granted.'[20] Within that framework, it is not necessary to

agree with or defend crime by alienated young blacks – still less to indulge in sophistry about it being a positive political act of some sort – to concede that its roots are political and that therefore the application of the law to deal with it is a political act as well. Apart from anything else, the state has made a choice to inject the Special Patrol Group into black areas rather than the resources needed to improve them. And again, we see reinforced the proposition advanced in the first chapter, that law cannot be divorced from the political economy of the environment within which it operates.

It is therefore crucial to acknowledge that whatever may be the legal niceties of the situation, and whatever are the abstract rights nominally enjoyed by blacks along with other British citizens, many black people *see themselves* as victims of the whole system of society. As one black writer and community activist explains:

... equality under the law is not a right Black people in this country could automatically expect, and ... the injustices Black people experience within the framework of social control and law and order cannot be attributed, as is customary, to the aberrations of the few exceptions to the rule. For if one looks at control institutions in the society and the way they act upon Black people, the important fact that emerges for us is that as a group Black people are victims of a systematic force of class and racial oppression carried out by the system through its institutions. The police, the courts of law ... all claim an over-representative number of Black victims. And the number grows increasingly in spite of the reformist programmes of various kinds.[21]

In other words, the whole operation of the law is politically biased so far as black people are concerned – and this notwithstanding the legislation introduced to outlaw racial discrimination.

· RACE RELATIONS LAWS ·

Efforts were undoubtedly made to improve legal protection for black people in the Race Relations Acts of 1965, 1968 and 1976. But their impact has been marginal, quite simply because they have stood isolated against a tide of institutionalized and ideological racism, in which formal legal rights were swept aside. The 1965 Act was in any case very weak and had little impact. Interestingly, its racial incitement clause was initially directed against black power spokesmen rather than white racists. The 1976 Act was tougher, but has also had little effect.

Indeed, the experience of race relations legislation in Britain underlines the need to question the value of a formal, legalistic strategy while the real causes of racism are left untouched. Moreover, the agencies set up under this legislation – initially the Race Relations Board and Community Relations Commission, both later merged into the Commission for Racial Equality – have served to mediate between the state and the black community. They have not had the power to challenge institutionalized racism, nor indeed could they be expected to do so: as part of the state they have been expected to remain 'non-political', hence restricting severely their ability to campaign against racism. Such a 'neutral' role has also meant that they have been denied the opportunity genuinely to *represent* the black community: for to do that would have meant taking the side of black people against the state. While the objectives of these agencies included both an altruistic commitment to non-racialism and to tackle discrimination, ultimately also they have served to co-opt dissent and channel it into avenues and procedures convenient to government. In this, race was no different from other crisis points – for example planning, housing and welfare – all of which in the 1960s and 1970s saw a series of sponsored agencies aimed at managing unrest and absorbing it into 'constructive' channels.[22]

Thus, while the anti-discrimination provisions of the Race Relations Acts were introduced in response to political pressure for Britain to be seen to have 'clean hands', in practice they have provided a cover for a continued failure to mount a *political* attack on racism. As we have seen also they have given Britain a respectable appearance of racial equality, while immigration controls in particular have been applied in a racist way going well beyond points of entry to the country and infecting the indigenous population.

The Acts have also been ineffective in achieving their stated objectives. For example, a study of racial violence and harassment in London's East End concluded: 'The 1976 Race Relations Act is proving quite inadequate to deal with the poison of racism.'[23] In particular the vaunted incitement to racial hatred clause of the 1976 Act has had a miserable record, as shown by research into the application of the clause.[24] During a five-year period since it came into effect, it has been applied in only 22 cases of which 16 resulted in convictions. This must be set against the fact that in two years, 1978 and 1979, one body alone, the Commission for Racial Equality, referred 43 and 31 cases respectively to the Attorney

General for prosecution. Referrals which were not prosecuted included a leaflet by the Nazi group, the British Movement, entitled 'Jews Bomb Themselves' which amounted to an incitement to organize attacks on the Jewish community.

The Act also failed abjectly in the 1977 case of ex-National Front leader John Kingsley Read, who, at a public meeting, made this comment about the death of an Asian student: 'One down, a million to go.' The failure of the prosecution case against British Movement members in Warwick in August 1978 was another example. They had made such public statements as: 'A nurse wiping froth off a coon's mouth and as a result dying of rabies. That is what these black bastards are doing to us.'

Although there is a strong case for strengthening the specific legal clauses on incitement to racial hatred,[25] the wider political climate cannot be ignored. The case of Joe Pearce, editor of the young National Front magazine, *Bulldog*, proved a salutary one for those placing their faith in legal redress against racism. He had been responsible for printing what by any standards were grossly inflammatory and racist statements. Yet he was only convicted (and sentenced to six months in prison) after three trials, the first of which produced a 'hung' jury, the second being halted on a technicality. Clearly, juries have reflected the wider racism infecting society as a whole, most of it the product of deliberate policies pursued over the years by the state and by private capital.

The weakness of the law and the reluctance of the authorities to act was illustrated in another case. In late autumn 1980 and early 1981, the Wandsworth and Lambeth branches of the National Front produced a publication entitled *South London News*. Both issues contained 'hit lists' of local anti-racists, giving their phone numbers and home addresses, and announcing: 'We believe that the time has now come to launch a "war of nerves" . . . against Anti Nazi League members . . . using "terror tactics".' In February 1981, shortly after it was circulated, rocks were thrown through the front windows of my Putney home. Others on the hit list were threatened, had their homes attacked or received excreta through the post. Yet despite the fact that we lobbied Scotland Yard, producing copies which included the address of the editor, the police were unwilling to prosecute or to take action to prevent the distribution of such material, even though a direct link between it and violent attacks had been proven.

·POLICE AND BLACKS·

Against this background it is not surprising to find that the police have
been seen as a hostile force by the black community. By and large the
police have tended to use their discretionary powers in a manner calculated to inflame relations with blacks – and this notwithstanding more
recent initiatives such as appointing police community relations officers
and recruiting black police officers. As the writer James Baldwin said of
the U.S.A. (though it is applicable here too), police in black areas are like
'an occupying soldier in a bitterly hostile country . . . Their very presence
is an insult and it would be, even if they spent their entire day feeding
gumdrops to children.'

Part of this is because the police have been charged by the state with
carrying out a specific social control function which is inherently racist.
As one police superintendent admitted, 'black and Asian immigrant
groups' tend to regard the police 'as outsiders and as the enforcement
arm of the white establishment'.[26] But police attitudes and practices are
a factor as well.

The same superintendent also gave an idea of thinking among senior
police officers when he argued that because of the fact that their 'cultural
background and social structure differed significantly from the indigenous community', 'these immigrants' do not 'readily recognize or accept
the traditional English view of the police'. Because the police do not
acknowledge the social control function they are playing, they tend to
rationalize conflict with blacks in terms of a collision with a 'foreign
culture', even though the vast majority of young blacks who have the
most fraught relationship with the police have been born in Britain.

Down on the ground, officers most directly in conflict with the black
community can be more forthright in their views. While there are many
police officers who are not racially prejudiced, the daily experience of
blacks tends to be one of being on the receiving end of racist attitudes
from the police. Many young blacks will recognize this kind of statement
made in a London police station by a detective constable: 'Shut up, they
will still find you guilty, Sambo, you can't win.'[27] Declaring that 'prejudice is a state of mind brought about by experience', one detective
superintendent automatically identified West Indians hanging around in
jeans and T-shirts as likely 'muggers'.[28]

In Reiner's authoritative study of police attitudes, it is clear that racism runs right through the force. But the significant point his research corroborates is that this is *inevitable*, given the hostile role the police are asked to play in relation to the black community. It is not a matter of individual failings by officers: racism flows automatically from the antagonistic stance the state has required them to adopt. Thus, as one uniformed sergeant said: 'The race aspect is so bad . . . I very rarely see a coloured man who is pro-police . . . So I don't exercise a colour bar, but I must admit that if my daughter wanted to marry a coloured man, I would most certainly object.'[29] In the city of Bristol, Reiner found that 23 per cent of police mentioned race as a worsening problem, with the figure rising to 35 per cent in the division containing the city's largest black community.[30] And that was in 1977, well before the outbreak of riots in the St Paul's area in 1980 and again in 1982.

The law does little to protect black people: indeed it acquiesces in their treatment as second-class citizens. This occurs in a number of ways. First of all, the police have been given a legal *carte blanche* to harass the black community, as has been well documented by the Institute of Race Relations. In their evidence to the Royal Commission on Criminal Procedure, *Police Against Black People*, they showed 'a consistent pattern of police suspicion against and general harassment of black communities throughout the country', manifesting itself in:

(a) police overmanning of black events
(b) police raids on black clubs, centres and meeting places
(c) police concentration in predominantly black localities including:
  (i) the operation of special squads
  (ii) operations whose pretext is to apprehend a particular offender
(d) information gathering and intelligence.[31]

Lord Scarman's report into the Brixton riots also found evidence of 'unlawful' police harassment of black youth especially,[32] confirmed by further documented evidence of abuses of police powers of arrest, detention and other invasions of individual rights, including police violence.[33]

The immigration laws specifically 'supply police with the discretion to go into houses and ask questions', reports Professor Stuart Hall, who points out that there are 'places in Britain where most adult blacks, especially Asians, will now carry a passport in order to provide ready identification on the street'.[34] This situation has developed with clear Home Office approval, quite apart from the operational agreement of local police chiefs. Before the 1971 Immigration Act had even come into force, the Home Office had set up the Illegal Immigration Intelligence Unit (I.I.I.U.), based at Scotland Yard, to coordinate a nationwide drive against suspected illegal immigrants. There was no prior parliamentary agreement to this, yet very soon widespread 'passport raids' into black areas occurred, involving abuse of individual rights. The evidence shows that 'few illegal immigrants have been discovered but many black people have been subjected to detention and harassment'.[35]

The other side of the coin of police–black relations is overwhelming evidence of the consistent failure to protect the black community from racial violence and harassment.[36] A Home Office study itself showed the disturbing extent to which such attacks occur in modern Britain – admitting that they were 'more common than we had supposed'.[37] Yet the police are usually unwilling to acknowledge their racial dimension. This has been characteristic even of the top of the force. Robert Mark, for example, refused to accept that the murder in June 1976 of an Asian student, Gurdip Singh Chaggar, in Southall was racially motivated, despite evidence to the contrary. Indeed, he expressed his exasperation at the community protest and concern which followed the killing: 'This racial unrest was stimulated and manipulated for their own ends by extremist elements,' said his 1976 Report.[38]

With such insensitivity at the very top, it is easy to see why similar attitudes prevail locally. Commenting, for example, on the refusal of Newham police to accept a racist motive in the killing of Kayumerz Anklesaria in London's East End in August 1979 – he had been kicked to death by three white racists in an underground train – the Indian Workers' Association stated: 'In East London racist attacks on the black population are an everyday phenomenon and are intensifying. When such attacks are reported to the police they ignore them. In the past all racist murders have been called non-racist by the police, who seem more interested in covering up racism than arresting the culprits.'[39]

The Institute of Race Relations shows how the police response to racial attacks includes:

(a) unwillingness to afford protection
(b) refusal to recognize the racial dimension of an attack
(c) delay
(d) unwillingness to investigate
(e) unwillingness to prosecute attackers
(f) misguided advice to victims

(g) hostility to complainants; and even

(h) treating the victim as the aggressor[40]

A clearer picture of the biased exercise of police discretion it would be hard to imagine.

Unfortunately, however, the story does not end here, as the case of Michael Ferreira illustrates. He was murdered on Hackney marshes in December 1978 by white youths, and a campaign around the case quickly gathered momentum, coordinated by the Hackney Black People's Defence Organization. But local police then started to harass the campaigners, conducting a series of raids on the homes of his friends and family, beating some of them up. At a protest outside a court hearing into the murder, some of the defence committee, including Michael Ferreira's mother, were arrested for obstruction. The defence committee later protested: '. . . not only will we get no justice within the courts, we will also get attacked by the police when we give support to our people.'[41]

This practice of the police switching the attack on to blacks who cross their path is illustrated by the arrest of an entire family in 1979. On 9 April 1979 Mrs Earlington and her son Trevor became involved in a domestic argument with their next-door neighbours. Other neighbours stated that there was no significant noise or disturbance, but police arrived on the scene shortly afterwards, shouted racialist abuse at Mrs Earlington and tried to arrest her. She was sick at the time, and others in her family came to her aid while the police were manhandling her. They too were arrested and later found guilty. During his detention, Trevor Earlington claimed he was called 'a black bastard' and a 'wog'.[42]

A disproportionate number of blacks are arrested and a Home Office study of arrests in the Metropolitan police area in 1975 suggested that this might 'lie partly in a greater impact on blacks than on whites of policing: support for this possibility lies in the fact that blacks are most heavily arrested for two kinds of offence in which there appears to be considerable scope for selective perception by police of potential or actual criminals'.[43] The two offences were 'Sus' and 'mugging'.

Finally abolished in 1981, after a long campaign, the 'Sus' law – the crime of being a 'suspected person' under the 1824 Vagrancy Act, which required a police officer simply to state that a suspect had been loitering with intent to commit an offence – had been widely abused against black people, particularly youngsters.[44] But it was replaced by provisions in the 1981 Criminal Attempts Act giving the police similar arbitrary powers if they suspect that someone is taking an undesirable interest in a motor vehicle. While it is unlikely to produce abuse on the same scale as the old law on 'Sus', one leading black activist has aptly commented: 'In a sense it will never be at an end, because Sus . . . is a name for racism within this society. By virtue of being black you are suspect in this society.'[45]

There is also evidence of considerable abuse of police powers against blacks during detention, of 'flouting of Judges Rules, use of brutality and intimidation, the fabrication of evidence, the forcing of confessions'.[46] Aside from any racial motive for this, the way the law is framed and operates makes such abuse virtually inevitable. In particular, the lack of a statutory basis for the Judge Rules on questioning and treatment of suspects while in detention has written what amounts to a blank cheque to the police to do what they feel is necessary to secure evidence to produce a prosecution. Police discretion here is compounded by judicial discretion.

The same picture can be seen over the charging of black suspects.[47] The police have some discretion over what charge to bring and this is very evident in the tendency to bring very serious charges when lesser ones could have been preferred. There has also been a tendency to bring 'frivolous charges' against black people. For example, blacks have been arrested on the street for having offensive weapons such as umbrellas, coins or screwdrivers; what is or is not an 'offensive' weapon is obviously highly subjective, and black people may be forgiven for thinking that a particular item is an offensive weapon if the police say so.

The differential treatment of black suspects is also evident in the thorny area of identification evidence. Notoriously unreliable in any case, identification evidence is particularly tricky when white eye-witnesses have observed an offence by a black. Research in the U.S.A.[48] suggests that whites are intrinsically prone to make a wrongful identification of blacks, and much the same picture emerges from British research.[49] But the police have not helped the prospect of obtaining reliable identity evidence by allowing for such practices as placing a black suspect in an identity parade when everyone else (save for one Asian) was white.[50] In 1980 it emerged that police had adopted the practice in London of holding 'parades' for black suspects at busy underground stations. Counsel for the Crown in a robbery case involving four young black men said it had been found 'wholly impossible' to find volunteers from the black community for a conventional parade. So police had adopted the procedure of placing black suspects on an escalator at a busy time of the day, leaving prosecution witnesses near the ticket barrier to make an identification if they could.[51]

There is also evidence of police exercising discretion in a discriminatory way in an area of the legal system especially vulnerable to this: the denial of bail, or the threat of such denial to 'bribe or induce a defendant to plead a certain way, or to otherwise cooperate with the police'.[52] The 1976 Bail Act gives wide discretion to magistrates over bail and, after the riots which hit Britain's cities in 1981, there was evidence of magistrates interpreting their discretion in an unusual manner, either to deny bail even to black defendants charged with a first offence, or to impose curfew restrictions as conditions of bail.[53]

The death in detention of Richard 'Cartoon' Campbell summed up black suspicion of a legal system they regard as fundamentally hostile. A Rastafarian, Campbell was arrested on 1 March 1980 in Brixton for attempted burglary of a sports shop. From the outset he strongly asserted his innocence, and remained in good spirits, confident that he would be acquitted. But after being on remand for ten days he was transferred to Ashford Remand Centre where it was claimed he was treated 'like an animal', partly because he was black. Soon after he went there he refused food and drink and eventually died on 31 March, after being force fed. An inquiry into his death convened by Battersea and Wandsworth Trades Council concluded that he was 'a helpless victim of a series of crucial failures, failures based on a lack of respect for Richard and on a racism that underpinned almost every aspect of the system'.[54]

·JUDGES, MAGISTRATES AND COURTS·

If police behaviour can be seen as reflecting the interests of a racism dominant in society, then so too can the role of the courts. On the whole, judges, magistrates and courts generally have not merely acted as agents of a system which as we saw at the beginning of this chapter has been used in a racist way; they have positively reinforced racism.

Magistrates' courts have been particularly criticized for 'sausage machine justice' in their treatment of black defendants, with one London court being described by a solicitor as a 'lynching court'.[55] Perhaps the most blatant – and maybe unusual – case of prejudice was of a magistrate hearing a formal application for bail. He asked the lawyer: 'Is your client black?' On being told he was, he replied: 'Then no bail.'[56] Moreover, it has been shown that magistrates in cases with blacks are 'only too willing to accept the police evidence as it stands'.[57]

In higher courts, many judges have also acted in a manner that is at best far from impartial and at worst racially prejudiced. For example, in January 1978 Judge Neil MacKinnon provoked an outcry when he summed up in a way that virtually directed the jury to acquit the fascist leader John Kingsley Read, who had been prosecuted for incitement to racial hatred. In a public speech following the death of an Asian student at the hands of white racists, Read had said, 'One down, a million to go', and had attacked 'niggers, wogs and coons'. Judge MacKinnon appeared to welcome such remarks when he summed up, saying that Mr Read had the guts to stand up in public for the things he believed in: '. . . we are allowed to have our own views still, thank goodness, and long may it last.' After the jury had returned a not guilty verdict, having been out for just ten minutes, the judge told Mr Read: 'By all means propagate the views you have but try to avoid the action which has been taken against you. I wish you well.'[58] In an interesting sequel a week after the case, the Labour Lord Chancellor, Lord Elwyn-Jones, made an unprecedented public statement implicitly rebuking the judge. Treading warily, since even the Lord Chancellor has no power to dismiss a circuit judge like Judge MacKinnon (unless he is incapacitated or misbehaves), Lord Elwyn-Jones tried to reassure the black community that the intention of race relations legislation to protect blacks remained intact. But his statement of confidence in the racial impartiality and fairness of the courts did not go anything like far enough for black leaders and for 113 Labour M.P.s who demanded Judge MacKinnon's dismissal (he was however retained). The incident revealed the gap between the liberal intent of the Race Relations law and the unwillingness of judges to carry it out.

The case of the Virk brothers was if anything even more extraordinary. They were attacked by several white racist youths and had to defend themselves. But when police were called to the scene, *they* were the ones arrested. They were later convicted solely on the basis of police evidence, and sentenced to varying terms of imprisonment by Judge Michael Argyle on 19 July 1978. Passing sentence, the judge condemned the brothers for trying to 'introduce racial prejudice' as a factor and rebuked the defence for asking the white youths whether they were members of the National Front.[59]

In exhibiting signs of racial prejudice, judges were perhaps reflecting public opinion. In some ways, weak though they have been, the Race Relations Acts have been 'ahead' of popular opinion on race, and judges may have seen their role as being to redress the balance. Thus, Judge Gwyn Morris, when sentencing five West Indian youths found guilty of 'mugging' to five years' jail or detention in May 1975, remarked of Brixton and Clapham:

Within memory these areas were peaceful, safe and agreeable to live in. But the immigrant resettlement which has occurred over the past 25 years has radically transformed that environment ... This case has highlighted and underlined the perils which confront honest, innocent and hardworking, un-accompanied women who are in the street after nightfall. I notice that not a single West Indian woman was attacked.[60]

But the public furore created by this kind of statement by a judge should not obscure the day-to-day way in which, away from the headlines, courts tend to work against the interests of ordinary black citizens. As one detailed analysis shows, the whole legal system is at fault: not only are the Judges Rules and bail procedures manipulated against blacks, but this has been compounded by a tendency to deny legal aid and for blacks to be represented by unsympathetic lawyers.[61] While many of these are problems more general to the whole legal system, regardless of race, the evidence is that blacks suffer disproportionately greater injustice as a consequence of them. Research by black community groups also shows that sentencing is on the whole heavier for blacks than for whites.[62]

· JUDICIAL DISCRETION AND RACE ·

The role of judicial discretion is sharply apparent over race, although it has come under increasing challenge by growing numbers of black lawyers. The Society of Black Lawyers has become more militant in recent years, manifested for example in a demand from its members for the removal of a judge in February 1982. In a three-day trial following from the Brixton riots the previous year, Judge Lord Dunboyne had repeatedly clashed with Mr Sibghat Kadri, counsel for a black defendant charged with assault on the police and with possessing offensive weapons. Mr Kadri had accused the Special Patrol Group of being the 'S.A.S. of the police', claiming that his client had been kicked and brutalized by the S.P.G. when they arrested him. Judge Dunboyne then intervened to say:

'It does not matter if the accused was maltreated. There are plenty of courses for alleging malpractice against the police. That is not the issue at the moment.'[63] Passing sentence later, he criticized the way Mr Kadri had handled the defence and, as legal etiquette rather quaintly puts it, 'provided guidance for the taxing officer' aimed at cutting Mr Kadri's legal fees. (The defendant in the case was acquitted of assaulting the police but found guilty of having an offensive weapon, a brick.)

It may be that as the numbers of black lawyers rise and more black defendants are represented by people who relate to their experience and interests, the courts will seek to curb their activities. By way of emphasizing this point, it is worth noting that the more radical white lawyers who emerged in the 1970s – one group of whom set up chambers outside the hallowed precincts of the Temple in an unprecedented move deemed by the legal establishment to be 'not quite cricket' – have also had regular brushes with judges, especially in political trials. I recall in my mistaken identity case how my legal advisers considered very carefully whom we might approach to conduct my defence. One of the factors we had to take into account was the likely prejudice of the bench against me. We concluded that it would be better to choose a barrister who, though roughly sympathetic to someone of my political standpoint, would nevertheless not be known as a 'radical lawyer' who might compound any existing judicial prejudice against me. The man we instructed, Lewis Hawser Q.C., was one of the top barristers in the country.

Turning to judges in their 'law function', we can find clear evidence of judicial discretion exercised in a way which, if not overtly racist, then at least has hardly furthered the cause of racial equality. Successive judgements over cases brought under the Race Relations Acts show that the House of Lords and the Court of Appeal have adopted a 'conservative' view of the law, so that its scope has been consistently narrowed.[64] An equally legitimate view for their lordships to have adopted would have been to interpret the law in a positive fashion, seeing their mission as being to root out racial discrimination wherever it appeared. But they chose consciously to adopt this restrictive position, which fell within an individualist legal tradition where the purpose of the law was not seen as being to intervene in what are deemed 'private' matters of social relations.

Furthermore, the courts have refused to challenge the derogation of power to administrative decisions over immigration control. Indeed, they 'have actively connived at a system of arbitrary and racially biased executive power'.[65] Analysis of a series of cases shows that judges have selectively interpreted immigration legislation in a manner prejudicial to the rights of black people.[66] The thrust of their judgements has been successively to erode the rights of immigrants who would otherwise be entitled to stay in this country, with Lord Denning's Appeal Court statement endorsing ministerial (and therefore in reality state official) discretionary power contrasting markedly with his attitude over executive power in other areas. All that was required for an exclusion order to be granted against an alien was the Home Secretary's opinion that this was for 'an authorized purpose', argued Lord Denning: 'I think the minister can exercise his power for any purpose which he considers to be for the public good or to be in the interests of the people of this country.'[67] That was certainly not the attitude taken by the law lords in 1976. Then they overturned the power of the Labour Secretary of State for Education to insist that the new Conservative-controlled Tameside Council proceed to implement the plans for comprehensive education agreed by the previous Labour administration in strict accordance with the 1944 Education Act. In that case, they were anxious to curb democratically authorized executive power; with immigration law they have been equally anxious to write a blank cheque for unaccountable administrative power. The phrases in Lord Denning's statement about 'public good' and 'the interests of the people of this country' are only capable of *political* interpretation. The only comparable discretion so enthusiastically handed to the executive by the courts is in the field of national security and official secrecy.

· POLITICAL TRIALS ·

So it should perhaps come as no surprise that blacks have faced a series of trials in the 1970s and 1980s which fully justify the prefix 'political'. By this is normally meant a trial where the whole motivation for the prosecution is to curb political activity which the state regards as disruptive. But it is clear with black defendants that 'political trial' takes on a looser definition capable of absorbing the racism running through the system.

Taking the *black community's* definition of a political trial, the list is a long one, with the characteristic number following the name to label each trial. Thus in August 1970 the Mangrove Nine were charged with riot and affray during a demonstration against police harassment of the Mangrove Restaurant – a gathering place for blacks in Notting Hill. In May 1971 the Metro Four were charged with affray and assaulting police when fighting broke out after police attempted to invade the Metro Club, also in Notting Hill. In March 1972 the Oval Four were charged with attempted theft and assault on police. In June 1973, the Brockwell Park Three were picked on at random in a running battle between police and black youths at a fair, and charged with affray and assault on police. The list continues with the Clapton Park Four: schoolgirls arrested in August 1974 after their headmistress had called police into the school and fighting broke out between girls and police officers. In September 1974 the Swan Disco Seven were charged with assault on police and possession of an offensive weapon after police had invaded a Stockwell disco club, provoking a running battle with black youngsters. The following month the Cricklewood Twelve were charged with affray, possession of offensive weapons and assault on the police, after officers had invaded the Carib Club in Harlesden, North London. Shortly afterwards, also in October 1974, the Stockwell Ten were arrested at Stockwell tube station and charged with affray, possession of offensive weapons, threatening behaviour and assault on police. In July 1974 the Dallow Road Seven were charged with threatening behaviour and assault on police when black youths tried to rescue one of their number, a fifteen-year-old girl, when police violently apprehended her. In November 1975 the Chapeltown Twelve were charged with affray, assault on police and criminal damage arising from a clash between police and local blacks.

These were all cases where vigorous campaigns were organized to support the defendants. Their other distinguishing feature is the nature of the charges brought. Every one involved assault on police, most involved possession of implements deemed 'offensive', and running through all were public order offences such as 'affray', 'threatening behaviour' or 'insulting behaviour', which are notoriously subjective and which invite political prosecutions.

But not all the trials went the way the police wished. None of the Cricklewood Twelve or the Metro Four were convicted, for example, while of the Stockwell Ten, nine were acquitted on all charges, with one conviction of possessing an offensive weapon; the judge directed the jury to find the defendants not guilty of affray and 'it was clear that a section of the jurors were unwilling to believe police evidence under any circumstances'.[68] Defendants in the 1971 Mangrove trial were acquitted on all the main charges, and again in 1979 the 'Mangrove Six' were all acquitted after another police raid on the club.

Moreover, all the cases followed police harassment, either of black clubs like the Mangrove or the Carib, or of black communities like the Leeds district of Chapletown. They tended to contain evidence from witnesses of racist remarks by police officers: for example, in the Cricklewood Twelve case, police invading the Carib club shouted 'Black whores' and 'Black bastards'. Alternatively, police appeared to simplify black politics in a way calculated to disadvantage the chances of defendants. Asked in court whether he knew what 'black power' meant during the 1971 Mangrove case, one constable replied: '. . . it is a movement planned to be very militant in this country'.[69]

By the late 1970s, trials of blacks began to take a different course. Conspiracy charges began to be brought, as in the 1977 case of the Lewisham Nineteen, charged after saturation police surveillance including use of new technology such as video cameras. They were all convicted. But the prosecution case in the 1977 trial of the Islington Eighteen, charged with conspiracy following the previous year's Notting Hill carnival, degenerated during a fifteen-week run at the Old Bailey. The jury were out for 170 hours, the longest in the history of the Central Criminal Court, and were only able to agree on three of the thirty-odd conspiracy charges – and those were not guilty verdicts. The trial cost the taxpayer over £¼ million and was variously described by court officials as 'a farce' and 'the biggest waste of time and money' they had ever seen.[70]

By the early 1980s, sections of the black community were interpreting almost any trial with a group of black defendants as a 'political trial', among these the charges brought against the Thornton Heath Fifteen and the Bradford Twelve in 1981. The latter contained all the ingredients of a full-scale political trial. The defendants, twelve young Asians, were either members of, or sympathizers with, a radical black group, the United Black Youth League. It had campaigned locally against harassment of blacks and manipulation of immigration controls; in a well-known case, the group had helped Anwar Ditta to force the Home Office to allow her to bring her children home to her in Rochdale.

In July 1981, during the summer riots elsewhere in British cities (there was virtually no trouble in Bradford), some bottles filled with petrol were found on a local waste ground. The Twelve were arrested and 'voluntary' statements of confession were extracted after lengthy interrogations. They were then charged with conspiracy 'to manufacture explosives with intent to endanger life and damage property'. All the defendants later retracted these statements, strongly asserting their innocence and complaining of racial abuse and harassment by the police. The solicitor for three of the defendants said in an early court hearing: 'It is the fear of the community that they may be on trial for what amounts to their political beliefs and their previous lawful actions in fighting racialism.'

The defendants were also the subject of unprecedented bail conditions. Initially they were jailed for three months, the prosecution opposing bail on the grounds that political demonstrations were taking place in their support. The Bail Act, however, makes no mention of such a reason for denying bail. When they were finally granted bail it was only on the basis of extraordinarily stringent conditions. These amounted to house arrest and were explicitly 'political'. Apart from large sureties, the Twelve were required to stay in their homes after 7 p.m. and could not leave Bradford. Nor could they attend any political meetings or take part in the activities of their defence committee. Clearly, the court recognized that the most effective defence in a political trial is to have a political defence committee coordinating legal tactics and arousing awareness about the issues involved.

Between the first day of the trial on 26 April 1982 and the verdict on 16 June, Leeds Crown Court was charged with political tension. There was controversy over the composition of the jury (described in Chapter 6). Outside, supporters of the Twelve demonstrated and chanted. Inside, it soon became clear that, in the words of the presiding judge, Christopher Beaumont, 'self-defence is a major, if not the central, issue in this case'.[71]

The accused did not deny they had made petrol bombs on 11 July 1981, at the height of the summer riots in Britain's cities. They had acted out of self-defence, with rumours rife of a skinhead attack on Bradford Asians that day. In the event no such attack occurred and the petrol bombs – milk bottles filled with petrol and rags stuffed in as wicks – were left abandoned until they were found six days later by police. The police claimed, without being able to produce direct evidence, that the Twelve planned a riot in the city centre.

So the crucial issue for the jury was the purpose for which the petrol bombs were made: in self-defence or as an offensive conspiracy? The defendants called a series of local black witnesses to prove how their community was terrified. Local Asians had been repeatedly stabbed, attacked, threatened and their homes firebombed. Yet the police had offered no real protection or even understanding of this.

Indeed the police response to the self-defence argument was to deny the existence of the pattern of the racial attacks documented in the evidence called. Where they did concede knowledge of, for example, the murder the previous November of an Asian taxi driver by a British Movement supporter, they still disputed any racial motive. In other words, their *political* attitude to such incidents prevented the police from acting in the interest of local blacks. Police political prejudices surfaced elsewhere during the trial. A detective sergeant claimed that one of the defendants was 'a man of extreme political views', citing his possession of, for example, the *New Statesman* as evidence of extremism. The same officer defined a left-winger as 'anyone who is against the police or against the general running of the country'.[72] But all twelve defendants were acquitted in a sensational verdict, the jury accepting both that the Twelve had acted out of self-defence and that the Asian community could not depend on police protection against racial attack. The police had staged a political trial and had come unstuck, primarily because the Twelve had staged a political defence, using committed lawyers and organizing a vocal supporting campaign.

The black experience sheds a sharper light on the role of the law, from the political trial that occurs on the street to some of the well-publicized trials referred to above. For blacks the law is politically biased because they are the targets of dominant economic interests for whom they have become surplus: there is therefore more of a problem in distinguishing between 'straightforward' criminal charges and those that can be shown to be politically motivated.

But if the law is a product of its political environment, then it follows that we should not rely on legalistic solutions to fundamentally political problems. Thus, while the intentions behind the Race Relations Acts have been admirable, their ineffectiveness in holding back the great tide of racist practice pouring through Britain these last few decades should not lead simply to calls for tougher anti-racist clauses in the legislation. For the record shows that, however tightly the law is framed, it can be undermined in a number of ways: by police and judicial discretion and by the countervailing pulls of racist immigration controls.

POLITICAL TRIALS

Our politics must be carried into the courtroom. We cannot resist
illegitimate authority in the streets only to bow politely before it in the
courtroom. We have to make clear in court that it is our identity, our
politics, and our life style that the government is attacking. We have to
appeal to the jury, outside and inside the court, to accept our politics as
legitimate . . . We should experiment with acting as our own lawyers as a
way to place our identity directly before the jury and the larger public.

(Tom Hayden, 'Thoughts on Political Trials', in *Trial*
(New York, Holt, Rinehart & Winston, 1970), p. 99)

In February 1982 a Conservative M.P. and solicitor, Delwyn Williams,
told a court that the hearing in which he was being sued for professional
negligence by a client was a 'political trial', implying that the case had
been brought to discredit him politically.[1] But while any trial involving
someone holding a position of public importance can obviously have
political consequences, the M.P.'s use of the term does rather confuse
the central issues identified in previous chapters.

It would be as well therefore to draw on the preceding analysis to
obtain a more precise understanding of what a 'political trial' is. Certain
trials are by definition 'political': those involving defendants who have
either broken the law in pursuit of their political objectives or who have been
prosecuted as part of an attempt by the state to control or repress political
unrest. Such trials have occurred regularly over the years, though more frequently in times of political and economic crisis. But underneath these 'high
profile' political trials have been others which also qualify for the description: what may be termed 'low profile' political trials. The best examples of
the latter concern the black community where, because of the racist nature
of British society, even the most trivial charge has political connotations.

Therefore, without doing serious injury to the term (and thereby
running the risk of obscuring the significance of prosecutions brought
for a purpose which is self-evidently political), the picture is of a *spectrum*

with clearly identifiable 'high profile' political trials at the centre, shading away through 'low profile' ones to cases which, although reflecting the political system, are not 'political' as such. To a large extent, the position of any case in this 'political trials spectrum' is dependent on the political circumstances at the time and the particular priorities then held by dominant interests in society. But leaving this question of definition aside for the moment, what are the advantages and disadvantages to the authorities in staging political trials?

·PURPOSE OF MODERN POLITICAL TRIALS·

The state in Britain has obtained a number of benefits from bringing 'high profile' political prosecutions in recent years. First of all, radical movements have undoubtedly been *intimidated* and their activity consequently restricted. The tempo of radical activism slowed during the 1970s partly because an example was made of groups or leaders by putting them on trial. The result was to reduce the numbers prepared to run the risk of indulging in demonstrations and so forth which might lead to prosecution. The forces of law and order can therefore take comfort in the fact that they have managed to constrain dissident political activity by prosecuting key groups and individuals. Indeed, such prosecutions have often provided a pretext for activity designed to break up radical groups – for example, when all the files of the British Withdrawal from Northern Ireland Campaign were confiscated after arrests of some of its members under the Incitement to Disaffection Act.

Secondly, political trials can have a *symbolic value* in enabling the state to signal to opponents that it is upping the stakes of political struggle. In a society such as Britain's – where the state does not act in a dictatorial way but is subject to democratic constraints and tries to secure legitimacy for its programmes rather than to rule by edict – political trials of all sorts can be a valuable way of exercising social control by making a public example. This is in keeping with the whole notion of using punishment under the law to act as a deterrent, and explains why it is 'leaders' (or at least those publicly prominent) who are invariably put on trial. Prosecutors have adopted a strategy of pursuing those they perceive to be 'ringleaders', even when thousands of others could equally have been charged with specific offences.

Third, high profile political trials can serve to *discredit* political opponents. They are in effect branded 'criminals', a categorization which makes it much easier to damage their credibility in the eyes of the public.

Fourth, even if they are not ultimately fully successful in the sense of securing a conviction, political trials can *exhaust* dissidents. For instance, although I gained a moral victory in being acquitted of the three more serious conspiracy counts I faced in my 1972 trial over sports apartheid, the whole affair literally exhausted me, and affected the level of my political involvement for some time afterwards. One of those most closely involved in the defence reckoned that he had been 'permanently drained' of some of his vitality. Apart from the length of the actual proceedings – four weeks in this case, though political trials have a habit of being even longer – which are themselves demanding and tiring, there are months of preparation (with the lawyers) for the defendant. Crispin Aubrey, one of the accused in the 'A.B.C.' official secrecy case in 1977–8, described how time-consuming preparation of the defence had been, and how the personal lives of all three defendants had been seriously disrupted.[2] They too obtained a 'moral' victory in the end, receiving trifling sentences. But the advantage to the state was to have made an example to all other journalists and investigators.

Linked with the exhausting factor is a fifth advantage: bringing a political charge forces political energy to be *diverted* on to a particular *legal* battle rather than the original *political* target. This may be double-edged, because while the practice (which became virtually the norm) during the 1970s of waging aggressive defence campaigns, with publicity, meetings and so on, serves to highlight the political bias of such trials, and can therefore be said to 'expose' the system, the fact remains that relatively large resources and levels of organizational energy are needed to wage such campaigns – and these could well have been directed into political struggle with more impact.

If then we can see these five advantages to the authorities in staging political trials – 'intimidating', 'discrediting' or 'exhausting' defendants, 'diverting' political struggle and acting 'symbolically' – what of the disadvantages?

Many of the 1970s political trials provoked serious public disquiet, even in circles not sympathetic to the views of the defendants. There was critical media comment on almost all of them, the exceptions being those involving the I.R.A.; even defendants in the Angry Brigade bombs cases won some sympathy from the press for the contradictory and oppressive nature of the conspiracy charge they faced. Indeed, the fashion for conspiracy charges in the early 1970s discredited the charge itself, and the ensuing political pressure forced a reform in conspiracy law under the 1977 Criminal Law Act. In short, there is a calculated risk in mounting a political prosecution, which helps to explain why such discretion has been exercised over who should or should not be charged.

Political trials have also had a habit of revealing themselves as oppressive, particularly when the defendants have chosen to defend themselves and to fight the case partly on political grounds by making a direct appeal to the jury. The very fact that a trial is 'political' leaves the prosecution vulnerable to having the tables turned on it by an astute defence. This occurred, for example, in the *Oz* case in 1971, my conspiracy trial in 1972, the Prescott–Purdie case in 1971 and the trial of the British Withdrawal from Northern Ireland Campaigners in 1975. Defendants taking their own cases are able to slice through the maze of court rules and protocol and get their message across to the jury, whether or not it is relevant or admissible under normal court criteria. Thus the jury can be made aware of the underlying political nature of the trial. For instance, three of the 'Mangrove Nine' who defended themselves in their 1971 trial 'gave the jury their view of police methods, race relations, colonial history, council politics, the prosecution's and judge's conduct of the trial and so forth – something lawyers could not attempt. The brilliance with which the three defended themselves over a ten-week long trial showed . . . that barristers, for a political trial at least, are not indispensable.'[3] (Significantly, the Mangrove defendants were acquitted on the main charges.) The 1982 'Bradford Twelve' trial was another example of a successful decision by some of the accused to defend themselves. By doing so they were able to describe to the jury the circumstances of racial tension during the summer of 1981 which led blacks in Bradford to feel they had to prepare to defend themselves against racist attacks. Given the technically strong evidence against them, it is difficult to see how they could have been acquitted without what amounted to a political appeal in court. The problem for the judge presiding over trials where the accused take their own defence in this way is to control them without antagonizing the jury into seeing the defendant as the 'underdog'.

The judge also has the added difficulty that defendants cannot be challenged as to what is their defence 'in law'. In my conspiracy case, for instance, I did not really have any defence 'in law' because of the oppressive way the conspiracy charge was framed, and this was one of the main reasons why it was decided that I should dispense with the services of counsel half-way through the case. As a non-lawyer I could not be asked to give opinion on the *legal* issues involved, as opposed to the *evidence*.

The same case illustrated another issue in weighing up the balance of advantage to the state in bringing a political charge. It would have been quite open to the authorities to have brought a conspiracy charge against me before or even during the campaign of direct action demonstrations mounted by the Stop the Seventy Tour Committee, of which I was chairman. I had been privately warned by a sympathetic solicitor about this danger, and in fact a former judge, Sir Wintringham Stable, had suggested in a letter to the *Daily Telegraph* in the middle of the campaign that such a charge be brought. But no prosecution *was* brought. This may have reflected a reluctance by the Labour government of the day to be associated with a prosecution against a movement widely supported by the labour movement among others. Furthermore, the modern fashion for conspiracy trials had not yet begun. But another factor must have been a political judgement that it would have been counter-productive to charge one or two leaders in what was a mass campaign in full swing.

It is not easy to make any definitive assessment of the advantages in practice won by the state in bringing particular political trials. Suffice to say that such trials must be seen in their historical context as part of a power battle between classes and groups – a battle in which such trials have been just one device employed by the state, in order to assert authority.

Historically public order control has been a reaction to protest, reflecting an underlying *political* conflict. But the picture is not so clear when protest assumes a 'criminal' rather than a 'political' form: then the issues can become confused, with a political cause being given a criminal label. Dissidence can then be presented as being 'against the law' or 'anti-police', with the grievances or issues that gave rise to it being submerged or pushed into the background. For the authorities there are obvious advantages in this, and it is clear that 'the "criminalization" of political and economic conflicts is a central aspect of the exercise of social control'.[4]

Political trials are part of such 'criminalizing' of political activity, just as the whole apparatus of the law can be used to tackle a political problem, for example, by 'criminalizing' the black community; or 'criminalizing' the basis of the conflict in Northern Ireland.

· POLITICAL ROLE OF THE LAW ·

It is therefore as well to re-emphasize that political trials should be viewed against the background of the role of the law and legal system in exercising political or social control. This controlling function is the key one. It makes a nonsense of the traditional view that the judge is 'like a political, economic and social eunuch'.[5] The evidence presented in this book supports Griffith's essential thesis on the myth of judicial impartiality, and confirms the fact that judges perform a key political function in society and one, furthermore, that is essentially reactionary, illiberal and conservative.

The law may act in a 'positive' sense to quell or control political dissent. Or it may act in a 'negative' sense to prevent powerless or disadvantaged groups from asserting their rights beyond a point which begins to challenge the basis of society: in a capitalist society, for example, tenants' rights are submerged under the weight of property interests.[6] Tenants enjoy legal protection only up to the point where the profit motive is severely threatened. Much the same points could be made of workers' rights. For although laws in Britain 'are established in a universal and abstract, rather than class-specific form', they are nevertheless 'circumscribed, with varying degrees of rigour, by capitalist relations of production'.[7]

But to acknowledge that the operation of our laws reflects dominant capitalist interests is not to suggest some crude model of how the legal system operates. For the law is a subtle animal.

Thus, while judges can act in a blatantly reactionary way, the judicial process may also 'put a check on arbitrariness or idiosyncracy which sections of the ruling class may exhibit in the exercise of power'.[8] This was seen, for example, in the farce of the A.B.C. official secrecy trial, where the judge was clearly unimpressed with the behaviour of the government in bringing the charge on such a clumsy basis. But judges are acting no *less* politically in seeking to ensure that unpopular or embarrassing errors are corrected.

Judges may also help to shape public opinion and social values by their closing trial speeches. This is shown in a series of 'mugging' cases where remarks by judges made headlines – behaviour which has been described as 'structuring public perception' of issues.[9] At the same time, judges may respond to popular moods if they feel that Parliament has gone 'ahead' of public opinion on an issue, as has occurred over some race relations cases. A comparable example was the judicial response to the undoubted concern about so-called 'permissiveness' in the late 1960s – the period of the Hippie movement and of experimentation by young people with 'alternative lifestyles', including challenging traditional sexual mores. It was also a time of legal reform under the Labour government, notably on capital punishment, divorce, homosexuality and abortion. There is clear evidence that judges started to clamp down despite these liberalizing measures. In 1969, for example, Justice Lawton questioned whether what he saw as 'leniency with the young' was 'best for the public'. He was worried by what he saw as 'all this violence that young people are indulging in today'. Significantly he added: *'Word has got to go around* that anyone who commits this kind of offence has got to lose his liberty'[10] (my italics).

Judges here have tended to reflect what has been described by one legal analyst as 'the morality of middle Britain'.[11] While it may well be suggested that this is perfectly reasonable given their mediating position in the system, it has political and social consequences which should be acknowledged. For instance, the trial under the obscenity laws of the young people who produced the 'alternative paper', *Oz*, and the vitriolic attitude of the judge and prosecutors to the defendants, contrasted starkly with the failure to act against pornography shops in Soho. As has been aptly said, 'the latter pandered to the tastes of established society, whilst the former wanted to eradicate this in favour of a counter culture'.[12]

The problem here is that judges may not simply be reflecting what they see as the values of 'middle Britain', but reinforcing them as well. Furthermore, since they have such huge discretion, they are able to determine on a selective basis which particular values they wish to project. In this respect it is interesting to note that one study of the police has argued that the behaviour of the force is 'governed more by popular morality than by the letter of the law'.[13] It would appear that this fits the behaviour of judges as well.

For it has to be remembered that the legal system has the dual function of exercising social control and helping to obtain legitimacy for the state's grip on society. And because there is such discretion built into the system, there is considerable scope for judges to act as they choose, reflecting their own beliefs. In this way, the state is not monolithic. For example, in Chapter 11, we saw how a private prosecution of National

Front members who had violently broken up a meeting in Manchester was successful in gaining a conviction, even though the police and the D.P.P. had previously refused to proceed. But if the state does not necessarily act in a machine-like manner over law enforcement, that is not necessarily as reassuring as it might appear. One key problem is the almost complete lack of parliamentary control over the judiciary, the police and the security services, especially in political trials – one of the most consistent themes running through the evidence reviewed in this book. The absence of democratic accountability is a key feature of the legal system, from decisions to do deals with 'supergrasses', to official secrecy prosecutions, to the way in which for fifty years judicial decisions have favoured natural parents over the rights of children as laid down in the 1926 Adoption Act.

However, under Conservative governments there is evidence of judges playing a much more supportive role. Statements by judges made at the time when the Tories were introducing what was to become the anti-union 1980 Employment Act suggested that they were keen to 'push the Conservative government in what they saw as the right direction'.[14] Delivering judgement in a case where transport workers had blacked a ship to try to get its workers paid decent wages, Lord Diplock spoke of the danger of wage demands bringing down 'the fabric of the present economic system'.[15] During the 1980 steelworkers' strike, an injunction was taken out to stop extending industrial action to the private steel companies, and Lord Diplock complained that the immunity given to trade unions was 'intrinsically repugnant', even though this immunity had expressly been granted by Parliament back in 1906.[16] In the same case, Lord Edmund-Davies described the law as 'unpalatable to many', and Lord Keith saw trade unionists as 'privileged persons' able to 'bring about disastrous consequences with legal impunity'.[17] By giving vent to their political views in this way, these senior judges appear to have been trying to increase pressure for further restrictions on trade unions – which duly occurred in 1982, union immunities being one of the main targets of the latest Tory measure.

But the tension between Parliament and the judiciary has been sharpest during periods when Labour has been in office. For example, both judges and the police took the view that Labour's reform of trade union law in 1974–6 had been too lenient on picketing. Criticizing pickets outside a hospital in 1979, Lord Salmon said that if the pickets were acting within the law then 'surely the time has come for it to be altered'.[18]

During the 1978–9 'winter of discontent', police chiefs lobbied the Labour government for a tightening up of the laws on picketing, their views being given wide media coverage which increased public pressure for such restrictions.[19] Again these were introduced by the Tories, in 1980.

· JUDICIAL INDEPENDENCE AND POLITICAL TRIALS ·

All this tends to confirm the view that the judiciary occupies an 'autonomous domain' between legislature and the executive which 'may become the site of conflicts within the ruling class'.[20] Another socialist critique of the judiciary refers to 'the autonomization' of the law in a capitalist society such as Britain,[21] suggesting the validity of the central theme running through this book of the judiciary as a state agency with its *own* political interests.

Political trials highlight the fact that the judiciary does have an 'independent' role – but not the kind of independence popularly supposed and officially projected. The conventional wisdom implies an impartial independence, and a judicial activity that is therefore solely a technical matter. By contrast this book has shown a different kind of independence: the judiciary is not merely independent of popular democratic accountability, it also has its *own political interests* to pursue. It is thus a political agency in its own right, constrained certainly by the rest of the state apparatus and reflecting broadly the dominant interests of capitalist society, but nevertheless 'independent' to pursue its own political and bureaucratic objectives. The police and the security services are similarly politically independent, generally, though not always, acting in concert with the courts.

Such political independence has become increasingly prominent over the past decade, as the storms of economic crisis have gathered. Looking back at the industrial revolution in the early nineteenth century, we can see that it produced a requirement for new laws and new state agencies, notably the police, to manage its socially disruptive results. It would appear that as the economic system is restructured in the 1980s – this time partly by a technological revolution – the agencies responsible for law enforcement and administration will be required to perform an even more powerful political function. If that occurs – and the development of the law and order state suggests that it has already begun – then there is every prospect of political trials becoming the norm rather than the exception.

In that event it will be necessary for the victims of political prosecutions to 'go political' themselves. Since there is a seamless web between the political objectives of the authorities and the use of the courts to advance these, defendants in political trials are justified in trying to pressure the courts politically. And the experience of the 1970s showed that political activity around such trials *does* influence the result.

The formation of defence committees, and, in the case of the black community at least, the mobilization of community campaign networks to support defendants, undoubtedly increases the pressure on the prosecutors and the courts to act with circumspection. It also helps create a political climate in which either an acquittal or a lighter sentence becomes more possible. Defence campaigns have been most effective when they have attacked either the charge itself or the motives for bringing it rather than the pros and cons of the evidence in question; for instance the busy campaign around the A.B.C. trial did much to discredit official secrecy charges.

While defence committees are obviously constrained by sub judice rules, they are not trapped by normal legal etiquette, which can be such an inhibiting factor on lawyers when defending clients in political trials: too many barristers and solicitors tend to play the defence in 'straight' criminal terms when their clients would be far better served by an openly political stance complementing a conventional legal defence.

Leafleting outside the court, organizing public meetings beforehand, producing background material, staging demonstrations, winning support from political groups and trade unions – all these have a role to play. For such activity has almost never been counterproductive. On the contrary, it has helped expose the reality of a trial that is political. Ultimately, if the state wishes to 'up the stakes' by bringing political trials to quell political opposition or to deal with a political problem, then defendants need to respond in kind. There cannot be one law for judges and prosecutors and another for defendants. If the former are prepared to carry their politics into the courtroom – as they clearly are – then so should the accused.

REFERENCES

CHAPTER I: LAW AND THE PEOPLE

1. *Time Out*, 14–20 December 1979.
2. For example, *Guardian*, 7 December 1979; *Daily Mail*, 7 December 1979.
3. For a good analysis of this see Francis Cripps *et al.*, *Manifesto* (Pan, 1981).
4. Richard Crossman, *Diaries of a Cabinet Minister*, Vols. 1–3 (Cape, 1975–7); Barbara Castle, *The Castle Diaries 1974–6* (Weidenfeld, 1980); Joe Haines, *The Politics of Power* (Cape, 1977); and Brian Sedgemore, *The Secret Constitution* (Hodder, 1980).
5. Sedgemore, op. cit., p. 11.
6. ibid., p. 32.
7. ibid., p. 34.
8. Keith Middlemas, *Politics in an Industrial Society* (Deutsch, 1979).
9. *The Journalist*, August 1980.
10. Ralph Miliband, *The State in Capitalist Society* (Weidenfeld and Nicolson, 1969), p. 120.
11. Miliband, op. cit., pp. 120–21.
12. E. P. Thompson, 'Introduction', *Review of Security and the State*, edited by State Research (Julian Friedmann, 1978), p. 5.
13. A. V. Dicey, *Law and Public Opinion in England during the Nineteenth Century* (Macmillan, 1914), pp. 12–13.
14. Miliband, op. cit., pp. 144–5. See also John Griffith, *The Politics of the Judiciary* (Fontana, 1981), Ch. 5.
15. Community Development Project, *Limits of the Law* (C.D.P. Inter Project Editorial Team, 1977).
16. ibid, p. 8.
17. See Patricia Hewitt, *The Abuse of Power* (Martin Robertson, 1981) and Barry Cox, *Civil Liberties in Britain* (Penguin, 1975).
18. C.D.P., op. cit., pp. 24, 47, 52.
19. See Stuart Hall, *Drifting into a Law and Order Society* (Cobden Trust, 1980).
20. Report of an Inquiry by Lord Scarman, *The Brixton Disorders*, Cmnd. 8427 (H.M.S.O., November 1981).
21. Kevin Boyle *et al.*, *Ten Years on in Northern Ireland* (Cobden Trust, 1980), pp. 107–8.

22. John Dearlove, *The Reorganization of British Local Government* (Cambridge University Press, 1979), p. 263.
23. William A. Robson, *The District Auditor* (Fabian Tract No. 214, June 1925), p. 3.
24. Noreen Branson, *Poplarism, 1919–25* (Lawrence & Wishart, 1979), p. 177.
25. Quoted in Robson, op. cit., p. 13.
26. David Skinner and Julia Langdon, *The Story of Clay Cross* (Spokesman, 1974).
27. *Guardian*, 15 February 1982.
28. *Labour Weekly*, 12 March 1982.
29. *Guardian*, 10 February 1982.
30. *The Times*, 3 April 1982.
31. *New Society*, 6 December 1979.
32. C. H. Rolph, in Dulan Barber and Giles Gordon (eds.), *Members of the Jury* (Wildwood House, 1976), p. 111.
33. Theodore L. Becker (ed.), *Political Trials* (New York, Bobbs-Merrill, 1971), p. xi.
34. ibid., pp. xvi, xi.

CHAPTER 2: POLITICAL POLICING

1. See Tony Bunyan, *The Political Police in Britain* (Julian Friedmann, 1976), Ch. 2.
2. Report of an Inquiry by Lord Scarman, *The Brixton Disorders*, Cmnd. 8427 (H.M.S.O., November 1981), para. 4.70.
3. Tony Gilbert and Kay Beauchamp, *Only One Died* (London, 1975), p. 107.
4. Quoted by Robert Reiner, *The Blue Coated Worker* (Cambridge University Press, 1978), pp. 108–9.
5. A. F. Wilcox, *The Decision to Prosecute* (Butterworth, 1972), pp. 47–60.
6. Scarman, op. cit., para. 4.58.
7. Gillian Susan Morris, 'The Police and Industrial Emergencies', *The Industrial Law Journal*, Vol. 9, No. 1 (March 1980), p. 3.
8. Reiner, op. cit., p. 220.
9. ibid., pp. 220–21.
10. ibid., pp. 225–6.
11. J. F. Robinson, *Catching Criminals* (Police Review Publishing Company, 1978), pp. 19–21.
12. David Powis, *The Signs of Crime: A Field Manual for Police* (McGraw Hill, 1977).

13. Remarks at a conference, 'What Sort of Police Force Does London Need?', 15 March 1980.
14. Institute of Race Relations, *Police Against Black People* (I.R.R., 1979), p. 30.
15. *State Research*, No. 13 (August/September 1979).
16. *Now!*, 16 November 1979.
17. *Guardian*, 17 March 1982.
18. *The Times*, 18 March 1982.
19. T. A. Critchley, *A History of the Police* (Constable, 1967), p. 50.
20. ibid., p. 127.
21. ibid., p. 138.
22. Bunyan, op. cit., p. 66.
23. ibid.
24. Critchley, op. cit., p. 163.
25. Tony Bunyan, 'The Police Against the People', *Race and Class*, Nos. 2/3 (Autumn/Winter 1981/2), p. 157.
26. Critchley, op. cit., p. 163.
27. Bunyan (1976), Ch. 3.
28. Sir Basil Thomson, *Queer People* (Hodder & Stoughton, 1922), quoted in Bunyan (1976), pp. 113–14.
29. Bunyan (1976), p. 121.
30. *New Statesman*, 1 February 1980.
31. Cmnd. 7863 (H.M.S.O., April 1980).
32. *Brownlie's Law of Public Order and National Security* (Butterworth, 1981), p. 307.
33. *Hansard*, 25 April 1978.
34. *Marxism Today*, April 1982, p. 10.
35. Quoted in L. H. Leigh, *Police Powers in England and Wales* (Butterworth, 1975), p. 415.
36. *New Statesman*, 1 February 1980.
37. ibid.
38. *Guardian*, 24 February 1982.
39. *Time Out*, 20 September 1974.
40. Bunyan (1976), pp. 141–2.
41. *Time Out*, 18 May 1979.
42. *State Research*, No. 12 (June/July 1979).
43. *New Statesman*, 20 August 1979.
44. *Guardian*, 20 September 1979.
45. *State Research*, No. 14 (October/November 1979).
46. *Evening Standard*, 4 September 1979.
47. Duncan Campbell, 'Society Under Surveillance', in Peter Hain (ed.), *Policing the Police*, Vol. 2 (John Calder, 1980), p. 120.
48. ibid., pp. 65–145.

49. Patricia Hewitt, *The Abuse of Power* (Martin Robertson, 1981), p. 32.
50. *Guardian*, 31 May 1979.
51. ibid., 19 March 1981.
52. Reiner, op. cit., p. 251.
53. *State Research*, No. 14 (October/November 1979).
54. ibid.
55. Reiner, op. cit., p. 19.
56. ibid., p. 33.
57. ibid., p. 34.
58. ibid., p. 46.
59. *State Research*, No. 5 (April/May 1978).
60. ibid.
61. Martin Kettle, 'The Politics of Policing and the Policing of Politics', in Peter Hain (ed.), op. cit., p. 14.
62. *Sunday Times*, 28 March 1982.
63. *New Society*, 18 March 1982.
64. *Guardian*, 11 March 1982.
65. ibid., 3 March 1982.
66. ibid., 27 February 1982.
67. ibid., 18 March 1982.
68. *State Research*, No. 13 (August/September 1979).
69. *Time Out*, 11 January 1980.
70. *Guardian*, 19 March 1982.
71. John Alderson, *Policing Freedom* (MacDonald & Evans, 1979).
72. B.B.C. Television, *Question Time*, 16 October 1979.
73. See Peter Hain, *Neighbourhood Participation* (Temple Smith, 1980).
74. Hain (ed.), op. cit., Vol. 2, p. 51.
75. *Guardian*, 11 February 1980.
76. *State Research*, No. 19 (August/September 1980).
77. ibid.
78. ibid.
79. See J. D. Devlin, *Police Procedure, Administration and Organisation* (Butterworth, 1966), p. 145.
80. Home Office Circular ES11 (22 March 1972), quoted in *State Research*, No. 19 (August/September 1980).
81. ibid.

CHAPTER 3: THE PROSECUTORS

1. For a fuller description see *Morning Star*, 25 January 1978.
2. John Brewer and John Styles (eds.), *An Ungovernable People* (Hutchinson, 1980), p. 18.

3. Douglas Hay, 'Property, authority and the criminal law', in D. Hay, *et al.*, *Albion's Fatal Tree* (Penguin, 1977), p. 48.
4. Michael McConville and John Baldwin, *Courts, Prosecutions and Convictions* (Oxford, Clarendon Press, 1981).
5. A. F. Wilcox, *The Decision to Prosecute* (Butterworth, 1972), pp. 41–2.
6. *New Society*, 13 May 1982.
7. McConville and Baldwin, op. cit., p. 189.
8. Wilcox, op. cit., p. 19.
9. ibid., p. 20.
10. *Guardian*, 2 June 1980.
11. Wilcox, op. cit., p. 18.
12. *Guardian*, 2 June 1980.
13. ibid.
14. *Sunday Times*, 13 January 1980.
15. *The Times*, 4 February 1982.
16. John Bull, Lewis Chester and Roy Perrott, *Cops and Robbers* (Penguin, 1979), p. 77.
17. *State Research*, Vol. 4, No. 21 (December 1980/January 1981).
18. *Daily Mail*, 6 June 1980; *Sunday Times*, 18 November 1979.
19. *The Times*, 9 October 1976; *Guardian*, 2 November 1976.
20. *Guardian*, 21 April 1978.
21. *New Statesman*, 18 January 1980.
22. *Guardian*, 21 June 1980.
23. Wilcox, op. cit., p. 20.
24. Robert Spicer, *Conspiracy* (Lawrence & Wishart, 1981), p. 147.
25. Peter Wallington, 'Criminal Conspiracy and Industrial Conflict', *The Industrial Law Journal*, Vol. 4, No. 2 (June 1975), p. 72.
26. Martin Bailey, *Oilgate* (Coronet, 1979).
27. Quoted in Wilcox, op. cit., p. 21.
28. Thom Young, *Incitement to Disaffection* (Cobden Trust, 1976), p. 19.
29. See Tony Bunyan, *The Political Police in Britain* (Julian Friedmann, 1976), p. 113.
30. Wilcox, op. cit., p. 25.
31. Bunyan, op. cit., p. 38.
32. Wilcox, op. cit., p. 22.
33. ibid., p. 29.
34. David Marquand, *Ramsay MacDonald* (Cape, 1977), pp. 365–70.
35. Wilcox, op. cit., p. 23.
36. ibid., p. 27.
37. *Guardian*, 10 January 1981.
38. Wilcox, op. cit., p. 112.

CHAPTER 4: JUDGES AND THEIR COURTS

1. See Peter Hain, *Mistaken Identity* (Quartet, 1976), pp. 90–102.
2. J. A. G. Griffith, *The Politics of the Judiciary* (Fontana, 1981), p. 19.
3. ibid., p. 20.
4. D. N. Pritt, *The Apparatus of the Law* (Lawrence & Wishart, 1971), p. 48.
5. Albie Sachs and Joan Hoff Wilson, *Sexism and the Law* (Martin Robertson, 1978), p. 42.
6. Griffith, op. cit., p. 26.
7. ibid.
8. See John Brewer, 'The Wilkites and the law 1763–74', in John Brewer and John Styles (eds.), *An Ungovernable People* (Hutchinson, 1980), pp. 157–60.
9. Robert Stevens, *Law and Politics* (Weidenfeld & Nicolson, 1979), p. 107.
10. ibid., p. 196.
11. *Listener*, 6 June 1974.
12. Griffith, op. cit., p. 27.
13. *New Society*, 22 November 1979.
14. *Observer*, 31 July 1977.
15. *Guardian*, 14 January 1978.
16. See Griffith, op. cit., pp. 27–32.
17. C. H. Rolph, *The Trial of Lady Chatterley* (Penguin, 1961), p. 17.
18. *Hansard*, 11 February 1982.
19. Christopher Bagley, 'The welfare of the child – An examination of judicial opinion about medical and social work evidence in adoption cases', *British Journal of Social Work*, Vol. 3 (1973), pp. 207–17.
20. Griffith, op. cit., p. 34.
21. Quoted in Ralph Miliband, *The State in Capitalist Society* (Weidenfeld, 1972), p. 139.
22. Quoted in Anthony Sampson, *New Anatomy of Britain* (Hodder, 1971), p. 344.
23. Griffith, op. cit., p. 34.
24. Miliband, op. cit., p. 142.
25. Quoted in Griffith, op. cit., p. 199.
26. According to a 'close colleague', *Guardian*, 26 November 1981. See also an article by Lord Scarman, *New Society*, 15 November 1979.
27. Lord Scarman, *English Law – The New Dimension* (Stevens, 1974), p. 3.
28. David Pannick, 'Why judges should stand up and be judged by the rest', *Guardian*, 13 August 1979.
29. Extracts from his speech reported in *Socialist Challenge*, 2 February 1978.
30. Bob Roshier and Harvey Teff, *Law and Society in England* (Tavistock, 1980), p. 57.

31. ibid., p. 5.
32. Barry Cox, *Civil Liberties in Britain* (Penguin, 1975), p. 57.
33. The Oxford case is described in the *Guardian*, 22 January 1982, and the Nottingham case in the *Daily Mirror*, 17 February 1982.
34. *Guardian*, 17 December 1973.
35. ibid.
36. *Morning Star*, 3 December 1975.
37. Quoted in David Leigh, *The Frontiers of Secrecy* (Junction Books, 1980), p. 158.
38. Quoted in Cox, op. cit., p. 71.
39. W. T. Murphy and R. W. Rawlings, 'After the Ancien Regime: The Writing of Judgements in the House of Lords 1979–80', *Modern Law Review*, Vol. 44 (1981).
40. *Sunday Telegraph*, 16 September 1979.
41. Sachs and Hoff Wilson, op. cit., pp. 14–22.
42. ibid., pp. 25–6.
43. See ibid., pp. 41–2, for an analysis of this point.
44. ibid., p. 48.
45. ibid., p. 136.
46. ibid., pp. 225–6.
47. Julia Brophy and Carol Smart, 'From Disregard to Disrepute: The Position of Women in Family Law', *Feminist Review* 9 (Autumn 1981), pp. 3–16.
48. See Patricia Hewitt, *The Abuse of Power* (Martin Robertson, 1981), pp. 171–86.
49. ibid., p. 172.
50. *Guardian*, 28 December 1979.
51. *Guardian*, 6 January 1982.
52. Quoted in *Spare Rib*, No. 114 (January 1982), p. 6.
53. See *New Society*, 4 February 1982.
54. L.W.T., *Weekend World*, 14 February 1982.
55. See Barbara Toner, *The Facts of Rape* (Arrow, 1977).
56. Leigh, op. cit., p. 136.
57. Quoted by Helenna Kennedy, 'Women at the Bar', in Robert Hazell (ed.), *The Bar on Trial* (Quartet, 1978), p. 158.
58. *Guardian*, 15 March 1982.
59. *Spare Rib*, No. 116 (March 1982).
60. Quoted by Kennedy, op. cit., p. 157.
61. ibid.
62. *Spare Rib*, No. 114 (January 1982).
63. *New Statesman*, 26 March 1982.
64. Ruth Hall, Selma James and Judit Kertesz, *The Rapist Who Pays The Rent* (Falling Wall Press, December 1981), p. 9.
65. ibid., p. 10.

66. ibid.
67. *Spare Rib*, No. 113 (December 1981).
68. Hall *et al.*, op. cit., p. 12.
69. ibid., p. 28.
70. ibid., p. 30.
71. *Guardian*, 21 December 1981.
72. Quoted in *New Statesman*, 15 January 1982.
73. *Guardian*, 12 December 1982.
74. 'Further Joint Opinion re: The Budget of I.L.E.A.' (I.L.E.A., 8 February 1982).
75. Justice, *Lawyers and the Legal System* (Justice, 1977), p. 4.
76. See Michael Zander, *Legal Services for the Community* (Temple Smith, 1978).
77. Howard Levenson, *The Price of Justice* (Cobden Trust, 1981), p. 81.
78. John Baldwin and Michael McConville, *Negotiated Justice* (Martin Robertson, 1977), p. 109.
79. Roshier and Teff, pp. 116–17.
80. Baldwin and McConville, op. cit., p. 19.
81. Roshier and Teff, op. cit., p. 116.
82. ibid., p. 223.
83. Quoted in Michael McConville and John Baldwin, *Courts, Prosecution and Conviction* (Oxford, Clarendon Press, 1981), p. 11.
84. Joanna Shapland, *Between Conviction and Sentence* (Routledge, 1981), p. 1.
85. Sachs and Hoff Wilson, op. cit., p. 226.
86. *Guardian*, 22 November 1978.
87. A. Bottoms and J. McLean, *Defendants in the Criminal Law* (Routledge, 1976).
88. Tom Hayden, *Trial* (New York, Holt, Rinehart & Winston, 1970), p. 73.
89. For example, Baldwin and McConville, op. cit., pp. 85–6.
90. Community Development Project, *The Limits of the Law* (C.D.P. Inter Project Editorial Team, 1977), p. 16.
91. A. Patterson, *Legal Aid as a Social Service* (Cobden Trust, 1970).
92. *New Society*, 15 November 1979.
93. Quoted in Griffith, op. cit., pp. 212–13.
94. See *Tribune*, 20 November 1981.
95. Griffith, op. cit., p. 215.
96. ibid., pp. 230–31.

CHAPTER 5: MAGISTRATES

1. Elizabeth Burney, *J.P.: Magistrate, Court and Community* (Hutchinson, 1979), p. 10.
2. W. R. Cornish, *The Jury* (Allen Lane, 1968), p. 139.
3. ibid.
4. Esther Moir, *The Justice of the Peace* (Penguin, 1969), p. 167.
5. Burney, op. cit., p. 53.
6. ibid., p. 57.
7. ibid., p. 58.
8. ibid., pp. 64–5.
9. ibid., p. 62.
10. ibid., pp. 65–9.
11. John Baldwin, 'The Social Composition of the Magistracy', *British Journal of Criminology*, Vol. 16, No. 2 (April 1976), p. 174.
12. *Coventry Evening Telegraph*, 13 November 1981.
13. T. A. Critchley, *A History of the Police* (Constable, 1977), p. 20.
14. Pat Carlen, *Magistrates' Justice* (Martin Robertson, 1976), pp. 129–30.
15. For example, Burney, op. cit., pp. 187–8.
16. ibid., p. 186.
17. *Bournemouth Evening Echo*, 22 June 1972.
18. *Guardian*, 9 January 1980.
19. *Guardian*, 15 January 1980.
20. Roger Hood, *Sentencing in Magistrates' Courts* (Stevens, 1962).
21. Radical Alternatives to Prison (Bristol Group), *A Scandal within a Scandal: Rates of Imprisonment in England and Wales* (Bristol, 1982).
22. *See Alternative London Guide* (Otherwise Press, 1982).
23. *Guardian*, 8 February 1982.
24. *Guardian*, 23 January 1982.
25. *Guardian*, 16 March 1971.
26. Burney, op. cit., p. 212.
27. Reported in *Socialist Challenge*, 1 November 1977.
28. See *Southall 23 April 1979* (National Council for Civil Liberties, 1980), and *The Death of Blair Peach* (N.C.C.L., 1980).
29. *Southall 342* (Bulletin of the Defence Committee, November 1979). But see the N.C.C.L. *Southall* pamphlet, op. cit., pp. 108–10, for qualifying comments on these figures.
30. *The Leveller*, November 1979.
31. Legal Action Group, Bulletin, December 1979.
32. *Observer*, 16 December 1979.
33. This was revealed at a meeting for Labour J.P.s called by the Labour Campaign for Criminal Justice.

CHAPTER 6: THE JURY

1. See John Griffith and Harriet Harman, *Justice Deserted* (N.C.C.L., 1979), p. 10. Also, Lord Devlin, *Trial by Jury* (Stevens, 1971), pp. 7–12.
2. John F. McEldowney, 'Stand by for the Crown', *Criminal Law Review* (May 1979).
3. Quoted in W. R. Cornish, *The Jury* (Allen Lane, 1968), p. 128.
4. ibid., pp. 128–9.
5. Quoted by Cal Winslow, 'The Sussex Smugglers', in D. Hay *et al.*, *Albion's Fatal Tree* (Penguin, 1977), p. 165.
6. E. P. Thompson, *Whigs and Hunters* (Penguin, 1970), pp. 74–8.
7. ibid., p. 151.
8. See John Brewer, 'The Wilkites and the Law 1763–74', in John Brewer and John Styles (eds.), *An Ungovernable People* (Hutchinson, 1980), p. 155.
9. Quoted by Phil Jeffries and Duncan Campbell, *New Statesman*, 28 September 1979.
10. ibid.
11. McEldowney, op. cit.
12. Home Office, *Report of the Committee on Jury Service*, Cmnd. 2623 (H.M.S.O., April 1965).
13. Devlin, op. cit., p. 20.
14. Quoted in Tony Bunyan, *The Political Police in Britain* (Julian Friedmann, 1976), p. 89.
15. National Council for Civil Liberties, Briefing Paper by Cedric Thornberry (mimeo, 1966).
16. *The Times*, 19 October 1966.
17. *Listener*, 8 October 1973.
18. Quoted in Bunyan, op. cit., p. 90.
19. *New Law Journal* (1966), pp. 1928–9.
20. *Listener*, 8 October 1973.
21. *Guardian*, 21 July 1977.
22. *Observer*, 16 March 1975, quoted in Bunyan, op. cit., p. 90.
23. Quoted in David Leigh, *The Frontiers of Secrecy* (Junction Books, 1980), p. 157.
24. *Daily Telegraph*, 5 October 1973.
25. See Derek Humphry and Michael Ward, *Passports and Politics* (Penguin, 1974).
26. Derek Humphry, *The Cricket Conspiracy* (N.C.C.L., 1975), p. 124.
27. See Michael Zander, *Guardian*, 12 April 1976, and David Leigh, op. cit., pp. 137–8.

28. Peter Hain, *Mistaken Identity* (Quartet, 1976).

29. *New Statesman*, 27 July 1979. See also David Leigh, op. cit., pp. 129–30 and 138–53.

30. See Lewis Chester, Magnus Linklater and David May, *Jeremy Thorpe: a Secret Life* (Fontana, 1979), and Barrie Penrose and Roger Courtiour, *The Pencourt File* (Secker & Warburg, 1978).

31. John Baldwin and Michael McConville, *Jury Trials* (Oxford, 1979). See also the criticism by Michael Zander, *Guardian*, 8 March 1979.

32. *Sunday Times*, 7 March 1976.

33. *Guardian*, 2 November 1977.

34. Quoted in David Leigh, op. cit., p. 135.

35. *Hansard*, 28 June 1977, clmns. 640–54.

36. *New Statesman*, 29 July 1977.

37. *Sunday Times*, 18 June 1972.

38. *Guardian*, 26 March 1974.

39. Griffith and Harman, op. cit., p. 22.

40. *Hansard*, Written Answers, 19 May 1975.

41. *The Times*, 11 October 1978.

42. *Observer*, 11 November 1979.

43. *Guardian*, 4 October 1979.

44. See David Leigh, op. cit., p. 163.

45. *Hansard*, 25 January 1979, clmn. 665.

46. *Sunday Times*, 1 October 1978.

47. *The Times*, 11 October 1978.

48. *Guardian*, 15 August 1979.

49. *Daily Telegraph*, 16 August 1979.

50. *Guardian*, 12 September 1979.

51. *State Research Bulletin*, No. 14 (October/November 1979).

52. For an account by one of the journalists involved, see David Leigh, op. cit., pp. 169–78.

53. *Guardian*, 10 October 1979.

54. *Sunday Telegraph*, 23 September 1979.

55. *Daily Telegraph*, 28 September 1979.

56. *Guardian*, 16 January 1979.

57. *Woman*, 29 May 1979.

58. ibid.

59. *Guardian*, 4 March 1980.

60. ibid., 25 April 1980.

61. ibid., 4 June 1980.

62. *Daily Telegraph*, 16 October 1979.

63. *Guardian*, 15 October 1979.

64. *State Research Bulletin*, No. 14 (October/November 1979).

65. *Hansard*, 13 February 1979, clmn. 469.
66. ibid., 22 June 1979, clmn. 18.
67. *Socialist Challenge*, 7 December 1978.
68. Baldwin and McConville, op. cit.
69. Quoted in Cornish, op. cit., p. 113.
70. D. Barber and G. Gordon (eds.), *Members of the Jury* (Wildwood House, 1976), p. 123.
71. Chris Ralph, *The Picket and the Law* (Fabian Research Series 331, 1977), p. 14.
72. *New Statesman*, 3 August 1979.
73. Quoted by David Leigh, op. cit., p. 132.
74. *Morning Star*, 27 November 1979.
75. *Guardian*, 15 March 1980.
76. *The Times*, 27 February 1982.
77. B.B.C. Radio, *The World This Weekend*, 28 February 1982.
78. *Daily Mail*, 3 July 1982; *The Times*, 6 July 1982.
79. Harriet Harman, N.C.C.L.'s legal officer, *Guardian*, 1 September 1980.

CHAPTER 7: CONSPIRACY: AN AGENT OF GOVERNMENT

1. Quoted by Lord Reid and cited in Robert Hazell, *Conspiracy and Civil Liberties* (Bell, 1974), p. 14.
2. Hazell, op. cit., p. 19.
3. See ibid., pp. 13–15, and Geoff Robertson, *Whose Conspiracy?* (National Council for Civil Liberties, 1974).
4. Hazell, op. cit., p. 15.
5. Quoted in Robert Spicer, *Conspiracy* (Lawrence & Wishart, 1981), p. 29.
6. ibid., p. 49.
7. Peter Wallington, 'Criminal Conspiracy and Industrial Conflict', *The Industrial Law Journal*, Vol. 4, No. 2 (June 1975), pp. 83–5.
8. ibid., p. 69, pp. 72–3.
9. Spicer, op. cit., p. 31.
10. ibid., pp. 62–3.
11. ibid., p. 66.
12. Geoff Robertson, 'All Our Conspirators', in Derek Humphry, *The Cricket Conspiracy* (National Council for Civil Liberties, 1975), p. 128.
13. See Humphry, op. cit.
14. ibid., p. 133.
15. Geoff Robertson, *Obscenity* (Weidenfeld & Nicolson, 1979), p. 242.
16. Chris Ralph, *The Picket and the Law* (Fabian Research Series 331, 1977), p. 15.

17. See Hazell, op. cit., Robertson (1974), Humphry, op. cit., Spicer, op. cit., and Tony Bunyan, *The Political Police in Britain* (Julian Friedmann, 1976), pp. 36–51.

18. Quoted in Robertson (1974), p. 40.

19. The Law Commission, Working Paper No. 50: *Inchoate Offences: Conspiracy, Attempt and Incitement* (H.M.S.O., July 1973).

20. Law Commission Report No. 76, *Conspiracy and Criminal Law Reform* (H.M.S.O., March 1976).

21. Peter Wallington, 'The Criminal Law Act 1977', *The Industrial Law Journal*, Vol. 7, No. 1 (March 1978), p. 40.

22. ibid., p. 42.

23. I. Brownlie, *The Law Relating to Public Order* (Butterworth, 1968), p. 90.

24. Wallington (1975), p. 71.

25. C. H. Rolph, 'The Uses of Conspiracy', *New Statesman*, 3 August 1973.

26. Spicer, op. cit., pp. 173–4.

CHAPTER 8: TRADE UNIONISM

1. Joe Rogaly, *Grunwick* (Penguin, 1978), p. 116.

2. Jack Dromey and Graham Taylor, *Grunwick: The Workers' Story* (Lawrence & Wishart, 1978), p. 195.

3. K. W. Wedderburn, 'Labour Law and Labour Relations in Britain', *British Journal of Industrial Relations* (July 1972), p. 25.

4. Chris Ralph, *The Picket and the Law* (Fabian Research Series 331, 1977), p. 9.

5. ibid., p. 10.

6. *Trade Union Immunities*, Cmnd. 8128 (H.M.S.O., 1981), para. 14.

7. Roy Lewis, 'The Historical Development of Labour Law', *British Journal of Industrial Relations* (March 1976), p. 2.

8. Quoted in Henry Pelling, *A History of British Trade Unionism* (Penguin, 1969 edition), p. 25.

9. E. P. Thompson, *The Making of the English Working Class* (Penguin, 1979 edition), p. 199. See also pp. 458–61.

10. Quoted in Lewis, op. cit., p. 2.

11. For a detailed account see Joyce Marlow, *The Tolpuddle Martyrs* (Panther, 1974), pp. 68–71.

12. ibid., p. 81.

13. Quoted in Pelling, op. cit., p. 41.

14. Ken Coates and Tony Topham, *Trade Unions in Britain* (Spokesman, 1980), pp. 268–9.

15. For analysis of this 'abstentionist' tradition in British trade unionism, see Lewis, op. cit., pp. 4, 8–9.

16. See Tony Lane, *The Union Makes Us Strong* (Arrow, 1974), pp. 92–3, and John Saville, 'Trade unions and free labour: the background to the Taff Vale decision', in A. Briggs and J. Saville (eds.), *Essays in Labour History* (Macmillan, 1967), pp. 317–50.
17. See Ralph, op. cit., p. 7.
18. Coates and Topham, op. cit., p. 275.
19. J. A. G. Griffith, *The Politics of the Judiciary* (Fontana, 1981), p. 76.
20. ibid., p. 77.
21. For accounts of the dispute see Dromey and Taylor, op. cit., and Rogaly, op. cit.
22. *Report of a Court of Inquiry under Lord Scarman*, Cmnd. 6922 (H.M.S.O., 1977).
23. Rogaly, op. cit., pp. 110–11.
24. See Counsel's *Opinion* to the U.P.W., 25 March 1977.
25. *The Times*, 4 March 1978.
26. *Guardian*, 16 May 1977.
27. See Brian Bercusson, 'Picketing, Secondary Picketing and Secondary Action', *The Industrial Law Journal*, Vol. 9, No. 4 (December 1980), p. 227.
28. W. E. J. McCarthy, *New Society*, 4 September 1980.
29. *New Society*, 20 November 1980.
30. *Guardian*, 5 November 1980.
31. Lord Wedderburn, 'Industrial Relations and the Courts', *The Industrial Law Journal*, Vol. 9, No. 2 (June 1980), p. 78.
32. Rogaly, op. cit., pp. 141–2.
33. *Socialist Challenge*, 15 October 1981.
34. Peter Townsend, *Poverty in the United Kingdom* (Penguin, 1979), p. 926.
35. Bob Hepple, 'A Right to Work?', *The Industrial Law Journal*, Vol. 10, No. 2 (June 1981), p. 81.

CHAPTER 9: OFFICIALLY SECRET

1. James Michael, *The Politics of Secrecy* (Penguin, 1982), p. 9.
2. *The Times*, 9 November 1979. See also Michael, op. cit., for a full analysis.
3. Tony Bunyan, *The Political Police in Britain* (Julian Friedmann, 1976), p. 11.
4. This is shown by Crispin Aubrey, *Who's Watching You?* (Penguin, 1981), pp. 14–16.
5. Tony Benn, *Arguments for Democracy* (Cape, 1981), p. 75.
6. See Barrie Penrose and Roger Courtiour, *The Pencourt File* (Secker & Warburg, 1978), p. 9.
7. Paraphrased in Aubrey, op. cit., pp. 17–18.

8. See Michael, op. cit., Bunyan, op. cit., Aubrey, op. cit., and David Leigh, *The Frontiers of Secrecy* (Junction Books, 1980).

9. *Report and Evidence of the Committee on Section 2 of the Official Secrets Act*, Cmnd. 5104 (H.M.S.O., 1972), Vol. 1, p. 123.

10. Quoted in Michael, op. cit., p. 34.

11. Bunyan, op. cit., p. 26.

12. See Jonathan Aitken, *Officially Secret* (Weidenfeld & Nicolson, 1971).

13. For an account of the trial, see Aubrey, op. cit.

14. Reported by Michael, op. cit., p. 54.

15. For an excellent exposé of this see Leigh, op. cit., pp. 1–35, and Michael, op. cit.

16. Harold Wilson, *The Governance of Britain* (Michael Joseph, 1976), pp. 167–8.

17. Tony Benn, *Arguments for Socialism* (Penguin, 1980), pp. 124–6, shows how prime ministerial power operates in this way.

18. See Leigh, op. cit., pp. 9–12.

19. Benn (1980), pp. 112–13.

20. See *State Research Bulletin*, Vol. 3, No. 18 (June/July 1980), p. 120.

21. *Report of the Committee on the Civil Service*, Cmnd. 3638 (H.M.S.O., 1968), pp. 91–2.

22. Leigh, op. cit., pp. 40–41.

23. Extracts from the *Security Handbook* were published in *The Leveller*, 9 January 1981, pp. 8–9.

24. See *State Research Bulletin*, Vol. 4, No. 23 (April/May 1981), pp. 102–3.

25. See Leigh, op. cit., pp. 71–8.

26. Christopher Price M.P., *Guardian*, 12 February 1982.

27. J. A. G. Griffith, *The Politics of the Judiciary* (Fontana, 1981), p. 121.

28. For an excellent analysis of this, see Geoff Robertson, 'Law for the Press', in James Curran (ed.), *The British Press: A Manifesto* (Macmillan, 1978).

29. Quoted in Brownlie's *Law on Public Order and National Security* (Butterworth, 1981 edition), p. 269.

30. See Leigh, op. cit., pp. 48–88, and Benn (1980), pp. 127–8.

31. *State Research Bulletin*, Vol. 2, No. 9 (December 1978/January 1979), p. 40.

CHAPTER 10: LESSONS FROM THE NORTH OF IRELAND

1. See John McGuffin, *The Guineapigs* (Penguin, 1974), and Peter Taylor, *Beating the Terrorists?* (Penguin, 1980).

2. See Carol Ackroyd, Karen Margolis, Jonathen Rosenhead and Tim Shallice, *The Technology of Political Control* (Penguin, 1977).

3. *Report of the Commission to Consider Legal Procedures to Deal with Terrorist Activities in Northern Ireland*, Cmnd. 5185 (H.M.S.O., 1972).
4. See Kevin Boyle, Tom Hadden and Paddy Hillyard, *Ten Years on in Northern Ireland* (Cobden Trust, 1980), p. 80.
5. Cited in Brian Rose-Smith, 'Police Powers and Terrorism Legislation', in Peter Hain (ed.), *Policing the Police*, Vol. I (John Calder, 1979), p. 112.
6. For a full analysis of this see Boyle, *et al.*, op. cit., pp. 24–5.
7. Liam O'Dowd, Bill Rolston and Mike Tomlinson, *Northern Ireland: Between Civil Rights and Civil War* (C.S.E. Books, 1981), pp. 190–91.
8. Tom Bowden, *Beyond the Limits of the Law* (Penguin, 1978), p. 217.
9. A short analysis of the role of the Special Branch is contained in Tony Bunyan, *The Political Police in Britain* (Julian Friedmann, 1976), pp. 102–51.
10. Ackroyd *et al.*, op. cit., p. 46.
11. *Guardian*, 18 February 1982.
12. ibid., 26 February 1982.
13. Liz Curtis, *They Shoot Children* (Information on Ireland pamphlet, 1982).
14. Rose-Smith, op. cit., p. 120.
15. Catherine Scorer and Patricia Hewitt, *The Prevention of Terrorism Act* (National Council for Civil Liberties, 1981), p. 12.
16. ibid., p. 19.
17. Quoted in ibid., p. 21.
18. ibid.
19. *Guardian*, 2 January 1980.
20. Thom Young, *Incitement to Disaffection* (Cobden Trust, 1976), pp. 12–18.
21. ibid., p. 58.
22. ibid., pp. 56–7.
23. ibid., p. 76.
24. ibid., p. 94.
25. ibid., pp. 93–4.
26. Boyle *et al.*, op. cit., p. 108.
27. See O'Dowd *et al.*, op. cit., p. 193.
28. Frank Kitson, *Low Intensity Operations* (Faber, 1971), p. 69.
29. Ackroyd, *et al.*, op. cit., pp. 68–77.

CHAPTER 11: PUBLIC ORDER

1. Quoted in *New Society*, 10 April 1980.
2. Tom Bowden, *Beyond the Limits of the Law* (Penguin, 1978), p. 21.
3. E. P. Thompson, *New Society*, 15 November 1979, p. 380.
4. See for instance E. P. Thompson, *The Making of the English Working Class* (Penguin, 1968).

5. V. G. Kiernan, 'Patterns of Protest in English History', in Benewick and Smith (eds.), *Direct Action and Democratic Politics* (Allen & Unwin, 1973), p. 32.
6. Bowden, op. cit., p. 215.
7. ibid., p. 225.
8. D. Philips, 'Riots and Public Order in the Black Country 1835–60', in J. Stevenson and R. Quinault (eds.), *Popular Protest and Public Order* (Allen & Unwin, 1974), pp. 159–60.
9. Tony Bunyan, *The Political Police in Britain* (Julian Friedmann, 1976), p. 36.
10. Robert Reiner, 'Forces of Disorder: how the police control riots', *New Society*, 10 April 1980, p. 53.
11. Robert Skidelsky, *Oswald Mosley* (Macmillan, 1975).
12. Robert Benewick, *The Fascist Movement in Britain* (Allen & Unwin, 1972).
13. See Stuart Hall's excellent analysis, *Drifting into a Law and Order Society* (Cobden Trust, 1980).
14. Bowden, op. cit., p. 262.
15. Carol Ackroyd, *et al.*, *The Technology of Political Control* (Penguin, 1977).
16. Bowden, op. cit., p. 271.
17. See Joanna Rollo, 'The Special Patrol Group', in Peter Hain (ed.), *Policing the Police*, Vol. 2 (John Calder, 1980), pp. 153–203.
18. See Peter Hain, *Don't Play With Apartheid* (Allen & Unwin, 1971), pp. 133–5.
19. Bowden, op. cit., p. 221.
20. Quoted in Patricia Hewitt, *The Abuse of Power* (Martin Robertson, 1981), p. 112.
21. ibid., p. 115.
22. ibid.
23. ibid.
24. Home Office, *Review of the Public Order Act 1936 and Related Legislation*, Cmnd. 7891 (H.M.S.O., 1980), and *Report* of the Home Affairs Committee, HC 756–1 (H.M.S.O., 1980).
25. Brownlie's *Law of Public Order and National Security* (Butterworth, 1981 edition), p. 6.
26. ibid., p. 9.
27. ibid., p. 8.
28. Report of an Inquiry by Lord Scarman, *The Brixton Disorders*, Cmnd. 8427 (H.M.S.O., November 1981), pp. 123–4.
29. Hewitt, op. cit., p. 120.
30. See Bowden, op. cit., p. 95.
31. See Hewitt, op. cit., pp. 109–11.
32. *New Society*, 10 April 1980, p. 54.

33. ibid.
34. ibid., and Ackroyd, op. cit., p. 225.
35. *Guardian*, 21 October 1981.
36. For a political science analysis of this, see P. Bachrach and M. S. Baratz, *Power and Poverty* (Oxford University Press, 1970).
37. Hewitt, op. cit., p. 122.
38. *Guardian*, 14 December 1982.
39. J. A. G. Griffith, *The Politics of the Judiciary* (Fontana, 1981), pp. 138–9.
40. ibid., p. 141.
41. Ron Bailey, *The Squatters* (Penguin, 1973), p. 156.
42. *New Society*, 8 March 1979, p. 552.
43. For a vivid account by Arthur Scargill, see *New Left Review*, No. 92 (July/August 1975), pp. 15–19.
44. Chris Ralph, *The Picket and the Law* (Fabian Research Series 331, 1977).
45. K. W. Wedderburn, *The Worker and the Law* (Penguin, 1971), p. 325.

CHAPTER 12: RACISM

1. *Guardian*, 1 December 1981.
2. Robert Moore, *Racism and Black Resistance* (Pluto, 1975), p. 37.
3. ibid., p. 5.
4. Andre Gorz, 'The Role of Immigrant Labour', *New Left Review*, No. 61 (May/June, 1970).
5. See Ceri Peach, *West Indian Migration to Britain* (Oxford University Press, 1969).
6. A. Sivanandan, 'Race, class and the state: the black experience in Britain', *Race and Class*, Vol. XVII, No. 4 (1976), p. 350.
7. A. Sivanandan, 'From resistance to rebellion: Asian and Afro-Caribbean struggles in Britain', *Race and Class*, Vol. XXIII, Nos. 2/3 (Autumn 1981/Winter 1982), p. 119.
8. ibid., pp. 119–20.
9. Sivanandan (1976), p. 358.
10. Quoted by Moore, op. cit., p. 40.
11. ibid., pp. 39–45.
12. *Guardian*, 30 January 1982.
13. Moore, op. cit., pp. 57–8.
14. Patricia Hewitt, *The Abuse of Power* (Martin Robertson, 1981), pp. 197–9.
15. *Hansard*, 26 July 1979.
16. Hewitt, op. cit., p. 200.
17. *Black and Blue* (Communist Party, 1981), p. 11.

18. Report of an Inquiry by Lord Scarman, *The Brixton Disorders*, Cmnd. 8427 (H.M.S.O., November 1981), para. 2.23.

19. Stuart Hall *et al.*, *Policing the Crisis* (Macmillan, 1978), p. 359.

20. ibid., pp. 186–7.

21. Gus John, in Derek Humphry, *Police Power and Black People* (Panther, 1972), p. 233.

22. See Peter Hain, *Neighbourhood Participation* (Temple Smith, 1980), pp. 54–9.

23. *Blood on the Streets* (Bethnal Green and Stepney Trades Council, 1978), p. 46.

24. Paul Gordon, *Incitement to Racial Hatred* (Runnymede Trust, 1982).

25. ibid.

26. Lawrence Roach, 'The Metropolitan Police Community Relations Branch', *Police Studies*, Vol. 1, No. 3 (September 1978).

27. *Race Today*, November 1975, p. 244.

28. *Guardian*, 14 September 1981.

29. Robert Reiner, *The Blue Coated Worker* (Cambridge University Press, 1978), p. 226.

30. ibid., p. 225.

31. Institute of Race Relations, *Police Against Black People* (I.R.R., 1979), pp. 5–18.

32. Scarman, op. cit., paras. 4.2, 4.67.

33. Institute of Race Relations, op. cit., pp. 30–40.

34. *Black and Blue*, op. cit., p. 8.

35. Institute of Race Relations, op. cit., pp. 14–16.

36. ibid., pp. 20–26; *Blood on the Streets*, op. cit.; Moore, op. cit., pp. 59–62.

37. Home Office, *Racial Attacks* (H.M.S.O., November 1981).

38. Quoted by Martin Kettle in Peter Hain (ed.), *Policing the Police*, Vol. 2 (John Calder, 1980), p. 38.

39. *Socialist Challenge*, 16 August 1979.

40. Institute of Race Relations, op. cit., pp. 20–26.

41. *People's News Service*, 20 February 1979.

42. *Socialist Worker*, 23 February 1980.

43. Quoted in *New Society*, 17 September 1981.

44. '*Sus*' (Runnymede Trust, 1978).

45. *Black and Blue*, op. cit., p. 12.

46. Institute of Race Relations, op. cit., pp. 45–57.

47. ibid.

48. Malpass and Kravitz, 'Recognition for faces of own and other race', *Journal of Personality and Social Psychology*, Vol. 13 (1969).

49. M. Billig and D. Milner, 'A spade is a spade in the eyes of the law', *Psychology Today*, Vol. 2, No. 2 (February 1976).

50. *Daily Telegraph*, 7 December 1977. See also Institute of Race Relations, op. cit., pp. 56–7.
51. *The Times*, 13 March 1980.
52. Institute of Race Relations, op. cit., p. 61.
53. *Legal Action Group Bulletin*, August 1981.
54. Battersea and Wandsworth Trades Council, *The Death of Richard 'Cartoon' Campbell* (1980), p. 23.
55. Humphry, op. cit., p. 85.
56. Moore, op. cit., p. 70.
57. Institute of Race Relations, op. cit., p. 59.
58. See *Guardian*, 7 and 14 January 1978.
59. Institute of Race Relations, op. cit., p. 27.
60. *Guardian*, 16 May 1975.
61. Humphry, op. cit., pp. 147–69.
62. For example, Hackney Black Peoples Defence Organization, *Morning Star*, 7 August 1979.
63. *The Times*, 2 and 3 February 1982.
64. J. A. G. Griffith, *The Politics of the Judiciary* (Fontana, 1981), pp. 101–6.
65. Hewitt, op. cit., p. 203.
66. Griffith, op. cit., pp. 106–10.
67. ibid., p. 110.
68. *Race Today*, November 1975.
69. Quoted in Stuart Hall *et al.*, p. 281.
70. *Time Out*, 5–11 August 1977, p. 10.
71. *City Limits*, 18–24 June 1982.
72. *The Leveller*, 25 June–8 July 1982.

CHAPTER 13: POLITICAL TRIALS

1. *Guardian*, 3 February 1982.
2. Crispin Aubrey, *Who's Watching You?* (Penguin, 1981), p. 13.
3. Derek Humphry, *Police Power and Black People* (Panther, 1972), p. 164.
4. Stuart Hall *et al.*, *Policing the Crisis* (Macmillan, 1978), p. 190.
5. J. A. G. Griffith, *The Politics of the Judiciary* (Fontana, 1981), p. 209.
6. Community Development Project, *The Limits of the Law* (C.D.P. Inter Project Editorial Team, 1977).
7. Goran Therborn, *What Does the Ruling Class Do When It Rules?* (New Left Books, 1978), p. 235.
8. ibid.
9. Hall *et al.*, op. cit., p. 32.
10. ibid., p. 34.

11. M. D. A. Freeman, *The Legal Structure* (Longman, 1974), pp. 47–9.

12. ibid., p. 48.

13. Michael Banton, *The Police and the Community* (Tavistock, 1964).

14. Griffith, op. cit., p. 225.

15. ibid., p. 223.

16. ibid.

17. Quoted in Lord Wedderburn, 'Industrial Relations and the Courts', *The Industrial Law Journal*, Vol. 9, No. 2 (June 1980), p. 91.

18. ibid.

19. See for example *Sunday Express*, 4 February 1979.

20. Therborn, op. cit., p. 235.

21. Hall *et al.*, op. cit., pp. 206–7.

Index